Windows to the Sun

Marcel Duchamp, *Nude Descending a Staircase, No. 2* (1912) (see 99–116). © 2008 Artists Rights Society (ARS), New York/ ADAGP, Paris/ Succession Marcel Duchamp; Philadelphia Museum of Art, The Louise and Walter Arensberg Collection, 1950. The same image is also shown on the dust jacket.

Windows to the Sun

D. H. Lawrence's "Thought-Adventures"

Edited by
Earl Ingersoll and Virginia Hyde

Madison • Teaneck
Fairleigh Dickinson University Press

Associated University Presses
2010 Eastpark Boulevard
Cranbury, NJ 08512

The paper used in this publication meets the requirements of the American National Standard for Permanence of Paper for Printed Library Materials
Z39.48-1984.

Library of Congress Cataloging-in-Publication Data

Windows to the sun : D. H. Lawrence's "thought-adventures" / edited by Earl Ingersoll and Virginia Hyde.
p. cm.
Includes bibliographical references and index.
ISBN 978-0-8386-4197-2 (alk. paper)
1. Lawrence, D. H. (David Herbert), 1885–1930—Criticism and interpretation. 2. Lawrence, D. H. (David Herbert), 1885–1930—Psychology. 3. Visual perception in literature. 4. Realism in literature. I. Ingersoll, Earl G., 1938– II. Hyde, Virginia.
PR6023.A93Z9547 2009
823′.912—dc22

2008029480

PRINTED IN THE UNITED STATES OF AMERICA

Contents

Introduction: Windows to the Sun: D. H. Lawrence's "Thought-Adventures" 7
VIRGINIA HYDE

"A New Continent of the Soul": Lawrence's Transcultural/Transhistorical Meeting with Herman Melville 21
EARL INGERSOLL

"Over Some Frontiers" at Monte Cassino: Lawrence and Maurice Magnus 50
JOHN WORTHEN

Women in Love: Sacrifice, Sadism, and the Discourse of Species 69
GERALD DOHERTY

Modernism's Fourth Dimension in *Aaron's Rod:* Einstein, Picasso, and Lawrence 99
KUMIKO HOSHI

Crossing Europe: Political Frontiers in Lawrence's *The Lost Girl* 118
THERESA MAE THOMPSON

Male Sexuality on the Frontier in D. H. Lawrence's *Kangaroo* 138
NANCY L. PAXTON

Keeping His Flag Flying: Censorship and Lawrence's Poetry 165
CHRISTOPHER POLLNITZ

Lawrence's De-patterning of America and Magical Realism 187
Jamie Jung Min Woo

How to Live?—The End of Lawrence's Quest 207
Keith Sagar

References 224

Notes on Contributors 239

Index 243

Introduction: Windows to the Sun: D. H. Lawrence's "Thought-Adventures"

Virginia Hyde

WHILE D. H. LAWRENCE IS OFTEN TAGGED AS AN AUTHOR OF "quest" literature, to whom travel was a staple both of his life and his writing, this volume is concerned even more centrally with what he called "thought-adventures" (1994, 279; 1988c, 197). Sometimes these advances in thought occur during actual journeys, like Lawrence's move out of England after the war, one of the major catalysts in his own thinking and works. The present volume includes texts that range over a broad scope of travels. Lawrence himself sails the seas vicariously with Melville in *Studies in Classic American Literature* (1918–23) and visits an Italian monastery in *Memoir of Maurice Magnus* (1924); his quests culminate in *Etruscan Places* (1932). European sites are profiled late in *Women in Love* (1920); Alvina Houghton moves to Italy in *The Lost Girl* (1920); Aaron Sisson explores Italy in *Aaron's Rod* (1922); Richard Lovatt Somers stops off in Australia in *Kangaroo* (1923); and Kate Leslie lives in Mexico in *The Plumed Serpent* (1926). These texts are sometimes called novels of pilgrimage, and all are represented in these essays. But the "thought-adventure" does not necessarily transport the readers to a new geographic location; rather, it moves them into a new perception of reality.

Lawrence's idea of creative purpose casts the artist as the one who continually disabuses society of the false world-views it creates for itself. The false "world," he explains, is an "umbrella" that people erect between themselves and the creative "chaos" of reality: "Man must wrap himself in a vision, make a house of apparent form and stability, fixity. In his terror of chaos, he begins by putting up an umbrella between himself and the everlasting whirl. Then he paints the under-side of his umbrella like a firmament" (2005a, 109). This simulacrum eventually becomes the "dome" of stultified beliefs and the "vault" of a deadened citizenry (109). But the artist is the "enemy of convention," who slits the umbrella and reveals "a window to the sun" (109). Lawrence realized that he lived in a time when the long-standing "world picture" was being overturned—a time for the artist to remove the shreds of "The Absolute Umbrella," whether "religious or moral or rational or scientific or practical" (113). Such an individual is "transgressive" in Lawrence's own terms—that is, transformative of a culture that he considered devastated by World War I; this artist also fits the "nomadic" definition by which Gilles Deleuze and Félix Guattari refer to one whose freedom of thought and action is not dictated simply by location.[1] The spirit of such freedom is voiced in Lawrence's essays on the novel as a form. In "The Future of the Novel," he relates the novelist's proper concern with the future, for the watchword should be "*What next?*" (1985b, 154).[2] He maintains that we can tell a good book by the criticism that nobody has yet thought this way; and moreover, "a really new novel will *always* hurt, to some extent" because of its departure from the past (1985a, 175). In part, he was thinking of the birth pangs of the postwar world.[3]

The "windows" to the sun that Lawrence imagined have a further meaning for today's computer-savvy reader: they suggest a whole bank of such "window" sites at our disposal, existing simultaneously, any of which may be opened, rather magically, at any time for a new outlook. Somewhat similarly, this collection is envisioned as a series of "windows" to new perspectives that Lawrence revealed in his texts. In these pages are nine essays by international scholars from four countries (four continents), including three Cambridge Edition editors. Sometimes the shift is one of location or "spirit of place," it is true, but always it is one of thought—a new "window to the sun." Issues Lawrence faces are not easy ones but include wartime and postwar malaise, fascism, eugenic marriage patterns, racism, sexism, ecological crisis, and the prospect of censorship that always attended him. Among his resources were Einstein's "relativity" theory (by which Lawrence somewhat explains his own shifting views); graphic arts, which offered models of new shapes and concepts, and a greatly broadened global time line that was informed by evolutionary theory (although Lawrence often claims to discount Darwinism). In almost all cases, he gauges the standard viewpoint and takes the side of the "other," beyond the "umbrella" of convention, moving his topic into new territory.

Lawrence's reputation has turned out to be more resilient than was often predicted. Assessments of his reception in the world (Iida 1999) as well as a new look at his place in Europe (Jansohn and Mehl 2007) show his significant followings through the years. In the latter, Lawrence is seen as "the only great writer of the last century" to work in virtually all the literary genres (2). A surprise of Jansohn and Mehl's study is the fact that "political" critical issues, sometimes said to threaten Lawrence's place in the academic setting, have never prevented him from having large numbers of adherents who read him with "genuine affection" (2). In Africa, too, Lawrence's influence in literature and art has been "vigorous and productive" (Phelps and Bell 2007, xv), and South Africa, for example, has produced major world-class Lawrence scholars, including a Cambridge Editor. Moreover, Gary Adelman's study of Lawrence's reputation with creative writers (2002) shows that his place among them has always been high and is so today.[4] The creators know creativity when they see it. In fact, Lawrence is specifically praised by well-known literary figures for standing far apart from an age of irony and cynicism today (Adelman 2002, 43). And mainline scholar Harold Bloom finds the best of Lawrence "astonishing" beyond all expectation; as we also suggest in our "window" metaphor, he amazes his reader by being "adept at . . . showing what cannot be shown" (Bloom 1986, 23).

Lawrence studies were not early to grapple with some of the contemporary theorists with whom he is now seen to have remarkable affinities.[5] Of course, he was not Foucauldian, Deleuzian, Bakhtinian, Derridean, or Lacanian; he was uniquely Lawrentian. But he and these later thinkers sometimes explored similar paths, and as a result he is well placed among them (as in some of the essays in this volume).

Lawrence was too strong a writer to follow standard critiques of his time, and his ideas and techniques remain characteristically his own today; this is one reason he has been difficult to "classify" in terms of one literary theorist or another—and also one reason that he transcends many topical critical skirmishes. Michael Bell and others have shown that Lawrence had his own form of dialogism, or "dialogue," independent of Bakhtin's terminology.[6] Lawrence also developed a "decolonizing" outlook that preceded (and often anticipated) postcolonialism (N. Roberts 2004, 16–41; Kinkead-Weekes 2001; Chaudhury 2003). Gerald Doherty (1987, 477–96) shows the "deconstructive turn" in Lawrence's own criticism and Earl Ingersoll (2001) demonstrates that he is explicable in Lacanian terms. In today's ecocriticism, Lawrence is the author of some of the original texts to be studied in terms of "deep ecology" (see Devall and Sessions 1985, 83; Forstner and Todd 1971). In fact, Dolores LaChapelle ranks Lawrence, in this field, with Henry David Thoreau and John Muir, and Lawrence is a cornerstone of Keith Sagar's *Literature and the Crime Against Nature* (see also his essay "The Resurrection of Pan"). Although it used to be said that Lawrence was not particularly innovative in genre, the publication of his edition—at more than forty-five volumes (scheduled for completion in 2008)—shows otherwise, revealing the effects of censorship on his work and allowing comparisons with unpublished versions that contributed to new generic directions. This is scholarship that is richly in evidence in the present volume.

Among the most vexed areas of Lawrence criticism has been feminist studies (see Milne 2001), but significant détente has appeared. It is some long conceptual distance from Kate Millett's hostile *Sexual Politics* (1969) to Marianna Torgovnick's statement that "we can modify the anger in Millett's critique to a new understanding of . . . Lawrence" (1990, 168). More recently, Torgovnick gives a nuanced look at Lawrence's writing about sex, crediting his ability to render "the ineffable surround of sexuality" (2001, 39). While Sandra M. Gilbert once called Lawrence "famously misogynistic" (1985, 141), she has more recently (2002) provided the foreword to *Reclaiming D. H. Lawrence* (by Gary Adelman) and also affirms Lawrence's particular appeal to women readers and writers (Gilbert 1990). Carol Siegel's landmark study (1991) relates Lawrence to the feminist movement itself and to a women's tradition in the novel. While he was once stereotyped by some readers as the titillating author of risqué sexual scenes (as acclaimed by Henry Miller and Anaïs Nin), recent studies like James C. Cowan's last book, *D. H. Lawrence: Self and Sexuality,* bring a more mature assessment to gender issues in Lawrence. Most of these critical topics are furthered in the present collection.

World War I has been mentioned as a particular watershed in Lawrence's development of a vision of the world. Surveying these essays, we may sense anew how early in his career it was (starting before he finished *The Rainbow* in 1915) and how many of his works are touched by it. Confined geographically as he was at this period, Lawrence was groping for a larger *weltanschauung.* Earl Ingersoll shows that Lawrence's essays for *Studies in Classic American Literature* are drawn on a broad canvas, both in space and time. They illustrate especially well how Lawrence interrelated geographic descriptions with expansive ideas, or "thought-adventures." It was during his wartime period in Cornwall, under national surveillance along with his German-born wife, Frieda, that he immersed himself in long-distance ententes with nineteenth-century American writers, especially Herman Melville. He associated the sailor-author with ancient seafaring Vikings and imagined the bracing voyage of the *Pequod.* The deep bond he formed with the other writer (perhaps his most successful *Blutbrüderschaft*) forms a fascinating look at literary influence as long-distance friendship and even as fulfillment of desire. Not only did Melville transport Lawrence to the South Seas and the geographic ends of the earth, he also introduced him to the "other" in terms of race, culture, and custom in the relationship between Ishmael and Queequeg in *Moby-Dick.* The sheer size of that novel—in exploring some of the farthest reaches of the globe and transgressing all borders—was salutary for the young Lawrence, whose surroundings were stultifying as he and Frieda waited for passports out of Britain.

Lawrence's Cambridge biographer and editor, John Worthen, reassessing Lawrence's *Memoir of Maurice Magnus,* brings new insight into the period that followed that long wait to leave England. The *Memoir* concerns Lawrence's visit in 1920 to the abbey of Monte Cassino—the original home of the Benedictine order—and to Magnus, who was staying there. In fact, the incident stands out as marking a mental frontier in his postwar life, and Worthen opens a window on this significant period. He makes use of little-known correspondence in which Magnus discusses the visit with great personal candor. (It seems he was actually hiding out from creditors and hoping that Lawrence would help him financially.) Lawrence, despite the war's end, was still sensing the continuous collapse of Europe—even of Christendom—along with its raisons d'être and all of its bonds of affection. In this, he resembled his character Somers in *Kangaroo,* who suffered "one of his serious deaths in belief" during the war, the more terrible because he "had always *believed* so in everything—society, love, friends" (D. H. Lawrence 1994, 247). Thus the visit to the enigmatic Magnus took on a particular importance from this postwar context, and Worthen is authoritative in stating that Lawrence was moved, as seldom before or after, by this encounter. Worthen's contribution provides new insights following upon his monumental biographies and editions.[7]

To a surprising extent, Lawrence seems to see Magnus as representing an old world of faith (that is partly why he was at Monte Cassino) and of love—spiritual and carnal, for the monk manqué was markedly bisexual. It is too little recognized (as Worthen recognizes) that, as Lawrence emerged from the war years, he felt himself "broken-hearted" (he refers to the heart remarkably often), jilted perhaps by what he called the "love urge" in all its unitary forms. Worthen portrays him, further, as something of a creative voyeur (like most artists), interested in "what he was not"; for Lawrence, both as an individual and as a writer, was interrogating the old theme that "love is enough." In Magnus, he observed a man whose lifestyle was clearly "other" than the standard domestic one in several different ways. Lawrence was entering the so-called leadership period, in which men were to come together and build anew.[8] But Magnus, rather "pompous" and conniving, was seemingly devoted to what Lawrence openly questioned: "the not-quite-dead past" (D. H. Lawrence 2005c, 22, 33).

One of the broadest "windows" Lawrence ever opened appears in Gerald Doherty's study in the present volume of "speciesism" in *Women in Love.* Other incidents in this "war novel" (that never mentions the war) may obscure the vast prepleistocene or postmodern prospect that Birkin views at times—from his apocalyptic thought of the dead ichthyosauri to the possibility of a future creation that is not androcentric: where "species passed away" and others sprang newborn from the "creative mystery" (1987c, 479). Doherty shows that the novel exposes an oppressive hierarchy in which men rule as humans (opposed to animals), as males, as masters of industry and heads of class structures. At the base of their destructive sadism is a denial of the animal body, and Birkin knows it can cause extinction. Doherty mines Derrida, Deleuze, and Nietzsche to show the dynamics of eroticism based on a *Wille zur Macht* over other living things. The iconic nature of Lawrence's chapters is fortunate for this study, and Doherty finds in them the "animal vignettes" that carry a central theme: the contrast between enmity with other species (like Gerald on his horse) and acceptance of life's nonhuman dimensions (as in "Excurse" with Birkin and Ursula in Sherwood Forest). The essay identifies Birkin's vision as more "theological" than "Darwinian." (And we may remember, after all, that he once welcomes "grass, and hares and adders, and the unseen hosts" [D. H. Lawrence 1987c, 128].) Without particularly mentioning the war years assumed in the novel, the essay goes far in demonstrating the roots of violence and destruction that often seem near the surface of the book.

Kumiko Hoshi takes the postwar setting of *Aaron's Rod* to anatomize Lawrence's relation to cubism as a means of expressing changing views of reality. She pairs Lawrence with Picasso and Duchamp in a study of modernist graphic art. Cubist art had turned from the fixity of an established representational style to the contingency of plural versions of its object. Similarly, says Hoshi, Lawrence sought to apply his brand of "relativity" to the developing options of characters like Aaron. Such multiple directions are illustrated visually by the Duchamp painting *Nude Descending a Staircase,* showing a figure with several different outlines at once. Hoshi looks at Aaron's action scenes—at the particular pattern of his movement—in the light of such art, relating it to the Einsteinian "relative" space that influences the novelist elsewhere. Lawrence depicts Aaron as an artist who is seeking the "slit" in the "umbrella" of false western European civilization. The competing directions suggest the urgency of his quest as he looks for a viable future. If Einstein's theory (and various "fourth-dimension" claims of the time) meant (to Lawrence) that the cosmos was without an axle—as he says in *Fantasia of the Unconscious*—at least Lawrence could rejoice in seeing the universe anew, as a freewheeling "cloud of bees" in active flight (D. H. Lawrence 2004a, 72). Some of this new sense of mobility emerges in the novels of world pilgrimage that, arguably, begin with this book.

The wartime (and prewartime) mood of elegiac questioning is captured in Theresa Thompson's analysis of *The Lost Girl* (1920) in terms of eugenic theories that sought to manipulate love and reproduction for a brittle society; against this current, the Englishwoman Alvina struggles to assert her own desire, only to leave questions at the novel's end as her chosen one, Ciccio, seems headed to the war. (Beyond that, it seems, America may offer a way out, but it stands far away on the horizon.) Thompson takes a feminist look at some of the conditions that women faced in Alvina's society, for the heroine explores middle-class expectations, employment, economic loss, and even reputed degradation in her choice of an "unsuitable" husband (becoming a "lost" girl). Thompson comprehends the context for Lawrence's negative response to these constricting mores as they relate to fascism and eugenics. He was bucking, through his character, some of the standard assumptions of the day and trying to reveal a "window" or a way out. The novel, like *Women in Love* and *Aaron's Rod,* is geographically bifurcated, and the essay details a peripatetic crossing of boundaries, national and personal. Its Italy is sometimes much brighter than its England but also sometimes much darker.

Lawrence's Australian novel *Kangaroo* offered a new opportunity for Lawrence to personify the Western "love urge" in a single figure, the homosocial political leader whose authoritarian schemes are rejected by the Lawrence-like Somers. Nancy Paxton's study follows Judith Butler's continuum of "gender melancholy," applying it to Somers's ambivalent responses to the charismatic Ben Cooley ("Kangaroo"). Cooley reveals a Jehovah-like appeal that continues to gain followers, even at the remote margins of a discredited Europe. But Somers has set his course for America and will not be detained. Paxton's is the third of these essays to indicate Lawrence's interest in gender as a more fluid distinction than he had always recognized. After the war, he believed, gender roles were in great flux, and he could not fail to be a rapt observer in the light of his signature topic of sexuality.

Among Lawrence's most significant roles as a pioneer was this one that has made him an "original" in the history of twentieth-century literature. Most of his works illustrate the bent toward transgressive innovation—none more so than those productions that were censored. Although we have long known about the historic censorship in his career—particularly that of *Lady Chatterley's Lover*—it has not been well known that his poetry, too, suffered from significant interference. But Christopher Pollnitz, an Australian critic who edits Lawrence's poetry for the Cambridge Edition, provides a view of a Lawrence who repeatedly challenged his editors—even in the poetry. Pollnitz understands the negative sense of the word "frontier," especially if it is the one where the censors ranged themselves against Lawrence's original texts. He shows how resolute Lawrence was to keep the "flag flying" in the face of the "censor-morons," and Pollnitz's essay makes news by providing specific details of this process.[9]

Jamie Jung Min Woo studies Lawrence as a precursor of a genre that developed fully only after his death, the novel of "magical realism." She uses both *The Plumed Serpent* and its earlier version, *Quetzalcoatl* (written in 1923, not published until 1995), to examine his place vis-à-vis the Latin American form of this genre that came to elevate indigenous mythology much as Lawrence attempted to do. She points to the recognition Lawrence has received from writers like Octavio Paz and Carlos Fuentes, but she is particularly concerned with the mode's original focus on the "magical" quality that resides within the natural. By this criterion, *Quetzalcoatl* can seem to fit the form better than its successor, which was more confined to the realistic world; but in terms of mythology, *The Plumed Serpent* clearly has a more elaborate register. Both versions are pioneering in the new genre and have only recently been recognized as such in Lawrence circles. Interestingly, it is a form particularly identified with a postcolonial or indigenous perspective. Arnold Odio, too, has shown how Lawrence's achievement differed from the "indianista" tradition that did not give its due respect to the native background. Lawrence's role as an opponent of the conventional status quo—as one who must puncture the "umbrella" of the times and open a "window to the sun"—enabled him to see beyond the Latinate Mexico of the tourists to the deep Indian foundations of the culture.[10]

Keith Sagar—whose attention to Lawrence's painting, biography, and literary texts has aided scholarship for a generation—returns us to the broader themes of Lawrence's quest and its relation to the "thought-adventure." He traces the author from the adventurer through the "married man,"[11] or "priest of love," and from the communal man to Lawrence the cosmologist. Sagar's strongest focus is on this ultimate Lawrence, the one who literally sought intimate contact with the universe. Modern people's "petty little love of nature" seems too paltry, Lawrence wrote, when actually "we have to get back the cosmos" and our lost responses to the sun and the moon (1979, 76). In fact, one is never really fulfilled without passing "further than every relationship: further than mankind and womankind" into connection with the surrounding universe (1988b, 375). This is the final meaning, perhaps, of a "window to the sun": it enables an intense relation between the individual and a dynamic universe that is usually hidden beyond society's "umbrella." Moreover, this is a Lawrence who fits well into today's literary approach through "deep ecology," a topic Sagar presents in his latest book about literature's ability to address the "crime against nature." Sagar places Lawrence firmly among those who have sought to preserve the environment—and thus among pioneers of biocentric and ecological criticism—and of regard for the "other." Doherty's work on Lawrence's stand against species subjection is related to this insight. Lawrence's concern for the living universe, in all its mystery, may have other meanings as well in philosophy and religion; but this environmental concern is a fundamental one.

One standard truism about art or literature is that it is intended to bring order out of chaos. Of course, this is true, and Lawrence himself discusses art that is "complete and consummate" (1972, 182). But this is not at all his own focus in the metaphor with which this introduction began—that of the artist's imperative to replace the last static construction, the decorative "umbrella," by revealing again the creative "chaos" outside as the stuff of life: "a strange and forever surging chaos" (2005a, 109). This is an aesthetic that thrives on the idea of creative chaos. Nor does the image of the "window to the sun" work quite perfectly. In "Education of the People," Lawrence posits a person who, in an odd version of Plato's cave, has lived "shut up in a hermetically dark room" and has emerged only in daylight: such a person would have no idea of the starry night sky and would miss much of the "fathomless multiplicity" of the universe (1988d, 135–36). The upshot of this anecdote is simply that one "window" to the universe will not do—or will not do for long. After all, "The chaos which we have got used to, we call a cosmos," says Lawrence (2005a, 109). The present volume has heeded such warnings and contains a variety of its own "windows" into major Lawrentian perspectives. Remarkably, this man who believed in a dynamic cycle of re-creation has retained his relevance to different ages. Our writers include scholars who are among the best qualified in the world to show us these directions that were daring in their own time and are still pioneering in ours.

Collections of essays like this one inevitably accrue debts. We thank Pollinger Limited as representatives of the Estate of Frieda Lawrence Ravagli for permission to quote passages from the Cambridge University Press editions of Lawrence's works and letters. For permission to print a reproduction of Marcel Duchamp's painting *Nude Descending a Staircase, No. 2* (1912) as frontispiece, we thank Arts Rights Society (ARS), New York/ ADAGP, Paris/ Succession Marcel Duchamp; Philadelphia Museum of Art, The Louise and Walter Arensberg Collection, 1950; the same image is shown on the book jacket. We wish also to thank our spouses, Mary Ingersoll and David Barnes, who not only generously offered help but bore with us patiently through the many hours of our labors. Finally all of us with any interest in the life and work of D. H. Lawrence owe a continuing debt of gratitude to James C. Cowan, who was more responsible than anyone else for the founding and fostering of Lawrence studies in America.

Notes

1. On "transgressive" theory, see Foucault 1978; on "nomads," see Deleuze and Guattari 1984 23–34, 53–54, 315–423, 492–99.

2. This is the essay previously entitled (not by Lawrence) "Surgery for the Novel—or a Bomb."

3. See also Delany 1978 and Wussow 1998.

4. Writers who have acknowledged Lawrence as a creative inspiration have ranged from Robert Frost to Joyce Carol Oates and Allen Ginsberg, from Aldous Huxley and H.D. to W. H. Auden and Seamus Heaney (see Meyers 1987 and Adelman 2002). His creative influence is well documented throughout the world. In the academic world, too, the Modern Language Association of America, the premier organization of language teachers and scholars, has published a book (namely Sargent and Watson 2001a) about the teaching of Lawrence, written by such teachers; and the MLA, which used to have one Lawrence session during its annual national convention, now has two. Of course, a main sign of Lawrence's academic recognition in our time is the Cambridge Edition.

5. See Cushman 1999, 160–61. The "opportunity for reappraisal" that Cushman and Ingersoll recognized (2003b, 17) is clearly advanced.

6. See Bell 2004, 2006, 2007. For Bakhtinian studies, see also Lodge 1990 and Fleishman 1990.

7. See Worthen 1991, 2005, see also Kinkead-Weekes 1996. Eggert discusses the significance of the Lawrence biographies of recent years—see especially "The Lawrence of the war years" and "Some reflections on the new Lawrence" (Eggert 2001, 163–68, 170–75).

8. None of our relationships "is quite so dead as the man to man relationship," wrote Lawrence in "A Propos of *Lady Chatterley's Lover*" (1993a, 331), for this lapse is "the ugly fact which underlies civilisation" (331, 332). This postwar period roughly corresponds to the period of what has elsewhere been called Lawrence's "turn against women" (see Nixon 1986).

9. See also Pollnitz 2005, 44–71, on another collection, *Pansies*.

10. See also Hyde and Clark 1993–94; Hyde 2001; Hyde 2003, 173–206.

11. This emphasis informs the title *The Married Man* for the English edition of Maddox's biography.

Windows to the Sun

"A New Continent of the Soul": Lawrence's Transcultural/ Transhistorical Meeting with Herman Melville

Earl Ingersoll

HALFWAY THROUGH THE FIRST WORLD WAR, D. H. LAWRENCE came to the decision that England and the rest of the Old World could not be saved. Energized by the promise of regeneration, both personal and cultural, he had offered the "Old Country" his writing, especially *The Rainbow,* in the hope that the possibility of new life could be recuperated by his society, one reader at a time. He became persuaded, however, that the Old World was hopeless—both without hope and beyond hope—because it was unwilling to acknowledge the "window to the sun" his writing had opened but preferred instead to hunker down under the deadening umbrella on whose underside his culture had painted an illusory firmament to replace the life-giving sun the umbrella obscured. Increasingly in that transitional year of 1916, as he conceived of the great novel that would become *Women in Love* and the volume of essays on American writers and their culture that would become *Studies in Classic American Literature,* Lawrence set his sights westward to New Worlds—not merely the Americas but beyond to the Pacific—as "a new continent of the soul" that would demonstrate yet another "window to the sun," or "thought-adventure," of his later life and art.

Among those American writers in whom Lawrence's energies became invested, including James Fenimore Cooper, Richard Henry Dana, Nathaniel Hawthorne, and Walt Whitman, Herman Melville was arguably the most important to

Lawrence the thought-adventurer. To the Lawrence who had already established his commitment to "thought-adventures," Melville was especially attractive as a crosser of boundaries, or frontiers. As Lawrence would later note in *Studies in Classic American Literature,* Melville was a variety of "thought-adventurer" by sailing into the South Pacific, by resisting the Old Country bias of identifying it as the "New World," by seeing the South Pacific instead as an Old World, whose peoples were more ancient than the Europeans. Melville would also offer the paradigm of a New World of the novel, stretching the limits (most notably in *Moby-Dick*) of what the novel could be made to do and perhaps most pertinent to Lawrence's concerns halfway through the "Great War," Melville, like other American writers such as Cooper and Dana, was pointing the way toward the potential for what Lawrence was beginning to call *Blutbrüderschaft,* but in the case of these American writers, a blood brotherhood between men of differing races and ethnicities.

Herman Melville came into Lawrence's life quite dramatically at a critical stage of his development. In 1915 the promising career initiated with the success of *Sons and Lovers* plummeted with the banning of *The Rainbow.* This censorship was particularly damaging because *The Rainbow* was the first major expression of Lawrence's mature style, and his disappointment was certainly exacerbated by this novel's having been freighted with high hopes and extravagant expectations. In his own mind Lawrence had created a sacred text—his "Bible," as George Ford called it in *Double Measure* a generation ago. Properly received, *The Rainbow* would allow his contemporaries, especially women, to shake off the integuments of a dead past and welcome the call to adventure in the Unknown, represented for its heroine Ursula by the promise of metamorphosis in the novel's closing paragraphs. Lawrence resisted the efforts to expurgate his "Bible" and generally ignored the novel's power to offend the British public by its depiction of his heroine's lesbian affair with her teacher as well as her psychic demolition of a British soldier with whom she makes more passionate love than had been described anywhere else in mainstream fiction. He pushed on for the publication of a text whose banning should have come as no surprise to anyone. Clearly, as Mark Kinkead-Weekes indicates in his biography, Lawrence appears to have had little understanding of the monolithic opposition to this novel. The biographer notes, for example, that Catherine Carswell lost her job after merely writing a positive review of *The Rainbow*. Had it been published before the war, this novel might have just as surely been banned, but probably with considerably less of the rancor and opprobrium heaped upon its author's head by those who saw it as not just an immoral novel but as something close to an act of cultural treason in its departures from traditional values.

Disgusted by the avalanche of recriminations resulting from his efforts to offer the British a Pisgah view of the promised land, Lawrence might understandably have just turned his back on his traduced novel as well as on his hopeless nation. He did not, however. Instead, he missed the opportunity to sail to the New World, specifically Florida—near Jacksonville or perhaps Ft. Myers. (Such a transplantation of a nascent Rananim to Jacksonville seems as much of a stretch of the imagination as the plan of Coleridge and his friends to establish their pantisocracy on the banks of the Susquehanna a century earlier.) How much the notion of moving to Florida was a practical option and how much it was Lawrence's daydream of escape from England is certainly a moot question. Despite, as Paul Delany reminds us, the unwillingness of the lending libraries to shelve his banned novel, Lawrence naively believed that *The Rainbow* might yet be "saved." He took heart from the news that the husband of his friend Ottoline ("Ott") Morrell would use his position as an MP to lodge a formal question of the Home Office concerning the banning of the novel and even raise the issue on the floor of Parliament. "Bloomsbury," in the form of Virginia Woolf's brother-in-law Clive Bell and others, seemed willing to speak out against the censorship of *The Rainbow*, although Lawrence was perhaps less confident of their efforts, following his earlier homophobic panic in reacting so strongly against the reality of sodomy among the "Bloomsberries."[1] But Lawrence continued to be optimistic about the eventual publication of *The Rainbow*, perhaps through private subscription, as he would one day publish *Lady Chatterley's Lover*. By the time it had become clear that all these efforts to rescue his fragile and vulnerable *Rainbow* were in vain, it was also clear that he had waited too long to make his escape from England. While it still might have been possible to get permission to go abroad—as Murry had, in order to accompany Katherine Mansfield to the South of France—he had passed up the opportunity to be certified unfit to serve in the military, perhaps from anxiety about the physical examination that such certification would have entailed. His biographer Brenda Maddox reminds us that he generally feared the medical profession, perhaps even the possibility of their certifying his incipient tuberculosis; at the same time, she indicates, with no discernible evidence, that he may have feared the possibility of gang rape among his fellow examinees. Interestingly, when he was eventually examined he was struck by the "camaraderie"—a borrowing from Walt Whitman, as Kinkead-Weekes suggests—although he was appalled that this comradeship was the product of a senseless war machine. Soon it became apparent that the conduct of the Great War was taking a decisive turn as the embattled nation accepted the inevitability of conscription, making it easier for the authorities to refuse Lawrence's application for permission to leave the country and later to persist in harassing him by subjecting his frail, nude body to humiliating "probings" of one kind or another.

Accordingly, Lawrence and Frieda headed "west," not to the New World but to Cornwall, a land he imaginatively constructed as about as close to the Americas as he could get in Great Britain *and* a land that was definitely *not* England. He had spent the holidays with his sister's family in the Midlands and rediscovered the life of the miners, to whom he responded tellingly: "God, how my boyhood comes back—so violent, so dark, the mind always dark and without understanding, the senses violently active. . . . These men, whom I love so much . . . still so living, so vulnerable, so darkly passionate. I love them like brothers . . ." (D. H. Lawrence 1981a, 489). The novelist J. D. Beresford generously offered the use of his house in Cornwall, and the Lawrences moved to Porthcothan with high hopes of starting afresh. January of 1916, however, found Lawrence desperately ill with the chronic respiratory ailment that would eventually be diagnosed as tuberculosis. Perhaps even more importantly, Lawrence was sick in spirit—Paul Delany speaks of a "nervous collapse" (Delany 1978, 191)—as is evident in his writing to Murry:

> Oh, my God, the horrible hopelessness of life! We've got to face it out. I feel now pushed to the brink of existence, and there remains only to fall off into oblivion, or to give in, and accept the ruck: or some way out, as yet undiscovered. I feel absolutely run to earth, like a fox they have chased till it can't go any further, and doesn't know what to do. I don't know what to do nor how to go on: like a man pushing an empty barrow up an endless slope. What good is it all. There is nothing but betrayal and denial, nothing at all: no trust, no faith, no hope from anybody, only betrayal and denial. (D. H. Lawrence 1981a, 500)

Frieda may have been joking when she reported, as Kinkead-Weekes notes, that she had "to hang on to L. on the rocks or he would be blown away like a little bit of foam," and yet she is also speaking to Lawrence's own sense of vulnerability in his rocky perch.

Later the next month, the Lawrences walked through the snow from Porthcothan to Zennor, where they were to settle for a year and a half, and more importantly where he was to write his masterpiece, *Women in Love.* Upon his return to Porthcothan, he wrote to Ott Morrell: "When we came over the shoulder of the wild hill, above the sea, to Zennor, I felt we were coming into the Promised Land. I know there will be a new heaven and a new earth take place now: we have triumphed. I felt like Columbus who can see a shadowy America before him: only this isn't merely territory, it is a new continent of the soul. We will be happy yet, doing a new constructive work, sailing into a new epoch" (D. H. Lawrence 1981a, 556). How may we explain this metamorphosis from paranoia and depression to an almost manic elation?

Certainly Lawrence was looking forward to the advent of Murry and Mansfield, with *both* of whom he was anticipating the establishment of a *Blutbrüderschaft* and the founding of his Rananim in Cornwall, if not Florida. Given that Murry had been about as hostile to *The Rainbow* as its most rabid detractors (such as Robert Lynd and J. C. Squire) had, it seems unlikely that Murry at least could have boosted

Lawrence's spirits to wax so eloquent as he did in the letter to Ott Morrell. Indeed, Lawrence's rapturous assertion of spiritual recuperation suggests the kind of "coming through" he experienced in the first months in the Tyrol with Frieda. A fuller explanation of his high hopefulness, I would argue, was the beginning of his acquaintance with Herman Melville.

That winter, as he was recuperating from both his physical ailments and his spiritual malaise, he had discovered Melville's greatest novel, *Moby-Dick*.[2] On February 7, 1916, he wrote Ott: "I am reading *Moby Dick*," adding, "It is a very odd, interesting book" and "I wish I were going on a long voyage, far into the Pacific" (1981a, 528). Lawrence wrote to others about his reading of Melville: to the Bloomsbury psychoanalyst Barbara Low he would write, "I loved Melville's *Moby Dick*"; and to the "Bloomsberry" friend he shared with Virginia Woolf, S. S. Koteliansky, he would pronounce the novel "a *real* masterpiece" (614, 615). It might be argued that as he moved to his rocky aerie at Higher Tregerthen he was beginning an imaginative journey to the America of Herman Melville and other American writers. Crossing the Atlantic frontier between the Old World and the New, he was initiating a figurative *Blutbrüderschaft* with Melville, who died in 1891, barely six years after Lawrence's birth. The openness of his letters to Ott Morrell and others associated with Bloomsbury may well be an index that Lawrence could trust his feelings of exuberance, stemming from his new acquaintance with Melville through novels such as *Moby-Dick*. It was in that novel in particular that Lawrence was to find a window to the sun in experiencing and representing the man-to-man relationship.

Melville quickly became extremely important to Lawrence as his forerunner in such "thought-adventures." Essentially imprisoned in wartime England, Lawrence was tremendously attracted to Melville the voyager, to his life as well as to his identity as a man in sailing westward to the South Pacific. In the 1919 Intermediate Version of *Studies in Classic American Literature*, he would link Melville to "those Vikings, inhuman, like sea-birds, creatures of the watery mystery, who sailed from their settlements in Greenland down past Labrador to Nova Scotia, and even to Florida. They were Northmen, ocean-born, seeking the sun" (2003, 334). Furthermore, Melville the voyager is an explorer of an "old, old world," whose "dark-eyed" inhabitants are the "children" of fire and earth. His voyages to the South Seas mark him as a frontiersman, sailing into the Pacific, "the great, original ocean" whose "mysteries are grander, profounder, *older* than those of the Atlantic" (335). For Lawrence, his American forerunner modeled the way to set out on "the great return" (335), for, as Lawrence writes: "The Pacific Ocean must have been the vast cradle of the civilisation of that geologically-incomprehensible world and what is now Europe must have been the hinterland" (335–36). Increasingly the trope of South Pacific exploration came to represent for Lawrence the opening of a window to the sun, opening to the bright prospects of blood brotherhood between individuals of differing races and ethnicities. In this context it should be no surprise that Lawrence was drawn to the microcosm of new and old worlds represented by Melville's *Pequod,* and particularly by the relationship between the narrator Ishmael, clearly an author surrogate, and that noble prince of the South Sea Islands, Queequeg. Lawrence writes that the "two swear 'marriage' in the language of the savages. For Queequeg has opened again the flood-gates of love and human connection in Ishmael" (348). And to take these issues of "thought-adventures" another step, as he was writing his own greatest novel—*Women in Love*—Lawrence probably could intuit his forerunner's state of being as Melville crossed those boundaries of approved gender identifications in the all-male community of the South Pacific whaling ship and explored at least in imagination those territories of experience between men traditionally hedged round with taboos at "home."

Lawrence's intuiting of Melville's mind-set ranged into other areas he came to share with his literary "brother" while he was reconstructing his intentions in writing *Women in Love.* With no external knowledge of Melville's circumstances or state of mind in writing *Moby-Dick,* Lawrence, for example, uncannily "understood" his brother's disdain for the marketplace in which his writing would have to sell in order to support himself. Similarly, Lawrence seems to have grasped Melville's impulse to write a novel beyond the bounds of conventional fiction, a novel for which he surely knew it would be difficult to find a publisher, even if he *had* developed a market as a writer of Tales of the South Pacific. Lawrence reports his own progress in writing *Women in Love* to Ott: "What I write now I write for the gods. I am useless to this mankind, and this mankind is useless to me" (1981a, 580). To Lady Cynthia Asquith he writes: "I can't write stories to make money, because I don't want to. Curse the idiotic editors and the more idiotic people who read: shall I pander to their maudlin taste. They bore me" (587). Clearly Melville's novel was encoded for Lawrence as the message of a literary giant who had grown restless with the Lilliputian restraints of the publishing world. Indeed, there is more than a touch of Freud's *unheimlich* in Melville's writing similar sentiments, speaking of two books he wrote before he took up the risky business of *Moby-Dick* as "two jobs, which I have done for money—being forced to it, as other men are to sawing wood" (Horth *Correspondence* 138). In a letter of June 1851, Melville summed up his situation in terms that Lawrence himself would have understood, if the Melville letters had been published during Lawrence's lifetime: "Dollars damn me. . . . What I feel most moved to write, that is banned,—it will not pay. Yet, altogether, write the *other* way I cannot" (Melville 1960, 128). Writing of *Women in Love* to Barbara Low, Lawrence would indicate that he had started to write "the second half of *The Rainbow*. But already it is beyond all hope of ever being published, because of all the things it says." He rails against "putrescent mankind," before returning to his commitment to this nascent *Women in Love* with a telling allusion to yet another artist from a different century and culture whose same-sex inclinations he probably intuited: "But a work of art is an act of faith, as Michael Angelo says, and one goes on writing to the unseen witnesses" (D. H. Lawrence 1981a, 602).

In these ways Herman Melville, especially the Melville of *Moby-Dick*, gave Lawrence permission to write *Women in Love*. As he sat down at Higher Tregerthen to write the novel he had originally planned to write in 1913, before both the Great War and *The Rainbow* intervened, Lawrence could not have "known" that his circumstances replicated those of Melville as he began *Moby-Dick*. Melville was thirty-one, as

Lawrence would be later in the big year of his writing *Women in Love*. Each had married three years earlier, based in part on the prospects of being able to support himself through writing—prospects brightened by early critical and popular success in writing novels. Both marriages had begun to disclose strains and fissures in their earlier connubial harmony, perhaps resulting from the Family Romance of their boyhoods. At the risk of appearing Freudian, it is worth noting that both writers had strong mothers and weak fathers: Melville's father failed in business and died when Herman was twelve, and as is well known, Arthur Lawrence was hardly a success in the eyes of Lawrence and his mother. More to the point, like Lawrence, Melville had a failed novel, his *Mardi* having dimmed the brightness of the popular and critical success of his first two novels, *Typee* and *Omoo*. With a characteristically Lawrentian dispatch, Melville had written two more novels, *Redburn* and *White-Jacket*, over seven hundred pages in a mere five weeks! Both of these novels enjoyed some moderate success, but it only persuaded Melville that he had little hope of recuperating the promise of the first two tales of Tales of the South Pacific, except by writing precisely what he no longer *wanted* to write.

Lawrence, we hardly need to remind ourselves, had achieved a genuine critical and popular success in 1913 with the publication of *Sons and Lovers*. That success provided him an entrée to the inner circles of London's cultural life. Soon he was on friendly terms with Lady Cynthia Asquith, the prime minister's daughter-in-law, and Lady Ottoline Morrell, arguably among the most powerful figures in earlier twentieth-century English cultural life. Ott, for example, offered her good friend Virginia Woolf the opportunity to meet Lawrence by inviting him and Frieda to Garsington when the Woolfs would be present, but Virginia demurred. To Woolf, Lawrence was a competitor in the novel, but even more important, Lawrence's origins were working class. Lawrence did enjoy a brief but strained friendship with another prominent member of Bloomsbury, E. M. Forster,[3] who may have been attracted to Lawrence in large part *because of* the latter's working-class origins. Lawrence also became the friend of Ott's lover, Lord Bertrand Russell, a member of the culturally elite Cambridge world that included Forster, Lytton Strachey, and other "Apostles."

Both Melville and Lawrence had witnessed the narrowing of their prospects when a novel for each failed in part because each writer was seeking a new departure in his writing. And because of the strains in their early married lives, each had begun to return to the possibility of recuperating earlier male friendships, but now in the context of something very like what Lawrence would conceptualize as "blood brotherhood." It is unlikely that Lawrence could have "known" of Melville's tragic friendship with Nathaniel Hawthorne before he completed *Women in Love;* however, Lawrence probably decoded the evidence of such a friendship through the representations of the powerful relationships between the men of *Moby-Dick*. Although we cannot allow the story of Melville and Hawthorne to distract us from the more important gender-bonding of Lawrence with Melville, that story is too instructive not to be related.

In July 1850 Melville moved his family to Pittsfield, Massachusetts. He had begun the composition of *Moby-Dick* two months earlier, and although he indicated to Richard Henry Dana that he was "half way in the work" his biographer Charles Haberstroh writes that whatever he had drafted was "still in its first, most unphilosophical stage of composition" (1980, 94). Later that summer, Melville wrote a review of *Mosses from an Old Manse* by Nathaniel Hawthorne, some fifteen years his senior. Another biographer, Edwin Haviland Miller, indicates that the piece Melville published on *Mosses* was less a review than a "love letter, a confession" (1975, 36). It marked the beginning of a brief and painful friendship with Hawthorne that was little short of idolatry on Melville's part. When Hawthorne responded very favorably to *Moby-Dick,* Melville wrote his friend an unspecific yet long and passionate letter of elation. This is the letter from which Melville's assertion, "I have written a wicked book, and feel as spotless as the lamb," has been frequently cited. More important, Melville's letter is also a clear gesture of deep affection for his brother-in-letters. He notes how important it was to him that Hawthorne "understood the book." Melville writes that he "felt pantheistic then—

your heart beat in my ribs and mine in yours, and both in God's." Moving the trope of fraternity one step further, Melville writes of this experience of "understanding" between the two writers: "I feel that the Godhead is broken up like bread at the Supper, and we are the pieces. Hence this infinite *fraternity* of feeling" (Melville 1960, 142; my emphasis). It may well have been, as his biographer speculates, that his reading of *Mosses* and his friendship with Hawthorne impelled Melville to become his "'own soul's emperor' regardless of what the ordinary literary public might think. . . . This time [in *Moby-Dick*] he seemed to feel he could create a piece of egotism that was so comprehensive that it might finally transcend any guilt, hostility, or insecurity he might feel about undertaking it" (Haberstroh 1980, 92). Clearly, for Melville the text he had written as *Moby-Dick* was a coded letter of "fraternity," or blood brotherhood, and he assumed that his friend "got the message." Apparently Melville grew confident enough to express his affection more directly; in any case, the two took a walk in the woods. What was said during that encounter was never recorded. Hawthorne, it has been speculated, was aghast at Melville's declarations. In any case, following the encounter, Melville and Hawthorne went their separate ways, and if there was further communication between the two writers, it has not survived. The paths of the writers crossed again only once, some five years after Hawthorne moved his family from the area in 1851; it was clear that the "ironical intimacy" of which Melville's biographer Raymond Weaver speaks (1961, 306) had clearly come to an end.

By the time he was working on the section on Melville in the Final Version of *Studies in Classic American Literature*, Lawrence was familiar with Weaver's groundbreaking biography of Melville. Weaver masterfully understates the impact of Melville's failed intimacy with Hawthorne. In his letter to Hawthorne, Melville indicates his awareness that he has reached the limit of his artistic powers. Melville was all of thirty-two years old. Weaver includes Melville's awareness of this doom at the end of a brief paragraph, beginning: "With the departure of Hawthorne from Lenox, Melville was left without companionship and without illusions" (1961, 340). Weaver ends this chapter—essentially the last, because the next is a kind of epilogue—with the dramatic assertions of the aging Melville: "[I]n his old age he was again to turn to prose: but before Melville was half through his mortal life his signal literary achievement was done. The rest, if not silence, was whisper" (348). It seems highly unlikely that Lawrence would have missed the biographer's intimation that it was Melville's failure to draw Hawthorne into a fraternal intimacy that condemned him to a life sentence of isolation and failed artistic accomplishment. As has been often observed, Melville's death was scarcely noted by the newspapers.

What matters here is the powerful example of "thought-adventure" *Moby-Dick* must have provided Lawrence, as he read that novel early in 1916, an ocean away from Pittsfield, Massachusetts, where Melville lived on into an early old age, and a continent as well as another ocean away from the South Seas where much of Melville's great novel is set. For the Lawrence who felt run to ground like a fox in Cornwall, Ishmael must have been an attractive figure—taking his name from the exiled son of Abraham and his servant Hagar, cast out by the jealous Sarah, whose long-awaited son Isaac would one day come within a hairbreadth of being sacrificed on the altar of his father's testament of faith. Melville's Ishmael seems his own midwife as he is his own baptizer, in the famous opening line, "Call me Ishmael." Scarcely is he born, when he becomes the "brother" and perhaps "wife" of the formidable Polynesian prince Queequeg, in whose bed he waits like a new bride for the husband she has yet to meet. Spying upon his prospective bed-partner as he undresses and then expressing puzzlement at the text of the harpooner's tattooed body, Ishmael understandably cries out when Queequeg joins him in bed, grasping a tomahawk between his teeth. Ishmael's cries rouse the landlord, Peter Coffin, who had earlier told him this was the very bed in which the Coffins spent *their* wedding night. Despite his early fright, Ishmael eventually admits his deep contentment, saying, "[I] never slept better in my life," and adding: "Upon waking next morning about daylight, I found Queequeg's arm thrown over me in the most loving and affectionate manner. You had almost thought I had been his wife" (1957, 25).

The marriage trope is further developed and then abandoned in the famous scene in which Ishmael joins his new "brother" in a ritual smoking session, followed by his worship of Queequeg's pagan idol. Ishmael's description betrays a Huck Finn-ish suggestion of boyish jocularity to mask any discomfort with the implications of this "bedroom" scene. Ishmael indicates that Queequeg "seemed to take to me quite as naturally and unbiddenly as I to him; and when our smoke was over, he pressed his forehead to mine, clasped me round the waist, and said that henceforth we were married; meaning, in his country's phrase, that we were bosom friends; he would gladly die for me, if need should be" (51). Although there is no evidence that Lawrence ever read that other American "boy's book," *Huckleberry Finn*,[4] the imprint of New World confidence-games is clear here in Melville's passing off as boyhood innocence what is clearly something more forbidden in the "adult" world. Lawrence could scarcely have missed how Melville was his forerunner in risking the dangerous waters of those "thought-adventures" involving brotherhood of men, here in a context of the "innocent" American baffled by the strange mores of this South Sea "Other." When Queequeg and Ishmael end up in bed again for something the narrative tropes as a matrimonial chat, Ishmael indicates: "Man and wife, they say, there open the very bottom of their souls to each other; and some old couples often lie and chat over old times till nearly morning. Thus, then, in our hearts' honeymoon, lay I and Queequeg—a cosy, loving pair" (52). As Leslie Fiedler argued a half-century ago, such "loving pairs" were possible in the boys' books of nineteenth-century American classics, from Cooper through Twain, in large part only when the "marriage" includes the further adventure of crossing the culturally imposed boundaries of race as well as challenging the sanctions against strong male friendships.

Another scene should suffice to point up what must have drawn Lawrence to the all-male company of the *Pequod*. One can only imagine what he must have thought about the barely covert homoerotic scene in which the members of the crew sit around a tub squeezing lumps of "sperm," or spermaceti, often squeezing one another's hands by mistake. Ishmael comments: "Such an abounding, affectionate, friendly, loving feeling did this avocation beget; that I was continually squeezing their hands, and looking up into their eyes sentimentally [wanting to bid them:] Come; let us squeeze hands all around; nay, let us squeeze ourselves into each other; let us squeeze ourselves universally into the very milk and sperm of kindness" (413). It must have seemed incredible to Lawrence, and others, that Melville could have managed to get this novel published with this talk of men sitting around squeezing "sperm," even if the term *was* short for "spermaceti," a secretion of sperm whales. And Lawrence did not in fact miss the chapter in which the mincer of whale blubber dons the skin of a whale's penis as though it were some priestly vestment. Indeed, in the Final Version of *Studies in Classic American Literature,* Lawrence speaks of this brief chapter, "The Cassock," as "surely the oddest piece of phallicism in all the world's literature" (2003, 142).

With the scene of Queequeg's preparation for death, Ishmael's focus in *Moby-Dick* shifts from his "brother" to the father figure Ahab. Although Queequeg's readying himself for death is somewhat premature, it is appropriate, because for all intents and purposes he is from this point dead for Ishmael—for both the Ishmael who is the story's narrator as well as its viewpoint character. Ishmael's role is subsumed by the first mate, Starbuck, who becomes locked in a loving conflict with Ahab, as Starbuck uses his powers as an avatar of the Handsome Sailor to attempt to dissuade Ahab from his hellish vengeance upon the White Whale. Whether it is the "marriage" of Ishmael and Queequeg or the strong bonding of Starbuck with Ahab, *Moby-Dick* must have astounded Lawrence with its apparent flaunting of taboos against man-to-man relationships. If Lacan was correct in his enigmatic axiom that the "letter always finds its destination," perhaps by *constructing* its addressee, there is little doubt but that *Moby-Dick* was a special delivery to Lawrence.

As I have indicated elsewhere,[5] echoes of *Moby-Dick* abound in *Women in Love,* especially in the development of Gerald Crich. Like Ahab, he is a captain (or at least a "captain of industry"), intent upon imposing his will on his world. That "will to power" scarcely needs rehearsing: it is evident in his brutal domination of animals (his horse in the famous scene at the railroad crossing or his sister's rabbit,

Bismarck, both associated with acts of cruelty performed for Gudrun's benefit), as well as in his virtual rape of Gudrun, and perhaps most tellingly in his expectation that his miners, like his coal, should be utterly in his control. The extensive portrayal of Gerald's capacity to command servile obedience among his workers, who voluntarily submit their wills to him as a "god of the machine," owes a great deal to Melville's drawing of the monomaniacal Ahab. Like his counterpart, too, Gerald is a wounded despot, a soul tormented from childhood by the guilt of accidentally shooting his brother and the pain of witnessing his father's failure of "manhood" in dealing with the miners' strike. In the powerful scene of his unsuccessful attempt to rescue his sister Di, the trope of wounding is more physical, for Gerald's efforts are partially hampered by a hand injured when it was caught in the machinery of the mines. And finally, of all the means the novel might have found to represent Gerald's eventual submission to death, the choice of his movement out into an immense, hostile, white wasteland of snow and ice is surely no coincidence, and may suggest Ahab's essentially solitary quest across perilous seas.

Perhaps an even less disputable site of Lawrence's relationship with Melville is provided by *Studies in Classic American Literature*. That collection of essays provides, among other things, a record of Lawrence's increasing estrangement from Melville. In that regard, Melville shares the dubious "privilege" with the rest of the American writers who are eventually treated with increasing bitterness and disdain. It is worth noting that the notion of writing these essays dates from 1917 as Lawrence's attention was directed westward toward the Americas for their promise of escape from the "dead letter" England had become for him.[6] By the time *Studies in Classic American Literature* appeared in 1923, Lawrence had transplanted himself to the "New World" and had seen enough of American culture for the blush to be off the rose of his earlier expectations that its "World" was indeed "New." His disillusionment points him to its roots in the very values he once found as a younger man in those "classic American" writers.[7]

The recent publication of the Cambridge University Press edition of *Studies in Classic American Literature* helps to clarify Lawrence's altered but still essentially steadfast loyalty to his literary brother, Herman Melville. This new edition allows readers for the first time to easily trace the changes from one version to another as a testimony to Lawrence's growing awareness that in many ways America was not the promised land he had dreamed of. Overall, we notice a very strong distinction between the First Version (1918–19) and Intermediate Version (1919), on the one hand, and the Final Version (1923), on the other. Much had taken place in Lawrence's life, and once he had moved to New Mexico he seemed to be self-consciously reconstructing himself as an "American writer," not only because England was a husk he had shed as Ursula does at the end of *The Rainbow,* when she finds herself bereft of her past—childhood, family, friends, lovers. And six years (1917–23) can be a long time in anyone's life, especially the life of a writer like Lawrence who had invested himself so fully in the concept of continual psychic renewal, aware as he was of the absolute need either to change or to risk being suffocated by the past. Before focusing on the changes in the Melville chapter(s), we might do well to explore at least some of the transformations of Lawrence's responses to the earlier versions of the essays in *Studies in Classic American Literature* and to note actually how *well* Melville fares in the context of the plunging approval ratings of these American authors in Lawrence's estimation as he lost faith in American culture.

A case in point is Hawthorne's most highly esteemed novel, *The Scarlet Letter.* In the First Version, Lawrence's commentary on this novel was part of the single essay, "Nathaniel Hawthorne," a fairly conventional piece of literary criticism, appropriate to British advanced secondary school or perhaps beginning university students with a desire to learn about nineteenth-century American (male) authors. For Lawrence *The Scarlet Letter* is a variation on the legend of the Fall, with Hester Prynne cast as the seductress of the hapless Arthur Dimmesdale, a kind of American Adam, self-deluded perhaps in believing the New World offered the possibility of recuperating original innocence, or at least a reasonable facsimile thereof. Lawrence is generous with his praise: "Hawthorne is a philosopher as well as an artist," "a master of symbology," "a master of serpent subtility," "a sorcerer, a real seer of darkness." Lawrence generalizes that *The Scarlet Letter* is "one of the wonder-books of the world"—even in the Intermediate Version he is still calling it a "profound and wonderful book, one of the eternal revelations"—but he does have his doubts, seeing it as "somewhat detestable, because of its duplicity" and faulting Hawthorne for his "pious preaching . . . whilst underneath is the lurid lust in sin, the gloating in the overthrow of that which is so praised." Some of the negative reaction toward Hawthorne, and especially *The Scarlet Letter,* might be understood in the context of the Lawrence who was returning to an earlier draft and measuring the change between the states of mind of the reviser and the earlier drafter of the text, and perhaps being impelled to shed an earlier conventionality and too-easy acceptance of the faults ignored in responding to authors not approached with sufficient critical acumen.

Even if we grant the effects of a writer returning several years later to an earlier draft, the Final Version of "Nathaniel Hawthorne"—now two essays—is blisteringly caustic, especially toward *The Scarlet Letter.* Here, as in the other essays in the Final Version, the voice of "Lawrence" seems a self-consciously constructed persona, similar to the narrators in *Mr. Noon* and *Fantasia of the Unconscious.* This is a persona with a propensity for polemics and bent on provoking—yea, even outraging—the reader through tirades that may be a "working through" or a performing of the author's own sense of anger and disappointment in recognizing that this promised land he longed for while languishing in England is actually no more than a whited sepulcher, and that the American soul is rotten to the core. Hawthorne comes in for the same hostile reaction as Fenimore Cooper, whose novel *The Deerslayer* Lawrence once loved but now casts aside as the "miserable story of the collapse of the white psyche" (2003, 65), or as Edgar Allan Poe, who is pilloried for the "inevitable falseness, duplicity of art, American art in particular" (80).

This persona of "Lawrence" is a disillusioned "innocent abroad," who can finally see the full dimensions of the duplicity in *The Scarlet Letter.* As American writers were once the embodiments of the New World of hope for escape from a dead England, Hawthorne's novel now reeks to him of "duplicity." The persona rants: "Always the same. The deliberate consciousness of Americans so fair and smooth-spoken, and the under-consciousness so devilish. *Destroy! destroy! destroy!* hums the under-consciousness. *Love and produce! Love and produce!* cackles the upper consciousness" (2003, 81). *The Scarlet Letter* becomes for this "Lawrence" an allegory of sin's entry into the world, but not in the form of sexual desire per se so much as the *knowledge* of its sinfulness, and even more the *pleasure* inherent in that knowledge, a kind of perverse epistemophilia, if you will.

Were this not enough, this "Lawrence" pushes *The Scarlet Letter* to perform his embarrassingly rabid misogynist sentiments as well. This is clearly the "Lawrence" Linda Ruth Williams has termed "feminism's *bête noire,* the monster it loves to hate" (1993, 16). The persona preaches: "Unless a man believes in himself and his gods *genuinely;* unless he fiercely obeys his own Holy Ghost; his woman will destroy him" (D. H. Lawrence 2003, 89). The specter of feminism further prompts him to divulge his nightmare that "the colossal evil of the united spirit of Woman . . . in the last war, was something frightening. As every *man* knows" (89). It leads him to look forward to the future of "the dark erection of the ithyphallic images once more, and the newly submissive women" (91). This is clearly a "Lawrence" unsettled by his postwar experiences with what he saw as the menace of feminism and his disappointment with America, both of which surface here in the context of his finalizing his discussion of the very same writers to whom he had once looked as offering the promise of "thought-adventures" for his life and art.

That disappointment is even more blatant in the Final Version of the essay in *Studies in Classic American Literature* devoted to Walt Whitman. Of these nineteenth-century writers Lawrence discusses, none was such an early and formidable literary "brother" as Whitman, whose poetry is generally acknowledged to have offered the young Lawrence a license to write himself out of the more formal verse patterns of the nineteenth century. For Lawrence, Whitman was probably of equal importance as a forerunner in representing taboo relationships between men within the coded term "camaraderie" in poems such as "Calamus" and "The Bathers," the same "camaraderie" Lawrence himself had struggled to encode as the love of Jonathan and David. And it was perhaps for these very reasons that Lawrence came to the writing of the Whitman essay somewhat later than the others, specifically in the 1919 Intermediate Version.

Thus, it is crucially important to our understanding of Lawrence's continuing respect and affection for Melville that we do not fail to note the vehemence with which Lawrence seems to be dismissing Whitman in the Final Version. In the Intermediate Version, Lawrence was at least ambivalent, beginning with respectful sentiments such as the view that Whitman was "the last and greatest of the Americans," adding that "In Whitman lies the greatest of all modern truths." He goes on to say, however, that Whitman was "the greatest of modern humbugs" (2003, 358). Whitman embraces "infinitude, Allness, the glory of infinite Light" (359), but because he does so *consciously* Whitman falls prey to the modern disease of allowing mind-consciousness to dominate and to suppress other modes of knowing and thereby to destroy blood-consciousness. In the Final Version, even Whitman seems to have turned "monstrous," like Hawthorne's Dimmesdale and Melville's Ahab. The soul in America sank with the crew of the *Pequod,* and only the body survives like a hot-air machine, going "CHUFF! CHUFF! CHUFF!" as Whitman mechanically repeats his familiar themes. The poet is denigrated through a parody of his own language:

> DEMOCRACY. EN MASSE. ONE IDENTITY.
> The universe, in short, adds up to ONE.
> ONE.
> 1.
> Which is Walt.
>
> (151)

Lawrence may assert, "Whitman, the great poet, has meant so much to me. Whitman, the one man breaking a way ahead" (155), making Whitman a kind of literary frontiersman. The tense of the verb "has meant," however, suggests at best ambivalence toward Whitman and at worst the loss of any meaning Whitman had for him. Like Hawthorne, Whitman has betrayed Lawrence's dream of America.

These "detours" into issues in the essays on Hawthorne and Whitman in *Studies in Classic American Literature* may seem of questionable value to the case for the importance of Melville as a "forerunner" to Lawrence, but they present crucial contrasts to the way the Final Version treats earlier avatars of the Melville essay(s). This is not to say that Melville entirely escapes the increased hostility toward *all* the authors in *Studies in Classic American Literature,* but only that more of Lawrence's affectionate regard for his literary "brother" persists than might be expected from this context of rabid reaction against these other fallen companions in letters.[8] Thus, Hawthorne may earn Lawrence's acrid criticism for his life-denying idealism and commitment to abstractions, and even old Walt becomes laughable as a tiresome old windbag. Melville has a better time of it coming through the sea-change of Lawrence's actually experiencing the New World.

First, it is important to note that Lawrence was still actively interested in Melville as the Final Version was being completed. The editors of *Studies in Classic American Literature* write: "His letters during the surrounding weeks were full of references to Melville's South Sea idyll in *Typee,* a preoccupation no doubt intensified by the fantasy he had developed with fellow writer Compton Mackenzie of chartering a boat for a cruise through southern waters" (Greenspan, Vasey, and Worthen 2003, xliv). The editors add: "The Lawrences arrived in America in early September 1922 after crossing the Pacific and calling at Raratonga ('very lovely') and Tahiti ('such a lovely sea and land—but the town all spoilt' iv. 284–5), Lawrence doubtless thinking of Melville in the South Seas" (xlix). And Lawrence was tellingly interested in the first biography of Melville. Not coincidentally, the first reference in Lawrence's letters to Weaver's biography appears in a letter to Thomas Seltzer: "Could you send me too that Herman Melville book—*Herman Melville, Poet and Mystic:*—I will go over the *Studies in C [lassical] A [merican] Literature* again:" (1987a, 306). It is worth noting that Lawrence has the full title of Weaver's book, and as a letter two weeks later indicates, he received the biography while he was planning to "go over [the manuscript of *Studies in Classic American Literature*] again." This concurrence of interest in the Weaver biography and a final return to *Studies in Classic American Literature* make it especially difficult to resist speculating that some of the increased disdain for Hawthorne's great novel was generated out of Lawrence's reading of Weaver's restrained rendition of Hawthorne's refusal of Melville's offer of fraternal intimacy.

Because the Final Version of the Melville essay on *Moby-Dick* had not undergone the extensive transmogrification of the earlier Hawthorne or Whitman essays, the changes that do appear are especially important. This version extends Lawrence's discussion of a novel that he still very clearly admires, even though his remarks have taken on the color of his often hostile responses to the other authors in *Studies in Classic American Literature.* To the lengthy passage of his discussion (but mainly quotation) of Ishmael and Queequeg's "first night" together, ending in the Intermediate Version with "Thus, then, lay I and Queequeg—a cosy, loving pair—" the Final Version adds this ironic comment: "You would think this relation with Queequeg meant something to Ishmael. But no. Queequeg is forgotten like yesterday's newspaper. . . . What's a Queequeg? What's a *wife?* The white whale must be hunted down. Queequeg must be just 'KNOWN,' then dropped into oblivion" (2003, 136; my emphasis). Clearly the irony of the Lawrence persona here marks disappointment at Ishmael's rejection of this offer of blood brotherhood, a rejection similar to Gerald Crich's turning away when Birkin reaches out to him in Lawrence's own narrative of a "loving pair." He appears to resist the temptation, however, to blame Melville for the weakness of his apparent viewpoint character, Ishmael, even though Lawrence is prone to read *Moby-Dick* biographically to an extent that might have infuriated *him* if his own readers of *Women in Love* had done likewise. He addresses the prospective reader of *Moby-Dick:* "There you are: you see Melville hugged in bed by a huge tatooed South Sea Islander . . ." (134) and later, as though to confirm that the earlier substitution of Melville for Ishmael was no slip of the pen, he speaks of "the moment's hearts-brother, Queequeg, the tatooed, powerful South Sea harpooneer, whom Melville loves as Dana loves

'Hope' . . ." (135). This biographical reading of the male friendships in Melville, and in Dana, exposes the coding of Lawrence's earlier enthusiasm for "classic American" writers whose fiction in general explores the potentially dangerous territory of intense male bonding, made possible in "frontier" communities, whether in Cooper's early-American upstate New York[9] or the newly discovered South Seas of Dana and Melville.

The mention of Cooper requires a brief digression, because the essays on Fenimore Cooper, as Lawrence chose to call him, offer a theme and variation regarding the man-to-man relationship that seemed to interest Lawrence in nineteenth-century American writers. In the First Version of *Studies in Classic American*, Lawrence notes: "Fenimore Cooper very beautifully gives the myth of the atonement, the communion between the soul of the white man and the soul of the Indian" (209). In Lawrence's reading of the writer of the Leatherstocking Novels, Cooper's "whole soul embraces the dark, aboriginal soul with unceasing, fertile love" (216), as perhaps Ishmael/Melville's soul embraces the soul of his racial other, Queequeg. Unfortunately for Cooper, at least in Lawrence's eyes, there is a *Mrs.* Cooper for the writer of the Leatherstocking Novels to deal with, a woman who is "impatient of her husband's Indian passion" (216), represented in Natty Bumppo and Chingachcook. Lawrence gives her a "tiny speech" in which she criticizes her husband thus: "It was a matter of course that he should dwell on the better traits of the picture rather than on the coarse and more revolting, though more common points. Like [Benjamin] West, he could see the Apollo in the young Mohawk" (216). Cooper might be writing his novels close to the "frontier" in upstate New York in the early nineteenth century, but he could "light out for the territory" only imaginatively to escape the jealous "Mrs. Cooper."

To return to Lawrence's Final Version essay on *Moby-Dick:* if Ishmael is "unfaithful" to Queequeg, as Gerald was to Birkin, the fault lies in the powerful attraction of the Ahab figure for Melville as well as for Ishmael and Starbuck. As we have seen, for Lawrence, the Ishmael/Melville of *Moby-Dick* is not content to affirm the richness of male bonding with a mere Queequeg. Perhaps there is the suggestion here that the culturally constructed "inferiority" of Queequeg as the darker and therefore attractive Other makes possible the open expression of intimacy, but at the same time it denies its permanence, for an Ishmael/Melville cannot entirely throw in his lot with someone who is not of his race. Where Lawrence stands here is difficult to establish. Clearly he is condemning Ishmael's redirecting of his attention from Queequeg to the Ahab whom Lawrence sees as locked into a hellish struggle to destroy blood-consciousness. One wonders how it plays itself out in Birkin's relationship with Gerald Crich, also perhaps fraught with ambivalence. Birkin is attracted to a figure who demonstrates a similar "monomania," the very term Lawrence uses to describe Gerald's behavior. Gerald is obsessed with imposing his own Ahab-like will on matter and men alike, and when it would appear that he succeeds in taking the mining enterprise as far as his technological grasp can manage, he turns to the impossible task of possessing Gudrun, who he must know will never be his, a White Whale of a different species. Where finally is the "betrayal" in *Women in Love?* Is it in Gerald's refusal to accept Birkin's offer of blood brotherhood, or in Birkin's decamping with Ursula to the warm South, leaving Gerald to his own devices in a white wasteland, or perhaps more accurately leaving Gerald to Gudrun's and Loerke's "devices"?

In any case, in this Final Version of *Studies in Classic American Literature* there is more than a hint that Melville, like Ishmael, may have thrown in his lot with Ahab in the mad attempt to destroy the Great White Phallos. Then, as earlier noted, there is Lawrence's new criticism of Ishmael's being unfaithful to his mate Queequeg, once he goes whoring after Ahab's pursuit of the Truth. Increasingly the "Lawrence" of this essay faults Ishmael for catching the contagion of Ahab's monomania. The earlier reading of the White Whale as the phallos is extended to an indictment of the West's obsession with abstraction and the Idea, with the mind-consciousness that now seems bent on not merely suppressing but also destroying the blood-consciousness encompassed in the mighty "symbol" of the phallic Moby Dick.

Unlike the work of, say, Hawthorne and Whitman, which seems to be vitiated for Lawrence by the authors' betrayal of his reverence for them as "thought-adventurers" of hope and promise in the New World, *Moby-Dick* at the end of this Final Version of the essay comes through as still "a very great book," in part because it announces for Lawrence the "Doom of our white day" (146). In its own way, Melville's great novel is very dramatically, as Lawrence said of his *Women in Love*, "so end of the world," or apocalyptic. Birkin seems an heir of that Melvillean vision of the apocalypse when he preaches to Ursula the need to bear—yea, even to anticipate with liberating enthusiasm—the prospect of a world from which humans have been eradicated and the rabbits have inherited the earth. Although Lawrence knew better than to attempt to emulate Melville's catastrophe of the *Pequod*'s destruction—perhaps with the collapse of the mines through Gerald's agency in some yet-to-be-imagined Götterdämmerung—there is ample evidence that the death of Gerald in his white wasteland will not free the miners and their families, along with Gerald's soul-mates, from the living death to which the extinction of blood-consciousness has condemned them all.

One fascinating "portal of discovery" of which the editors of the Cambridge edition of the *Studies in Classic American Literature* offer a reminder (JoEllyn Clarey explored it two decades earlier) is the truncated text of *Moby-Dick* on which Lawrence based his reading of Melville's masterpiece. This is the Everyman edition, which for some incomprehensible reason *omits* the epilogue.[10] We recall that Ishmael begins the Epilogue by citing the report of the single survivor of the calamitous scene of Job's family's annihilation: "And I only am escaped alone to tell thee." Suddenly readers who are reminded of Lawrence's truncated knowledge of *Moby-Dick* are made aware that to Lawrence *all* the members of the *Pequod*'s little world of man were drowned, including Ishmael. No wonder this Lawrence seems fixated on the "Doom" in Melville's world. Can he have escaped the feeling that Melville's despair was so great that he included his own "son," Ishmael, a sacrifice to his vision of lost humanity? Was that misapprehension on Lawrence's part, we cannot help wondering, one root of his continuing admiration for a literary brother who could imaginatively fashion an ending in which even his surrogate narrator perished with the remainder of humanity? Interestingly, Lawrence could not follow that path in *Women in Love,* since obviously Birkin and Ursula survive, even though the silence following the narrative's final words—Birkin's rejoinder to Ursula's assertion that man-to-man love is something he cannot have: "I don't believe that"—may seem an ominous suggestion that Art may have its end here, but Life will propel this conflict into the future.

We return to the salient fact of Lawrence's continuing affection for Melville, clearly marked by his insistence that Seltzer send him a copy of Weaver's biography, whose title he accurately indicated in the letter. We search the letters for some indication of how carefully he read *Herman Melville, Mariner and Mystic* or how he responded to finding in Weaver some of his own admiration for Melville's genius. Even more specifically, we wonder how well Lawrence decoded Weaver's narrative of Melville's risky reaching out to Hawthorne as a blood brother and Hawthorne's apparently frigid response, consigning Melville to "old age" at thirty-two. In any case, the descent into hostility toward Hawthorne and even Whitman in the Final Version highlights Lawrence's continuing admiration and affection for Melville as a literary brother. As a brother across the boundaries of history and culture, Melville licensed Lawrence's "thought-adventures" into the dangerous territory of exploring the potential for new relationships between men and larger possibilities in the novel.

More than any of the other writers explored in *Studies in Classic American Literature,* Melville was central to Lawrence's continuing interest in the series of essays. As Americanists in the later twentieth century often acknowledged, Lawrence was himself a variety of frontiersman in believing in "American literature" as a meaningful subject of study. *Studies in Classic American Literature* was probably a very provocative title for its first readers. As the editors of the work indicate, few readers in 1923, even if they were Americans, would have interpreted the term "classic American literature" as much more than an oxymoron, since "American literature" was not yet a field of study. Interestingly, the editors posit Lawrence's awareness of his role as a pathfinder in establishing American writing as a respectable field of study, although he chose an alternative to that metaphor when he wrote in the foreword to the American *Studies in Classic American Literature* that he saw himself as a "midwife to the unborn homunculus" of American literature, a role he clearly enjoyed, perhaps in part as a certification of his commitment to the New World of professional investment in America.[11]

Perhaps what Lawrence learned in his long "relationship" with Melville was something about the possibilities and the limitations of his relationship with another man. Much as he may have longed for a physically intimate bond with another man, in the end such a relationship may have been possible only at a distance, as though the relationship required the restraining force of distance to survive. And survive it did, for we have only to recall how *many* animal poems Lawrence wrote in his later years, particularly poems such as "Whales Weep Not!" Although he had written works about animals as early as "Rex" and "Adolf" and, of course, the poems of *Birds, Beasts and Flowers,* many of the later poems seem expressions of a continuing affection and admiration for Melville's writing. As Kinkead-Weekes so usefully describes it, Lawrence's aspiration for something beyond male friendship was painfully conflicted.[12] Murry and even Hocking were probably too near at hand, too put off by Lawrence's "dominating" persona, or too timid about the repercussions of "crossing the line" for either of those two friendships to survive. Melville, from another time and another culture, outlasted those of Lawrence's contemporaries who once had the potential to become "brothers." And perhaps having read Weaver's biography, with its sad chronicle of Melville's long existence after the failure of his friendship with Hawthorne and its corollary disintegration of his literary productivity, Lawrence found in this nineteenth-century American blood brother another role: as the pathfinder toward resignation and compromise. For neither Melville nor Lawrence would there be another *Moby-Dick* or *Women in Love*—although there would be a *Billy Budd* and a *Lady Chatterley's Lover,* like those exquisite and tender blossoms on old cherry trees as they near the end of their productivity.

Notes

1. Mary (Mrs. Desmond, later Lady) MacCarthy has been credited with coining the term "the Bloomsberries" in a letter, probably written in 1910 or 1911.

Yet another disappointment of 1915 for Lawrence was his observing David Garnett, a major model for Gerald Crich in *Women in Love*, moving toward one of the leading "Bloomsberries," Duncan Grant. As part of Lady Ottoline Morrell's cultural matchmatching, Lawrence was invited to Garsington in part to meet E. M. Forster, next to whom Ott seated him at dinner. Grant and Garnett were also at the table; they had met some weeks before, and some weeks later would become lovers. What Lawrence (as well as Frieda) would have seen as the tragic loss of "Bunny" Garnett to "Bloomsbury" may well have generated an interest in the construction of Gerald Crich's tragedy.

2. More recent Americanists have restored the hyphen in the American title of Melville's *Moby-Dick*. Lawrence apparently never saw an American edition of that novel.

3. Dixie King argues provocatively, but probably not conclusively, that Forster risked the consequences of disclosing his sexual orientation by sharing the manuscript of what would become his posthumous novel *Maurice*. She mentions this on her way to arguing that the Forster novel influenced Lawrence's conception of *Lady Chatterley's Lover.*

4. In her tremendously helpful catalog of Lawrence's reading, Rose Marie Burwell notes that in his introduction to *Max Havelaar* Lawrence "[i]ndicates knowledge of the misanthropic tone in the writing of Gogol, Mark Twain, and Jean Paul Richter." Twain's "The Mysterious Stranger," however, is perhaps a better candidate for "misanthropic tone" than *Huckleberry Finn*. Perhaps not coincidentally, there is no essay on Twain in *Studies in Classic American Literature*.

5. See Ingersoll 1989.

6. The plural "Americas" seems justified by Lawrence's willingness for a short time to entertain the possibility of following his friend Dr. David Eder, a London psychoanalyst, to the jungles of Brazil as a venue for Rananim.

7. The Cambridge University Press editors write: "With this goal (a final revision of the essays) in mind, Lawrence, who had evidently decided not to take any copy of *Studies* in the pile of trunks and suitcases which he and Frieda had carried halfway around the world, wrote to Seltzer just eleven days after his arrival in Taos to request a copy of the complete set of essays, as well as of Raymond Weaver's recent pioneering biography of Melville" (Greenspan, Vasey, and Worthen 2003, li).

8. Clearly Lawrence still had a large investment in Melville and his writing. As the Cambridge University Press editors write: "Early in December Lawrence finished work on the ninth *Studies* ('Dana') and, setting his sights on Melville, asked Seltzer to bring copies of *Mardi* and *Pierre* with him when he came down for his planned Christmas visit to New Mexico in 1922" (vi. 345) (Greenspan, Vasey, and Worthen 2003, lii).

9. Richard Chase, one of the molders of "American literature" in the mid twentieth century, wrote in 1957: "Opinion about Cooper during the last twenty years, when it has been interesting at all, had to be in one way or another an elaboration or revision of Lawrence" (Chase 1969, 44n).

10. Armin Arnold offers the crucial reminder that Lawrence used the 1907 "Everyman's Library" edition of *Moby-Dick*, one of two based on the original English version of the novel, omitting the epilogue (1958, 29).

11. The Cambridge editors provide an extremely useful context for Lawrence's writing on American literature: "At the time of his writing, the field of American literature was not yet part of the curriculum in most American universities, while the first professorship in American letters had not been established until 1919. Similarly, the founding of the American Literature Group of the Modern Language Association did not take place until 1921, and its journal, *American Literature*, began publication only in 1929. . . . Almost predictably, therefore, the very title of Lawrence's work [namely, *Studies*] was certain to raise eyebrows, as it did . . ." (Greenspan, Vasey, and Worthen 2003, lix–lx).

Clarey claims (but does not document her claim) that Lawrence's "observations on Melville have been proclaimed by some the best in *Studies in Classic American Literature*" (1986, 195). Clarey also stresses how important Lawrence's reading of *Moby-Dick* was in shaping the understanding of that novel. She notes that Anthony Beal writes: "Since his death Lawrence's importance as a critic has been increasingly recognised. Many of his judgments and comments have passed into critical parlance and any discussion of the novel or the relation of literature to morality must heed his views" (Beal 1955, ix–x). She also cites Richard Chase's generalization that "Lawrence's approach to American literature, which may be described variously as historical, cultural, or mythic, has been congenial to those modern critics who have not devoted themselves merely to textual analysis" (Chase 1969, 44n). In addition, she points readers to a 1975 essay by Michael J. Colacurcio in which he asserts: "[T]he time seems right to suggest that the critical response to D. H. Lawrence's *Studies in Classic American Literature* has changed over the last ten years. It may be too academic to say that there is a 'School of Lawrence,' but clearly there are many avowed disciples. And it is probably a melodramatic exaggeration to say that Lawrence's passionate impressionism (disseminated, it may be, by Leslie Fiedler [especially in his 1960 *Love and Death in the American Novel*]) is 'everywhere,' but it is certainly showing up all around. So much so that it may now be time to admit that Lawrence's well known, often maddening, and seldom verifiable series of literary and cultural *aperçus* are now part of the received critical wisdom" (Colacurcio 1975, 488).

12. See Kinkead-Weekes for perhaps the sanest and most sensitive analysis of this vexed issue of Lawrence's sexual orientation. He writes, for example: "In fact our culture is seriously at fault in having no language for the whole spectrum of possibility and satisfaction that lies between the admission of sexual attractiveness between men, and the fulfilment of sexual desire in acts of sodomy and mutual masturbation. The word 'homosexual'—especially if opposed to 'heterosexual' as though these were categorically exclusive—is of confusing span and hence of intolerable crudity" (1996, 381).

Paul Delany provides a biographical reading of the parting of the ways between Somers (the Lawrence figure) and John Thomas, for whom Hocking may have served as a model in *Kangaroo*. Thomas deliberately keeps Somers waiting two hours in St. Ives, barely excusing the lightly disguised gesture of distancing himself from efforts of Somers to draw him into a closer relationship. Somers "quietly" says: "'I shall never come with you again.'" Delany notes the drawing apart of Lawrence and Hocking after the Lawrences left Cornwall: "So the episode ended; and Lawrence, having failed to achieve a homoerotic solution to the painful and exhausting conflicts of his sexual life, would never be so close to a man again" (1978, 315), an assessment strikingly similar to the evaluation of biographers concerning Melville's situation after Hawthorne refused his gesture of blood brotherhood.

"Over Some Frontiers" at Monte Cassino: Lawrence and Maurice Magnus

John Worthen

IN MY RECENT BIOGRAPHY OF LAWRENCE, *D. H. LAWRENCE: THE Life of an Outsider,* I wrote at length about the relations between Lawrence and the American writer Maurice Magnus in 1919 and 1920. I now think that I was wrong in some of my assertions there; but I also suspect that my failure to stress what was most interesting in that relationship (and in Lawrence's subsequent account of it, in his *Memoir of Maurice Magnus*) was significant. I underrated Lawrence's wide-ranging and exploratory imagination: the way he crossed frontiers and reported back on what he found. And I did what many biographers do: I normalized my subject. I did not allow for the width, the range, and at times the sheer strangeness of Lawrence's imagination. Let me start by setting out what I wrote in my 2005 book:

> The war lay like a crevasse across Lawrence's life; he felt caught between an irrecoverable, beloved past, in which he had believed, and a present in which he was in danger of believing in nothing at all. Experiences like the one at Monte Cassino triggered once again a realization of the gap which for him never lay far below the surface of the everyday.
>
> The fact that he was with Magnus may well have contributed to this feeling. Magnus was homosexual: Lawrence had even been subjected to an appreciative chat-up line when they had first met in Florence—"How lovely your hair is—such a lovely colour! What do you dye it with?" (D. H. Lawrence 2005c, 18). But Magnus was not the kind of predatory homosexual whom Lawrence,

back in 1915, had felt [Maynard] Keynes to be and with whom he had feared Bunny Garnett had become entangled. The "Memoir" constantly stresses Magnus's yearning, tenderness and vulnerability; Magnus was a man to whom Lawrence could "open his 'heart,'" and he did so on at least one occasion. He may have gone to Monte Cassino in hope of a warm response, even love, from his new friend. But at Monte Cassino, in the company of Magnus—a deeply troubled, sensitive man—Lawrence was struck once more by feelings of his own irretrievable loneliness, and realised once again that homosexual love was, for him, a road not to be taken, in spite of his sympathy with Magnus. Lawrence usually felt that "most people one can hardly bear to come near," but here he found no problem with the fact that Magnus "seemed to walk close to me, very close." [Thornycroft 1991, D. H. Lawrence 2005c, 34]. Yet this in turn made Lawrence realise that his own "heart," his whole emotional life, belonged to his original love for his mother and then to his love for Frieda. And those past loves now seemed lost; the heart which had loved them broken forever. A couple of years later, thinking specifically of his mother, he would confirm this by writing how love "belongs to the old life"; and in October 1921, feeling that Europe "was dying under my eyes," he wrote, revealingly: "It's almost precisely as if somebody were dying: one's mother, for example" [D. H. Lawrence 1987a, 327, 102]. All he could now do, stoic and courageous, was assert: "One can't go back." And it was at Monte Cassino in February 1920 that he said to Magnus something like: "I think one's got to go through with the life down there—get somewhere beyond it." There was no going back to the comforting past. Rather, he felt that "one must strike camp, and pack up the things, and go on"; he now imagined his own life would now be a matter of "some sort of action and strenuousness and pain and frustration and struggling through" (D. H. Lawrence 2005c, 33; 1987a, 327, 154].

Magnus was a rather unsuccessful American writer, magazine editor, translator, and journalist, born in 1879, whose literary contacts had dried up during the First World War, leaving him professionally helpless after it; he was living by his wits and occasional journalism when Lawrence arrived in Italy in November 1919 and met Magnus in the company of Norman Douglas (who had known Magnus for years). The three men spent some days together in Florence. Magnus and Lawrence next saw each other again in February 1920 when Lawrence went up to the monastery at Monte Cassino where Magnus had invited him. Magnus at this stage was actually in hiding from the police after a check he had given to an Italian hotel had bounced (though he did not tell Lawrence that); he was in serious financial trouble. In the late spring of 1920, Magnus most unexpectedly turned up in Taormina in Sicily, where the Lawrences were then living, hoping that Lawrence would lend him some money. Lawrence felt obliged to pay his hotel bill and lent him some other sums of money, too. Lawrence and Frieda went for a trip from Sicily to Malta in June 1920 (Mary Cannan had asked them to accompany her for a week's visit); Magnus turned up again on the journey, and scrounged a bit more cash from Lawrence; but when the Lawrence party went back to Sicily Magnus stayed on in Malta and settled down there (in the British Empire, thus hopefully out of reach of the Italian police). And it was on Malta—after being threatened with deportation to Italy, because of the original bouncing check—that Magnus committed suicide in November 1920, at the age of forty-one. By then he had appeared recreated as Mr. May in Lawrence's novel *The Lost Girl;* and between October 1921 and early 1922 Lawrence would write a long memoir of him.

In the biography I describe how, while the Lawrences and Mary Cannan were on Malta in the summer of 1920, "Lawrence's homosexual friend Maurice Magnus wrote to Norman Douglas that Lawrence 'opened his "heart" (!) to me here accidentally,' in another of those 'uncritical intimacies' which Frieda so distrusted" (Worthen 2005, 190). I then reproduce part of Magnus's letter to Douglas. Lawrence, Magnus wrote, "is looking for bisexual types for *himself.* Spoke of his innocence when he wrote 'Twilight' and 'Il Duro'. Evidently innocent no longer. Didn't like Malta because he thought that the religion or something prevented their sexual expression! I didn't elucidate [enlighten] him as I could have done even after a few days stay! He revels in all that is not just within his reach. He wants it to be within his reach. Arrived too late—regrets it. Never speaks of it unless bored to tears by women as here by Mrs Cannan and his wife" (Worthen 2005, 190, quoting Kinkead-Weekes 1996, 855).

And I comment, in the biography:

> Magnus is an unreliable reporter: always with an ear cocked for scandal, he is writing to his gossipy, boy-loving friend Norman Douglas, who would much have enjoyed hearing such things about Lawrence. There is no other evidence that Lawrence was on the lookout for "bisexual types," though such people undeniably intrigued him (both Douglas and Magnus were married homosexuals, and he certainly enjoyed their company). But by 1920 Lawrence seems to have regretted that he had spent so long refusing to acknowledge his attraction to men. His friendship with Hocking in 1917 shows him starting to do this. (Worthen 2005, 190–91)[1]

Although I still agree with some of that, I now think it unimaginative. I have started to understand how Magnus was someone to whom Lawrence talked about sexuality as to very few other people: and for that reason I would like to give far more attention to that extraordinary phrase about Lawrence—"he is looking for bisexual types for himself"—which, in my biography, I effectively dismissed as the kind of unreliable gossip that a man like Magnus would maliciously pass on to a man like Douglas.

For it was in a man like Magnus that Lawrence could really start to imagine what he himself was *not,* and what he might have been *more* like. Magnus offered him a kind of road not taken:

> Two roads diverged in a yellow wood,
> And sorry I could not travel both
> And be one traveler, long I stood
> And looked down one as far as I could
> To where it bent in the undergrowth. . . .[2]

But one thing I did not suggest in the biography—and certainly ought to have done—is that giving Magnus to understand that he was "looking for bisexual types for himself" may well not have been a confession on Lawrence's part so much as a strategy. It would have been a way of getting Magnus to talk about his *own* experience of moving between the heterosexual (Magnus had married in 1910) and the homosexual (which Magnus certainly was in 1920). Like Lawrence, Magnus was a man who risked himself: but where Lawrence's risks were thought-adventures, and the risks of a man publishing up to and over the limit of the acceptable, Magnus's risks and adventures had been sexual as well as financial. We need to understand how such a man was an irresistible invitation for Lawrence: a provocation for that exercise of stretching the imagination, extending over and across the borders and boundaries of what he felt he himself was like, and into the alien territory of the other. For it seems undeniable that—just as Magnus put it—Lawrence as a man and as a writer reveled "in all that was not just within his reach. He wanted it to be within his reach." And that would have applied to Lawrence's desire to know more about Magnus's experiences too, as well as his thinking aloud about his own missed chances.

Magnus was in that way a rare opportunity for Lawrence. There is little evidence anywhere else in the biographical record of the kind of intimate conversation Magnus records having had with Lawrence in that letter. Many of the people who knew Lawrence—at times it feels like nearly all of them—wrote memoirs of him and reported what he said. But there is nothing anywhere quite like this. Murry recalls Lawrence talking about the problems he and Frieda had when he wanted to make love to her and she did not want him; Compton Mackenzie has an extremely unreliable account of Lawrence talking in Capri about the problem for a married couple of reaching simultaneous orgasm (Mackenzie was almost certainly influenced by his reading of *Lady Chatterley,* eight years later) (Kinkead-Weekes 1996, 156, 551; see D. H. Lawrence 1993a, 201–2.) But they are not nearly as odd or interesting as this brief account of what Lawrence discussed with Magnus.

I think Lawrence might well have wanted to know what it was like to have sexual relations with a man, after having been heterosexual; how you felt about yourself; what sex was like without love being involved; how it might be for a man who was married to have an affair with another man; and in particular what it was like for a man primarily attracted to men to have an affair with a woman. Magnus could tell him about all these things, and no one else probably could. And for that reason, if no other, he would have been important to Lawrence. He went—as Lawrence said about him in the *Memoir*—to places which Lawrence had not himself gone; and that was why Lawrence valued him so highly.

It strikes me, too—and this is not in the biography, either—that Magnus's semiexplicit account of homosexual behavior in the Foreign Legion, in the book that he would call *Dregs*, was very likely written at Lawrence's particular instigation. Magnus certainly wrote it after talking about the book with Lawrence in February 1920—and, what is more, he sent the rewritten version to Lawrence at some point, either in the spring or more likely in the summer of that year, after he had moved to Malta.[3] And those passages in *Dregs* took Magnus well beyond what was actually publishable. For a writer as canny—and hard up—as Magnus, who needed to seize every publishing opportunity he could get, writing a text that publishers would insist on censoring, or might simply reject outright, would really have been very odd: though of course it was exactly what Lawrence himself had always done . . . and had paid the price for. I think it really rather likely that Lawrence provoked Magnus to do such writing. Norman Douglas would certainly not have done so. There is also the odd fact that after Magnus killed himself, the person who bought up Magnus's remaining manuscripts and typescripts (Michael Borg) sent the typescript of *Dregs* straight to Lawrence, while himself hanging on to all the other unpublished Magnus materials. Borg certainly linked the typescript of *Dregs* with Lawrence. He probably knew that Lawrence had previously read it, and had tried to help get it published, and that may be sufficient reason to have sent it to him. But it seems possible that Magnus had told him that it was in its own way *for* Lawrence: provoked by him, and interesting *to* him. I cannot in any way substantiate that, but I now think I might have speculated along those lines in the biography.

I also wonder now whether it would not also have been worth speculating about Lawrence's behavior during the rest of 1920 and 1921; whether, in his turn, Lawrence's affair with Rosalind Baynes in September 1920 (and his heart-wrenching account of Aaron's affair with the Marchesa in *Aaron's Rod* the following spring) may not also have owed something to those conversations with Magnus, and their frontier-crossing exploration of sexual experience normally beyond Lawrence's reach. What it was like for the man attracted to men to have an—unloving—sexual affair with a woman? And *Aaron's Rod* was the place where Lawrence took his chance to explore that at length and in terrifyingly depressing terms. Again, I cannot prove that it was Lawrence's contact with Magnus that provoked him to do that; but I think it likely.

But there *is* something else that I didn't really bring out in the biography and certainly should have done. Lawrence's trip up to Monte Cassino to see Magnus in the monastery in February 1920 was unlike any other journey I think he ever made. For one thing, he only seems to have written about it in his memoir of Magnus, and never mentioned it to anyone on any other occasion. If the memoir did not survive, we would have no reason for imagining Lawrence had ever made such a journey. Conscious that I needed a way of thinking about its obscurity in the surviving record, I borrowed from Lynn Talbot and Mike Squires the word they used in their biography: "veiled."[4] But even that is not quite right, I now think. It was really very odd. It was an eleven-hour journey; it took place on foot, by funicular, and then by small boat from Capri, and then three hours by passenger steamer across to Naples; then a three-hour wait: then a three-hour train journey, followed by a long journey by carriage up to the monastery at Cassino. Lawrence left Capri at six in the morning, on Thursday, February 19, and arrived at Monte Cassino at around five in the afternoon. He stayed that Thursday night (when Magnus showed him round the monastery church, Lawrence buttoned up in Magnus's sealskin overcoat against the cold), and Lawrence stayed at the monastery all the following day, Friday; but the day after that, Saturday, February 21, Lawrence went all the way home again. He had promised Magnus to stay two days, and Magnus begged him at least to stay over until that Sunday, when the services in the monastery chapel would have been especially interesting: but Lawrence stayed just one complete day and two nights, and then went home. Leaving as he did on Saturday at midmorning, he would have got back to Capri pretty late on Saturday night, after two whole days spent traveling and just one at the monastery. And all this to see someone who was by no means an old friend. It is a bit extraordinary. Lawrence had clearly wanted to see the monastery, or to see Magnus, very much; but he had also found that he wanted to leave, or had to leave, almost as quickly as he could.

I suspect that he had an instinct that being with Magnus might help him over those frontiers of imagination that he wanted to cross. I think Lawrence was fascinated by Magnus. Not in love with him; in fact probably rather disliking him, the more he saw of him; but all the same drawn to him as someone who—sexually—was (or had been) actively bisexual, and who was obviously prepared to share intimacies about his experiences, and who could be encouraged into making such disclosures in the writing of his Foreign Legion book. Lawrence would, I suspect, have argued strongly that Magnus *owed* it to his readers to be explicit about those sexual things. Which is, again, why Lawrence valued them so highly when he read them in the typescript of *Dregs*, and why he worked so hard to try to get the book published after Magnus's death, and praised Magnus so strongly in the introduction he wrote for it. This really was new experience.

But, for Lawrence, Magnus and the monastery together also had—and he says this time after time—the most heartbreaking impact. This is the other thing that makes this odd winter journey up to Monte Cassino so special. I cannot think of another place in his writing where Lawrence uses such language about his experience as he does about his single, long day up at the monastery, and about the day he left. He describes feeling agonized on his first morning there, Friday, the twentieth; he accounts for it as the reaction of a modern person in a place that was still the Middle Ages, but he says, "[It] took hold of me till I could hardly bear it": "It was really agony to me": "this was almost a violation to my soul, made almost a wound" (D. H. Lawrence 2005c, 26, 38). This is an extremely powerful reaction if it is *simply* to the experience of something stuck in the past. And then, on the sunny Friday afternoon, going for a walk with Magnus on the hilltop and looking out over the panorama of the modern world down at the foot of the hill, which Lawrence hated, he described feeling again "the poignancy of the not-quite-dead past," something that was—somehow—even worse than the modern world down below: "The beautiful, the wonderful past, it seems to prey on my heart." And then he walks back across the hilltop with Magnus, after an afternoon's talk, with the sun going down, "I feeling as if my heart had once more broken: I don't know why." Finally, the next afternoon, back in Naples and waiting for the steamer to take him over to Capri, he describes that experience again: "I sat in a bit of sunshine, and felt again that the world had come to an end for me, and again my heart was broken" (2005c, 33, 34, 36).

How are we to understand this? Lawrence says that *he* doesn't know what had happened. What could have been so heartbreaking about being up at the monastery, which might have made him want to leave almost as soon as he had arrived?

I think that I was quite wrong about Lawrence wanting love from Magnus: it was not that which disturbed him so much at Monte Cassino. He may have gone there hoping for some kind of comradeship, some intimate shared friendship. Although he did not love Magnus, I think Lawrence would have welcomed some tenderness *from* Magnus, and may even have got a little of it: those constant (and for the usually untouchable Lawrence, very striking) references to Magnus putting his hand on his arm and to the way Magnus walked so close convey something of the tenderness that he was clearly allowing Magnus to show toward him (at least in memory, and perhaps actually at Monte Cassino).

But it was while with Magnus that Lawrence would also have seen just the kind of person he himself might easily have been reduced to being: a sexually undecided writer-as-outsider, writing unacceptable books, desperately hard up, and on the run—with a sensitive intelligence, but filled with a stultifying reverence for and belief in the past. That was *exactly* the person who Lawrence—in his time—had been. One only has to read those astonishing letters of his from late 1915 about the "great wave of civilisation, 2000 years, which is now collapsing," especially those written from and about Garsington Manor—"So much beauty and pathos of old things passing away and no new things coming: this house of the Ottolines—It is England—my God, it breaks my soul—this England, these shafted windows, the elm-trees, the blue distance—the past, the great past, crumbling down, breaking down . . ." (1981a, 431) to realize Lawrence's intense, almost paralyzing attachment to the past in 1915, against which he had struggled.

And for Lawrence the old world was now ending, or "had come to another end in me." He had come to live at the edge of old Europe, and would shortly go even further, down to Sicily; and there he would feel "my heart—and my soul are broken, in Europe. It's no use, the threads are broken" (1984, 486; 1987a, 90, 125). And then he would set off into the wilds, consciously putting the old world and—ideally—all his links with it behind him.

However, it was more than just the European past that made him feel heartbroken up at Monte Cassino, and turned Magnus into the figure of someone who hopelessly clung to the past. Lawrence's own feelings were, I think, about the absolute death of his own capacity to love. I would now say that his heartbreak was that of believing he had nothing to which he would turn, and no one whom he could ever love, ever again in his life. He would write very powerfully in the autumn of 1922 how "[l]ove is not a fundamental thing. As life drives us deeper and deeper, we pass certain borders, and love ceases to be of first-rate importance. It comes to an end. . . . The world of love fades into rubbish: like a dead empire" (2003, 429, 430). That is in the culmination of the 1922 version of the Whitman essay. And such a feeling was what he perhaps first coherently realized on that trip to Monte Cassino. He could see in Magnus, exactly, someone who still adhered to the past, to love, to religion, to belief: that was why Magnus was up at Monte Cassino, of all places: because of his beliefs, rooted as they were in so many traditions and in so much of the past. And that would have driven Lawrence still further into his rocky, isolated, unloving independence: and horribly painfully too, so that he just wanted to get away and be by himself; and to write and say nothing about the experience for nearly two years.

I think the visit to Monte Cassino probably *was* a turning point in Lawrence's life and writing, and a great deal more crucial than I ever suggested in the biography. It left him lonelier than ever: emotionally, personally, culturally, religiously. You can see something of the consequences of his subsequent attitude to religion and the past in Ceylon in 1922, when the Brewsters would take off their hats and shoes and go into Buddhist temples, and come out to find Lawrence with his shoes on, and his hat "tight on his head," saying that there was no use *his* going in (Brewster 1997–98, 260–61). Religious beliefs—and their links with the past—were a real problem to him, until he got to New Mexico; and even there it took him a very long time to come to terms with what he experienced.[5]

As if to confirm the importance of the occasion up at Monte Cassino, and the importance of the person, Magnus would become the only man to whom Lawrence ever devoted a long biographical account: the *Memoir of Maurice Magnus*. There were of course reasons for Lawrence to have written such a piece: he told everyone that he wanted to write an introduction that would help sell Magnus's book about the Foreign Legion, *Dregs*, and thus pay some of Magnus's posthumous debts (and get back what Magnus owed him, too). But the difference from his other introductions is enormous. In April 1928, for example, full of friendliness and gratitude toward Harry Crosby, he wrote Crosby an introduction for his poetry book *Chariot of the Sun*. In the pagination of the Cambridge University Press edition, it is quite a lengthy introduction: eight pages (D. H. Lawrence 2005a,

109–16). In January 1930 Lawrence wrote another longish introduction for the translation that his old friend Koteliansky had done of Dostoevsky's Grand Inquisitor episode, another act of pure friendship; and again it was eight pages long (D. H. Lawrence 2005b). These were the two other longest book introductions he ever wrote. The introduction to Magnus's book is, however, sixty-one pages long, in the identical Cambridge University Press pagination (2005b, 11–72). It is far longer than it needed to be to do the job of getting Magnus's work into print. It was not just an introduction. It was the only time outside his fiction, I think, in which Lawrence attempted to lay this particular ghost, of what had happened to the past and to belief and to love, in his own case, and to state how he would henceforth live without it. His heart would stay broken.

It is interesting that Magnus himself was clearly impatient with Lawrence and does not seem to have liked him particularly, though he could feel tender toward him and also reckon (rightly) that Lawrence would come in handy as a useful soft touch when one needed cash. Magnus by 1920 had grown to be an expert in people he could get money from: he had spent a good deal of his recent life looking for them. And Lawrence—pretty hard up himself—nevertheless handed over various sums amounting to some twenty-three pounds between January and July 1920 (coming close to $2,000 in modern money, so a very tidy sum). And he would have got absolutely none of it back if he had not taken on the writing of the introduction and the selling of Magnus's book. No one else ever took money off Lawrence like this.

But Magnus's impatience is there in the letter to Douglas about bisexuality that I quoted earlier. He was amused at Lawrence's ignorance—after being on Malta for a week—of sexual behavior on the island, but says, "I didn't elucidate him as *I* could have done, even after a few *days* stay!" Magnus had obviously explored the Maltese homosexual scene and its possibilities. Lawrence had no idea it existed (but then *he* was not gay). And Magnus's amused impatience is there in the memories recounted in Lawrence's own memoir. Magnus was impatient with Lawrence for being (*he* would have thought) such an awful innocent: innocent about sex, innocent about homosexuals, and dreadfully—or in another way wonderfully—naïve about money and loans and banks and bills. Magnus found Lawrence absurd in his attitude about how to deal with the problem of being poor. In the *Memoir,* Lawrence has just described telling Douglas and Magnus in Florence in November 1919 that he is never going to let himself run out of money, however poorly he has to live. He says he is determined never again to " 'be penniless while I live—I mistrust the world too much.' 'But if you're going to live in fear of the world,' said Magnus, 'what's the good of living at all. Might as well die.' " And Lawrence comments: "I think I give his words almost verbatim. He had a certain impatience of me and of my presence. Yet we had some jolly times—mostly in one or other of their bedrooms, drinking a whisky and talking" (2005c, 16).

I think that Magnus would have been amused by Lawrence, as someone so stupidly independent as to fear that the world might interfere with his freedom. If you were Magnus, you knew that you had to take the world on, and you had to know how to win. (Magnus eventually killed himself because he found that he had lost.) But above all I think Magnus would have been amused by the huge value that Lawrence's *Memoir* would place on Magnus's Foreign Legion experiences, in remarks such as "Magnus carried the human consciousness through circumstances which would have been too much for me. I would have died rather than be so humiliated. I could never have borne it" (2005c, 69). I can imagine Magnus saying to Lawrence, if somehow he had lived to read that: "Well, my dear chap, if you *really* want to know the fearful kinds of thing a homosexual man goes through in the twentieth century, let me give you a few choice details." And I can imagine Lawrence being correspondingly aghast; but also fascinated with the choice details, and wanting to know more. At the back of my mind here is the sixteen-year-old Lawrence going to work at the factory in Nottingham in the autumn of 1901, and who was seen before work on Monday mornings standing "on the outskirts of groups of girls chatting about their boyfriends . . . listening to them with a kind of fascinated horror" (Worthen 1991, 100). That was just how he reached out to all that was alien to him, in Magnus's terms, so as to bring it within his reach. Magnus, too, was someone who filled him with fascinated horror.

Lawrence could not report on his own homosexual or bisexual experiences, because he had not had any, beyond describing his own unwitting attraction to men like Il Duro in *Twilight in Italy* and Birkin's rather more witting attraction to the Cornishman in the *Women in Love* prologue. But in the *Memoir* Lawrence does write about the "gironds" described in Magnus's Foreign Legion book—these are passive male homosexuals, exploited by the active ones—with exactly the kind of fascination he had shown at the age of sixteen, outside the factory. He also actually knew a little more about homosexual experience than he puts into the *Memoir*. He questions the word Magnus uses for a passive homosexual, "girant"—that is how Magnus typed it and spelled it, and how Lawrence wrote it and repeated it in his memoir, but, says Lawrence, "one wonders what the actual word is." How ever did Lawrence *know* that it was not the actual word? Because it should be "girond": Magnus's American ear had not registered the French properly.[6] And Lawrence knew enough about that homosexual world to know it was the wrong word, at least. Someone must have told him that Magnus had got it wrong. Douglas, gay and cosmopolitan to his fingertips, might have known. But Lawrence was not going to let on that *he* knew.

With the Magnus piece in print again, first in Keith Cushman's edition of 1987, and now in the Cambridge University Press edition of *Introductions and Reviews*, there is a chance that people will realize its importance. I think it is even more significant than my biography makes it; and it is immensely revealing, far more than my biography shows, about how Magnus really fascinated Lawrence.

For Magnus invited Lawrence where he could not easily go himself; and Lawrence partly responded, and partly did not. There is a kind of impressive rhetoric in the last part of the *Memoir of Maurice Magnus* that is rather unusual in Lawrence; it provides some sense (to me, now) of his covering his tracks, of his disguising behind the rhetoric his fascination. I quoted just now the kind of passage I mean: the one about carrying the human consciousness through circumstances "which would have been too much for me" (2005c, 69). The very end of the piece is impressive but also (something always intriguing when it comes in middle and late Lawrence) a little bit overwritten. He is forcing the significance of Magnus rather hard, as he makes Magnus that hero, that strange, quaking little star (70), who goes so boldly through the extremes of experience. It was one of Lawrence's deepest kinds of self-honesty *always* to register what he had experienced clearly in words: so that he makes Magnus a kind of paragon of honest reportage of extreme experience. The Magnus book that is supposed to contain all this marvelous honesty is in reality rather (or mostly very) dull; it is a great deal better in Lawrence's account of it than it is in reality. All the last part of the *Memoir* is really Lawrence talking about what he believes in, rather than what Magnus had actually written.

It was Wittgenstein who remarked, "The frontiers of *language* . . . mean the frontiers of *my* world."[7] Lawrence, like every ambitious writer, was determined to push back the barriers of—whereof—we cannot speak. He was setting out to be—thereof—as little silent as possible.[8] On the one hand, he was at times very conscious of what he thought those frontiers were. "*I dare do all that may become a man,*" he once quoted, and sardonically commented: "It's the becoming" (D. H. Lawrence 1989a, 199). He would put it very pointedly himself in his poem "Fish," for which (Mark Kinkead-Weekes reminds us) the given location is "*Zell-am-See*" but which was actually written in Nellie Morrison's flat in Florence in September 1921 (Kinkead-Weekes 1996, 671). The narrator of the poem presents some brilliantly anthropomorphic poetry about a fish—like this little paragraph:

> A slim young pike, with smart fins
> And grey striped suit, a young cub of a pike

Slouching along away below, half out of sight,
Like a lout on an obscure pavement
—Ah, there's somebody in the know!

But the narrator then realizes,

I had made a mistake, I didn't know him,
This grey, monotonous soul in the water,
This intense individual in shadow,
Fish-alive.

I didn't know his God.
I didn't know his God.

Which is perhaps the last admission that life has to wring out of us.

I saw, dimly,
Once a big pike rush,
And small fish fly like splinters.
And I said to my heart, *there are limits*
To you, my heart;
And to the one God.
Fish are beyond me.

(1972, 338)

But—just as in that poem—Lawrence habitually wanted his writing to go beyond: beyond me, beyond those limits: in fact to go off-limits.[9] The *writer's* job may perhaps be defined as trying to go off-limits and attempting to redefine both the needs to which the limits relate and the human nature that feels itself to be limited. When, for example, Lawrence got the news in Taos of the death of Sallie Hopkin, the wife of the Eastwood socialist and freethinker Willie Hopkin, and thought back to his own early years in Eastwood, it was natural for him to say to Hopkin in his letter of condolence: "[Y]ou two led me over some frontiers . . ." (D. H. Lawrence 1987a, 327). That was very high praise from Lawrence. There are ways in which his writing was a constant and regular temptation and opportunity for him to go well beyond the limits of what was allowed; to cross a series of frontiers, to pass (as he put it in 1922) "certain borders" (2003, 429). Writing may be a thought-adventure, as his memorial in

Westminster Abbey reminds us; but the adventure is no good unless it really goes out into the wilds, crosses the frontiers, on its way to the bounds of the wild and the waste. And this Lawrence did, in (for example) politics and his attacks on democracy; in his thinking about women, especially between 1917 and 1923; in his rejection of love; and in his savage attacks on ordinariness and living in the human world. He was not just a radical thinker and writer. He was a violently extreme one: in part to provoke, but also out of what he drove himself to imagine. His desire to separate himself in most ways from ordinary people, to become (and crucially to write the books of) a savage outsider, is at times very sharply articulated. I think of him in New Mexico late in September 1922, having learned to ride, and being tempted (like the Woman in his story) just to Ride Away: "[T]he desert has a fascination—to ride alone—in the sun in the forever unpossessed country—away from man. That is a great temptation . . ." (1987a, 314). And there is nothing comfortable or comforting about that temptation. If you really cross that borderline, that frontier, you may well go where no one can go with you.

The painter Francis Bacon once remarked that half his painting life he spent trying to disrupt what he could do with ease (Sylvester 1975, 91). The same is true for some writers. By 1918 or so Lawrence had written extensively about the thought-adventures he had previously had. He could *do* dialogue, he could do systole and diastole: he was an easy master at it. He could describe the natural world vividly. And at that point he initiated almost a decade of writing in which he really began to disrupt what he could do with ease. He set himself to write the unthinkable and the unwritable; to go off-limits. You can see him starting to do this, I suggest, in the esoteric parts of the first draft of *Studies in Classic American Literature* written in Cornwall; and then in the revisions to the "Excurse" chapter of *Women in Love;* some of the odder things in *Fantasia;* and then spectacularly in the weird original ending to *Studies,* which I quoted from earlier, and which he removed after Seltzer objected to it.[10] And then in *The Boy in the Bush,* and again in *The Plumed Serpent.* And then finally in *Lady Chatterley's Lover* when he attempted to find a narrative technique for writing the language of bodily experience.[11] The experimentation of Lawrence's writing (in particular his novels) from 1918 onward is what really distinguishes it. The extremity of it is often the reason for its existence. It is the work of a man determined to push back the boundaries, to write about living independently, without love, about finding a language (or languages) for bodily experience. It is often fairly unattractive writing, and it has made him few friends. It often feels like fantasy: at times it is not—to use Lawrence's own wonderful phrase from 1913—"sufficiently inrooted."[12] But that is not the point (or would not have been, for Lawrence). When he wrote to Edward Garnett about "The Sisters," "It is not perfect, because I am not expert in what I want to do," he was annoyed to the breaking point with Garnett not because the latter had criticized him but because he had criticized "the thing I *wanted* to say: not me, not what I had said, but that which I was trying to say, and had failed in" (1981a, 183, 164). But the thing Lawrence *wanted* to say, by 1920, was a good deal further on than what he had wanted to say in 1914. Pushing out the frontiers was, more and more, what he came to believe his novels should do. It is one of the reasons why his novels of the 1920s are in so many ways the least appealing things that Lawrence has bequeathed to us, for all their brilliant writing. He hated the writer whom he described as happy to be spending his time "playing word-games around the camp fire." Lawrence believed that "[s]omebody has to jump like a desperate clown through the vast blue hoop of the upper air" (2005b, 233). And he was prepared to be that desperate clown: for he was, just as he had been in 1916, in pursuit of "the great articulate extremity of art" (1981a, 661). Over the frontiers: and well beyond.

Notes

1. Worthen 2005, I continue: "What is most illuminating about Magnus's comment, however, is the way it shows how profoundly Lawrence

was fascinated by experiences and feelings outside the grasp of his own intuitive understanding. He was an extremely detached person, in spite of his friendships and his marriage; and in his attraction to men he had at least three times been disappointed or let down. Bunny Garnett had flatly rejected his loving friendship in 1915; by the end of 1916 Murry and he were estranged; in the winter of 1917 William Henry Hocking would stop answering his letters. In *Kangaroo,* Somers feels taken advantage of by John Thomas Buryan, rather as Lawrence came to feel he had been by Hocking; and Lawrence may well have come to feel the same about Magnus, who took advantage of him financially because of Lawrence's interest in him" (191).

2. "The Road Not Taken" (1916), lines 1–5, in Frost 1995, 131. NB, "bent" in the sense of "homosexual" only dates to 1957, according to *OED,* 2nd ed.

3. See D. H. Lawrence 2005c, 36.

4. I owe the word to Squires and Talbot 2002, 223.

5. See Worthen 2003.

6. D. H. Lawrence 2005c, 63. "Girond": French slang (first recorded 1872) for a passive male homosexual.

7. In the preface of the *Tractatus* he noted: "It will therefore only be in language that the limit [to thought] can be drawn"; and at 5.62 he wrote, specifically, "The world is *my* world: this is manifest in the fact that the limits of *language* (of that language which alone I understand) mean the limits of *my* world." (Wittgenstein 1961, 3, 57).

8. Cf. the language of C. K. Ogden's first (1922) translation of Proposition 7 of the *Tractatus* ("Whereof we cannot speak, thereof we must be silent"); the Pears-McGuiness translation prefers "What we cannot speak about we must pass over in silence" (Wittgenstein 1961, 74).

9. A phrase however originating with the U.S. military and first recorded during the Korean War in 1952. This is DHL in 1929, for example, writing about the ways in which man was limited: "What are the limits to the nature, not of Man in the abstract, but of man, mere men, everyday men? . . . Mankind in the bulk can never be 'free,' because man on the whole makes three grand demands on life, and cannot endure unless those demands are satisfied" (2005b, 128). Dostoevsky's Grand Inquisitor defines those demands as for miracle, mystery, and authority, and Lawrence agrees with him: "Surely it is true", says Lawrence: "We have to . . . agree that men are like that" (2005b, 129). Lawrence is, however, explicitly not limiting *himself* to those demands (nor, therefore, to those limits). It is explicitly "everyday men" that he is talking about, mankind "in the bulk," "man on the whole." And that is not where he places himself.

10. See D. H. Lawrence 2003, 429–30, final readings.

11. I would like to draw attention to Nakabayashi 2006, in which the attention to the narratives of the novel is exemplary.

12. D. H. Lawrence 1981a, 99. "Inrooted" means "Deeply rooted, fixed, or established" (*OED,* 2nd ed.).

Women in Love: Sacrifice, Sadism, and the Discourse of Species

Gerald Doherty

As a modernist "frontier" novel, D. H. Lawrence's *Women in Love* issues its own formidable challenge to what it means to be human that sets it apart from its contemporary rivals—James Joyce's *Ulysses,* Virginia Woolf's *Mrs. Dalloway,* and E. M. Forster's *A Passage to India,* for example. While they predicate human being in terms of the full measure of how their protagonists engage with each other (they accept their status as human as, more or less, already given), *Women in Love* refuses such an easy acceptance. Through its remarkable forefronting of animal presence (no fewer than five major vignettes, a species-debate chapter, and numerous more incidental discussions), it seeks to articulate human being along the precarious fault line where the human and nonhuman intersect. Such a continual redrawing of fault lines at once interrelates and separates off the main protagonist pairs from each other. Repudiating their own animality, Gerald and Gudrun effectively corral it off in their desire to negate and destroy it. Incorporating the animal other as the nonhuman core of the human, Birkin and Ursula, by contrast, become fully human in those terms for which Birkin is spokesman. Through a sequence of vignettes that engage human with nonhuman being, a new kind of species discourse locates acceptance or rejection of the animal other as the vital hinge upon which the human struggles to realize itself and come into being.[1]

Of course, species discourse is only one among other ideological discourses—sexual, class, aesthetic, technological—that deploy one another in their struggle for dominance, but its presence has been hitherto underestimated. Critical appreciation has been largely reserved for the purely human dimensions of the ideological drama. If, as Giorgio Agamben puts it, "the caesura between the human and the animal passes first of all within man, then it is the very question of man—and of 'humanism'—that must be posed in a new way" (2004, 16), then *Women in Love* poses the question of man precisely in the manner that sets it off from other major contemporary novels in the English tradition. Through its radical upending of Enlightenment humanist assumptions that privilege human autonomy, and through its blinding focus on the animal body[2] in man, it continually redraws the fault lines that separate human from nonhuman, in the process shaking their very foundations.

To frame these particular fault lines, and as a prelude to close readings of these animal vignettes, I shall juxtapose two antithetical concepts across which *Women in Love* insistently plays in its quest to articulate the human through its highly complex detours through the nonhuman other. Situating man at the center, the anthropocentric (first concept) and, by extension, the anthropomorphic[3] reinforce the Cartesian mind/body as its carnal leftover, thus safely divorcing man from his or her own animality. Fixing the species barrier absolutely in place, the Cartesian mind/body represses the animal body by means of a culture of sacrifice that denigrates and denies it. Such a culture, as Derrida shows, not only organizes a hierarchy of subjects (man/woman/animal): it also founds the differential concepts of subjectivity that help to sustain it (1991, 114). At the lowest rung of the hierarchy, animals are "sacrificial offerings to our need for ritual confirmation of our peculiar self-understanding" (Wood 2004, 139). A sacrificial ethos that practices a disciplined sadism toward the animal body is complicit with an anthropocentrism that pursues its drive toward transcendence—toward noncorporeal or virtual or spiritual being. Bataille has succinctly unraveled these interconnections: "Man has, in a sense, revealed and founded human truth by sacrificing: in sacrifice he destroyed the animal in himself, allowing himself and the animal to survive as—noncorporeal truth" (Bataille 1990, 18). Through ritual sacrifice, man institutionalizes the logos as spirit, as that impenetrable barrier that keeps languageless animals always on the far side of being. In *Women in Love*, Gerald and Gudrun are compulsive sacrificers who kill off the animal body to secure a human ascendancy over each other.

The biocentric (second concept), by contrast, radically shifts the fault line in the direction of that animal being common to human and nonhuman alike. In positing a continuum, not a split or a break, it forefronts embodiment itself as that irreducible material base that all creatures share, celebrating the instinctual over the rational, bypassing a culture of sacrifice that invents punishingly cruel rituals to ensure a species ascendancy.[4] As part of man's evolutionary inheritance—the "shared community of life with other living beings" (Steiner 2005, 250)—and as index that man has no need of scapegoats or victims upon which to project his own insufficiency, the biocentric embraces bodily being. Renouncing fault lines or caesuras or splits, it posits a web of interdependencies that bind all life species together, enmeshing man in a cosmic network of energies of which he forms a not very significant part. Because they share the same root identity, the nonhuman is directly intuited as a constituent part of the human—an ever-present "within" upon which man constructs a precarious species identity. In the end a cosmic holism shrinks human being to an infinitesimal moment in a vast evolutionary history that existed before man emerged and that will survive his departure.[5] As an idiosyncratic apostle of a biocentricity that foregrounds the animal body, Birkin quests for new modes of integrating the nonhuman into the human—for that final dissolution of the props that undergird the old humanist self.

As the drive that most resists acculturation, and that threateningly confronts man with his own animality, the sexual maps out that highly unstable, forever mobile, supersensitive caesura, where the question of what constitutes the human is incessantly renegotiated. Cultural swings between repressive denials and tentative affirmation posit the erotic as a node around which these constitutive tensions revolve.[6] In its celebration of (what Birkin calls) the "dark sensual body of life" (D. H. Lawrence 1987c, 42), *Women in Love* also revolves around this node, constantly shifting the treacherous fault line between the nonhuman and human, where the sexual drives come into play. This is the "terra incognita" Birkin and Ursula ceaselessly navigate in their quest for erotic fulfillment, and that Gerald and Gudrun refuse to recognize as "terra incognita" at all, since they relate to each other through its violent repudiation, which reflects humanism's own self-destructive potential.

Women in Love has thus a double thrust: Birkin's biocentrism reinstates the animal body as integral to full human being, as opposed to Gerald and Gudrun's anthropocentrism that sacrifices that same animal body in their attempts to transcend it. Of course, Gerald and Gudrun do not ritually kill animals in obedience to a biblical injunction (note God's preference for Abel's animal sacrifice over Cain's vegetable one: Genesis 4), nor in the Girardian way of the scapegoat who restores communal peace, nor in the Bataillean way of overcoming one's own fear of death.[7] Instead they practice a wholly secularized form of sacrifice where the calculated infliction of pain acts as a catalyst for erotic arousal. Being sexually turned on by the pain of the other is precisely the aspect of sacrifice *Women in Love* calls "obscene" and "abhorrent" (242), since it violates the traditional notion of sacrifice as essentially sacred—a hallowed victim offered up to a god. Locating sacrificial death "at the base of eroticism," Bataille speaks of "the excitement sacrifice," which does not just dismember the animal body, but which opens "on to a realm beyond this world" (Bataille 1990, 21–23). Gerald and Gudrun experience something like this excitement in the episode "Rabbit." As opposed to the "profound innocence" of animals who do not recognize their own cruelty as such (Derrida 2003, 132), Gerald and Gudrun cultivate a mediated, self-conscious sadism that needs the gaze of the other as proof that the rite is efficacious. Unleashed on the animal body, pain is the "perverse" expression of the erotic desire that compels them, but whose source they disguise from each other.

Because it draws on a species continuum that integrates the nonhuman into the human, Birkin's biocentrism circumnavigates a redemptive culture of sacrifice of which the animal body itself is the traditional victim. In renouncing a corporeal transcendence that abjects the body and leaves it behind, Birkin also renounces the biblical God, who approves of animal sacrifice (the Cain/Abel syndrome), in favor of the dark gods of the blood, where the word "blood" signifies that material liquid that flows unimpeded across species boundaries. In place of a sadistic economy that represses the flesh to lift up the spirit, Birkin's erotic economy mobilizes desire, not through the infliction of pain, but through desire's intimate conjunction with bodily being—the "vital, sensual reality" (D. H. Lawrence 1987c, 320) all animals share.

In *Women in Love*, as this essay suggests, the discourse of species assumes a centrality that marks it off from other major modernist novels and locates the human in closest proximity to its nonhuman roots in defiance of those established humanist barriers that would keep them apart. As such, species discourse takes its proper place alongside those other discourses—gender, class, aesthetic, and so on—deploying and modifying their force in its repeated attempts to articulate what it means to be human. The remainder of this essay tracks this discourse in action, both in those dramatic vignettes where animals play the lead roles and in its submerged presence in other scenarios whose surface appears to reflect exclusively human preoccupations.

I.

As a prelude to the first major animal vignette—Gerald's violent reining in of his Arab mare—a sequence of minor indicators point up the species divide, presaging the lines of its future development. Gudrun's initial recognition of Gerald as a "smiling wolf" is the symbolic precursor of those "real" animal scenarios shortly to follow, highlighting the flagrant contradiction between Gerald's "good-humored" public mask and the harsh repression required to keep the facade in place. Gerald's disposition as "wolf" (traditionally a fierce, predatory, pack-hunting beast, unlisted among Nietzsche's and Lawrence's "noble" animals)[8] already evokes cruel energies kept under harsh restraint: lacking the spontaneous discharge that marks "noble" animals, these are subtly deflected, diverted from their paths of natural fulfillment. Already the "lurking danger of [Gerald's] unsubdued temper" masks a sadistic cold-bloodedness his outward demeanor conceals. Gudrun's near-orgasmic reaction —her "paroxysm of violent sensation"—gets straight to the core connection in the callous "strangling" of the animal body as the clue to erotic arousal (D. H. Lawrence 1987c, 14–15). In its theatrical initiation into the sacrificial refinements of a sadism that draws Gerald and Gudrun together, this little vignette carries a vivid premonitory charge.

As it emerges in their first slightly fraught conversation at Shortlands, the difference between Birkin and Gerald turns on two of Lawrence's favorite terms to characterize animal being: the "hardest thing," Birkin declares, is to act "spontaneously" and in "singleness," though he omits to add its (for him) natural corollary—"as animals do." Already a species discourse infiltrates the basic argument between the two characters. While Gerald, like the wolf, is an instinctive pack animal, at once an industrial magnate and "high priest" of the machine that sacrifices the working bodies of the miners (231), disfiguring them to the point where they no longer look human, Birkin is a lone ranger, a solitary, nonsocial creature, though paradoxically in search of a mate to share his own isolation. Gerald's "collective thing," as Birkin points out, involves a ruthless violence toward others as its foundational principle: "cut[ting] another man's throat" is Gerald's sacrificial strategy for securing an always precarious hold on a human identity, incessantly under threat from the animal other. Birkin, as it were, is more consciously aware of the collusion in a sacrificial sadism that binds the collective body together than is Gerald, who is its virtuoso practitioner, and in the end, its unwitting victim (32–33).

Whenever the species issue emerges into the open, as it does for the first time in "Class-room," its connection with cruelty is never far off. Hermione's phobic attitudes toward her own animality fuel the bitter fracas that brings her essential difference from Birkin to its confrontational crisis. While Hermione's insistence on the therapeutic benefits of "spontaneous" animal reactions (especially in children) is close enough to Birkin's position to incite his spontaneous aggression against her, it differs radically from it. Exemplifying the Cartesian mind/body split that in turn mirrors the human/animal one, Hermione cordons off her own animality, keeping it safely behind bars. A purely symbolic conception of the animal secures her distance from the real thing. A cold, dispassionate observer of her own instinctual life, as Birkin perceives her, she cages her circus animals, which perform their mindless routines only to "thrill" and entertain her.[9] This "animalism . . . in your head," as Birkin puts it, is at the opposite pole to "be[ing] an animal," as he will later come to define it. The "pornography" of "watching [her] naked animal actions in mirrors" marks Hermione down as a violently repressed (and repressive) narcissist, who triumphantly secures her social identity as *Kulturträger* by observing the animal other within her in the certainty it cannot observe her in return (40–42). (Later Hermione takes her revenge on the repressed animal body by hitting Birkin over the head with a lapis lazuli ball [105]).

Hermione's anthropocentric devaluation of animal being in turn provokes the first part of Birkin's biocentric manifesto, a partial unfolding later completed in his first tea party with Ursula (146). Birkin's diagnosis of her lack of "any dark sensual body of life" already locates corporeal existence, not as a Cartesian supplement, an accidental appendage, but as the raw-material essence from which all species diversity springs. Though clearly not meant as a simple regression to the animal state (a proposition Lawrence always rejected), Birkin's insistence that "*[e]verything* [human] must go" (my emphasis) involves apocalyptic catastrophe—the "death" of the humanist self that excludes recognition of the animal being that constitutes the core of the human (42–43). Through such recognition, Birkin implies, humans become different types of animals from the "spiritual" ones they ideally conceive themselves to be. In the first of the major animal vignettes (to which we now turn), Gerald literalizes the repression of the animal body that Hermione's treatment of her circus animals symbolically threw into relief.

In shifting the context from the cruelty humans inflict on each other (Birkin and Hermione) to the cruelty humans inflict on animals, the "Coal-Dust" vignette insinuates species difference as the catalyst for a kind of sexual excitation, signified entirely by coded gestures and looks.[10] Species supremacy, as it were, unleashes that harsh abjection of the animal body that acts as a turn-on for humans, raising the pain to a high pitch of erotic intensity. It also organizes that "hierarchy of subjects" (Derrida's phrase) that locates the male at the top rung of the ladder: Gerald displays his male mastery to two female spectators, whose complex "responses" to his brutality separate them off from the animal who can only "react."[11] Indeed, the shadow of a sacrificial violence hangs over the scene: in his "mechanical relentlessness," Gerald is not only "keen as a sword pressing into [the mare]": his whole body becomes, in Linda Ruth Williams's graphic phrase (1993, 81), "a devouring set of teeth"—a chewing machine, greedy to kill off and then eat up his hapless victim. (In the "Rabbit" episode, as we shall see, this carnivorous compulsion is at last made explicit.)

The "quantitative reiteration" Deleuze locates at the core of sadism (1989, 134)—the increase in the stimulus to intensify the effect—also marks the mare's reactions: from her initial "winc[ing] away" from the thunderous noise of the colliery train, through the "mad clamor of terror" that overwhelms her, on to the "repulsive sight" of her frenzied nostrils and eyes. The sight of the blood flow from the spurs signals the crisis of difference between the two sisters' responses. In her urgent cross-species identification with the Arab mare's pain, Ursula's Benthamite anthropomorphism[12] gives voice to the suffering body, conflating a species with a gender rhetoric in her accusatory onslaught on Gerald: "Does he think it's manly to torture a horse?" Gerald's cruelty, Ursula implies, is his mode of asserting his male ascendancy by subjugating the female animal body.

Gudrun's rapturous identification, by contrast, is not with the suffering body but with the abstracted potential of pain to shatter her consciousness: "The world reeled and passed into nothingness" (D. H. Lawrence 1987c, 112). Indeed her hysterical declaration from the side of the road—"I should think you're proud"—resonates with suggestions of the absolute species mastery Gerald has just displayed: Gerald is proud to be human, and not an animal, where being human means forcing an animal to recognize its proper place in the ontological hierarchy. Like Gerald's, Gudrun's sadistic resistance to internalizing the pain of the animal is the core element in her still-latent power to transmute pain into erotic pleasure. Thus, her immediate replay of the vignette screens out all those pain indicators the original narrative highlighted: the mare is neither frantic nor frenzied nor lacerated, but merely softly "palpitating" between Gerald's energized thighs. In identifying her own female flesh with that of the mare, Gudrun not only slips down a notch on the ontological hierarchy (she becomes the "palpitating body" of the mare, locked "into pure control")[13] she also (momentarily) succumbs to the masochistic logic of domination that transmutes the pain of subjugation itself into rapturous pleasure. At the same time, the text subtly masks this intimate association between human and nonhuman bodies (it relies entirely on the reader to make it), focusing exclusively on Gerald's "magnetic domination," which forces the mare "into unutterable subordination" (110–13).

What Gerald and Gudrun share, in effect, is a "sadistic *apathy*" (Deleuze 1989, 134), not so much in the face of, but produced by, intolerable distress—a nonchalant unconcern that allows Gerald to "smile" his way through his performance, and Gudrun to feel "cold and indifferent" at the sight of the blood flow from the spurs. As the following episode ("Sketch-Book") makes abundantly clear, it is their capacity to focus this sadistic drive on each other that institutes the "diabolical freemasonry" between them (D. H. Lawrence 1987c, 122). The Arab mare vignette is thus "primal" in the Freudian sense of conflating sex with sadistic aggression (the child's view of parental intercourse) and of acting as thematic prototype for all the subsequent encounters between Gerald and Gudrun.

Given the primal significance of the species hierarchy in articulating the Gerald/Gudrun relationship, it comes as no surprise to find the next episode ("Carpeting") given over to locating each of the main protagonists vis-à-vis the species divide, shifting the fault line back and forth in response to some basic questions: Why should Homo sapiens so insistently set himself off from the animals? On what grounds (if any) should he perceive himself as superior? What is the nature of animal consciousness, if there is such a thing? A Watteau-style open-air picnic by a pond sets the scene for a compendium of conflicting views that nevertheless share a common denominator: the disputants all uphold the anthropocentric belief in a species hierarchy that locates man at the top, thus implicitly rejecting a biocentric commonality of interests and aims with other sentient beings. Castigating Gerald for his "unnecessary torture" of the Arab mare, for example, Ursula is not only a good anthropomorphist, who, Bentham-like, identifies with animal suffering: she also moves tentatively toward a biocentric position, perceiving all living creatures as "teleological centers of life," each pursuing its own way (Steiner 2005, 250): the mare, as Ursula puts it, has "as much right to her own being" as Gerald has to his. In addition, her shrewd use of the term "unnecessary" penetrates to the hidden motive behind Gerald's excess—his secret compulsion to prolong the mare's pain to intensify Gudrun's pleasure. Yet, in the end, Ursula too clings to a traditional biblical hierarchy that sanctions man's superior power over what she calls an "inferior creation." As a utilitarian hard-liner, Gerald, by contrast, thinks exclusively in terms of the use he can make of animals, politely ridiculing Ursula's biocentric notion of each creature "fulfil[ling] its own marvelous nature." At the same time, he suppresses his own "perverse" motivations in the interests of a rational justification. Withholding his own personal "manifesto"—which, in effect, dissolves all species hierarchies, till the next episode ("Mino"), Birkin appears at his most priggish, at once putting down Ursula's positive anthropomorphism (it is "detestable"), while exploiting the species divide to bolster a sexist one (like horses, women have two choices—either to subject themselves "utterly," or to "bolt") (D. H. Lawrence 1987c, 138–43). Clarifying conventional anthropocentric positions without seriously challenging them, the debate stands as entrée to a much more radical set of propositions—Birkin's biocentric "manifesto," which shakes the species foundations upon which humans seek to establish themselves as superior beings.

Up to this point, the protagonists have analyzed the symbolic presence of the nonhuman within the human, witnessed an animal mistreated, and debated the species divide, but no character has suggested that humans might learn something from a "real" animal performing freely and without restraint on its own territory. In fulfilling that function, the "Mino" episode takes its cue from Nietzsche's Zarathustra, who not only contemplates his animals, but takes his philosophical lead from them in relation to the question especially of what human beings lack. Because, like Zarathustra, Birkin too is a "sick animal"—as Ursula notes, he is "very thin and hollow, with a ghastly look in his face" (124)—immersed in a pathological culture from which he cannot escape, he needs an animal example as a mode of overcoming the limits of his own human nature. Just as Zarathustra's animals teach him this mode of self-overcoming, so Mino reveals an "inhuman" otherness—that strange "beyond" without speech to which Birkin aspires.[14] Delivered in a voice of "pure abstraction," and as an overture to Mino's appearance, Birkin's manifesto gives verbal shape to that "impersonal" dimension of contact Mino embodies, as opposed to Ursula's humanist belief in the redemptive power of personal love. As a silent theatrical spectacle, Mino's knowing-without-knowing enacts that nonhuman dimension of being for which Birkin is forced to find words in order to communicate it to Ursula.

The most remarkable aspect perhaps of the manifesto itself is that all its "wild" stipulations apply with more validity to nonhuman than to human being, though, as Birkin implies, their realization in humans will be different. Restoring the "sapiens" to "Homo," Birkin's appeal to the "inhuman" dimension embraces animal being as the lost component a civilized language of culture and ethics represses. In his new dispensation, there is "no speech" (no logocentric foundation), no "terms of agreement" (no legal or institutional backup), no "understanding" (no personal reciprocity), no "calling to book" (no sacrificial self-castigation)—in short, there is an absence of all those elements that secure human ascendancy through the arts of symbolic substitution. Incorporating a new "inhuman" power into themselves, the two "utterly strange creatures" Birkin projects point at once backward to what is already "known" but repressed, and forward to an "unknown" whose evolutionary contours are as yet undeciphered. To remedy this defect in "not-knowing," Mino now takes center stage.

Though Mino embodies the "unknown" in a weak sense of that term—for three brief moments he looks distantly into the landscape or toward the sun, "oblivious of the two human beings"—nevertheless the overwhelming narrative emphasis is on his engagement with Birkin and Ursula, and with the stray cat.[15] In the Deleuzean sense of the term, Mino is a classic oedipal "pet," disdaining mama (Ursula), fixated on papa (Birkin), putting on for his benefit exactly the kind of exhibition of masculine potency he knows his master approves of.[16] A theater of exorbitant anthropomorphisms mixes class, gender, and species discourses together in a manner that instantly alerts Ursula's (and the reader's) suspicions. Does Mino merely act as narrative catalyst for the squabble between the two humans that immediately follows his exit?

From the start, this aristocrat among cats—"kingly," "lordly," full of "manly nonchalance"—exercises his male territorial rights over a deterritorialized female, who solicits the light paw-cuffing Mino promptly delivers. Configuring the "superior wisdom" Mino possesses, this little pastoral drama pushes anthropomorphic projection to its metaphorical limits. Yet, once again, it is the issue of species difference—the gratuitous cruelty to animals—that propels the verbal spat between Birkin and Ursula to its crisis, precipitating the first of Lawrence's many revisions of the meaning of Nietzsche's *Wille zur Macht.*[17] As Ursula perceives him, Mino is the Gerald of the feline brigade, compelled by a real will to power, bullying a female "inferior" to impress his human spectators. For Birkin, by contrast, Mino's aggression represents an exuberant discharge, an overflow of natural vitality to which the stray responds by submitting. The term "bullying" concentrates the distinction between them: while the first involves a sadistic mastery designed to secure male ascendancy (like Gerald with his mare), the second communicates a natural force and authority, a potency of being that the other does not possess (145–52).

In the end the "Mino" episode is most notable for its introduction of a galaxy of new metaphors—"superfine stability," "transcendent and abiding *rapport,*" "two single equal stars balanced in conjunction"—that establish the basic species rhetoric upon which Birkin subsequently redraws the boundaries of the human relationship: animal being, as it were, forms the basis for a new theory of love that includes *it* in its human reckoning. In the "Man to Man" episode, Birkin's extended meditation shows this collocation in action: the "superior wisdom" animals possess without effort humans must strive for by incorporating the nonhuman other. Thus the stable star equilibrium that two cats achieve is the prototype for the "two single [*human*] beings, constellated together like two stars"—the condition Birkin aspires to with Ursula, binding nonhuman and human sexuality together to make a continuous whole. In its embrace of a "primal desire" (146)—its freedom from civilizing constraints—the animal prototype stands in direct opposition to the oedipal model (from whose symbolic proscriptions animals are free) which exalts the "Great Mother" who sacrifices her son to satisfy her "lust for possession."[18] In sum, Birkin's desire to reduce human sex to a purely "functional process" mirrors his image of the way animals practice it (199–201), though the two are not necessarily identical.

II.

At this point, *Women in Love* shifts into a different register—a new kind of species rhetoric that greatly complicates the Gerald/Gudrun relationship vis-à-vis their violent encounters with animals. Two major scenarios open up complexities of response merely hinted at in the Arab mare vignette, linking Gerald and Gudrun's cruel baiting of each other to their ruthless repression of animal being. Sacrificing the animal in themselves unleashes a force whose erotic potential subserves their desire to annihilate each other.

Gudrun's terrorizing of the Highland cattle (in the episode "Water Party") is, in effect, a reversed mirror image of the Arab mare vignette, with Gudrun imposing her compulsive will to ascendancy over the nonhuman as index of her symbolic mastery over her own animal being. Her aggression toward the cattle fuels her aggression toward Gerald, intensifying the sadistic erotics through which they provoke and excite one another (to Gerald's "You have struck the first blow," Gudrun replies "And I shall strike the last"). Inflicting pain on the animal acts as spur to their inflicting pain on each other.

Gudrun's "palpitating dance"[19] toward the cattle—"her breasts lifted . . . her throat exposed as in some voluptuous ecstasy" (D. H. Lawrence 1987c, 167)—exploits a rhetoric of seduction to camouflage a despotic need to subjugate the animal other. Indeed, Gudrun's subsequent becoming-animal—"the electric pulse from [the cattle's] breasts running into her hands"—is a kind of parodic rehearsal of a Deleuzean "becoming," which, in dissolving nonhuman and human identities, precipitates the free flow of libidinal energies across species bounds.[20] In her act of unbridled ascendancy, Gudrun's "rushing" the cattle, by contrast, puts the maximum distance between them and her. In the end, galloping off into the evening, "becoming tiny in the distance," the cattle take shape as manikin figures, mirroring Gudrun's own sculptures of "tiny" animal forms (169–71).

The reductive effect Gudrun achieves on the animal body, Gerald, as "industrial magnate," achieves with the human body, through his collective subjugation of the coal miners themselves. In this calculated violence toward his own species, the miners are surrogates for the violence he instinctively directs against animals. In a modified sacrificial economy, Gerald "crucifies" the collective mining body itself, disfiguring them to the point where they no longer look human, in order to secure his own transcendental identity as "the God of the machine." Instead of to a biblical God, Gerald makes his sacrificial offering to himself, thus secularizing the idea of sacrifice through its purely anthropocentric orientation. As a Nietzschean "high priest" of the miners, who "represented the religion they really felt," Gerald is species-indifferent, violating the symbolic cultural law that decrees that animals, and not humans, should be immolated to appease a god. In transforming humans into Cartesian biomachines, sacrificing nonhumans and humans alike, Gerald asserts his ascendancy over the carnal body itself in all its species permutations (223–31).

That Lawrence was well aware of the close association of sacrificial transcendence with carnivorous practices the first reference to Bismarck, the pet rabbit, makes abundantly clear. In Derrida's terms, Gerald is classically "carnophallogocentric," a human for whom the killing and ingesting of animal flesh is "foundational for [his] social and cultural self-definition" (Wolfe 2003a, 100). If only because they are, at least partly, humanized, oedipal pets like Bismarck are not usually eaten by humans. Since, however, Bismarck retains his feral nature intact, he is not quite a "pet," as Gudrun discovers when he lacerates her arm as she lifts him out of his hutch. Even before Bismarck appears on the scene, Gerald already "sacrifices" him in anticipation. Indeed, his initial suggestion to Gudrun that Bismarck be "draw[n]" and "quarter[ed]," and then "dish[ed] up" incites the first seductively intimate look "of knowledge" between them. Carnivorous sacrifice, Gerald implies, is a more appropriate way of dealing with animals than treating them as art objects, as Gudrun and Winifred do. The prime means to erotic transcendence, as both Gerald and Gudrun now recognize, is through torturing and killing off the animal body both in themselves and in others. Through the species abyss that exalts the human over the nonhuman, they seal their erotic bond through the violent repudiation of their own animal being.

Throughout the "Rabbit" vignette, the rhetoric of the "hellish recognition" between Gerald and Gudrun is geared repeatedly to exposing the unconscious substratum behind the public display, stripping away rational self-justification to reveal the "obscenity" of sacrificing the animal body as a means of heightening sexual pleasure. While immolating an animal, the text implies, to propitiate a god or to bring peace to a divided community is culturally acceptable, the same ritual is "obscene" when its cruelty acts as a spur to erotic excitement. Indeed, contrasting implications of cruelty open up the gap between the nonhuman and human infliction of pain: while Bismarck's laceration of Gudrun's arm is a purely defensive discharge of energy without ulterior intent to wound her, Gerald's deathblow to the animal's neck secures his erotic at-one-ness with Gudrun—their accession to a special kind of transcendence. At this point a close-up of these strange transferential dynamics across species bounds may be of interest.

At precisely the moment Bismarck wounds Gudrun ("her wrists . . . badly scored by the claws of the beast"), the rhetoric shifts from a species-neutral description ("great, lusty rabbit") to a brutally species-reductive one (Bismarck's "mindlessness" and his "bestial stupidity"). As a "heavy cruelty well[s] up" in Gudrun, species subjugation is for the first time openly linked to erotic excitation. Bataille suggests that, "[i]nitiations [and] sacrifices" unite human beings with one another "through rents or wounds," making "sexual laceration and ritual laceration" coterminal (1985, 251), and Gerald and Gudrun's "white-cruel recognition" is of exactly this kind. The literal "long red rent" on her forearm becomes the inflamed sexual wound—the "shallow red rip" that sears his "ultimate consciousness." The transference of pain from one vulnerable body to another not only acts as a sexual stimulus: it also fuels the transcendental drive that underwrites sacrificial substitution—the body tortured in order to make the spirit appear. For the first time, Gerald catches a glimpse of a world other than the one he daily inhabits. As a writer finely attuned to the secret motivations of sacrificial activity, Bataille once again puts it well: the "excitement of sacrifice . . . is a sacred horror . . . which does not limit itself to dismemberment but which . . . opens itself . . . onto a realm beyond this world" (Stoekl 1990, 21). In Gerald's case this "sacred horror" involves the letting through of what the text mysteriously calls the "unthinkable red ether of the beyond, the obscene beyond," and at the same time refigures this aerial or heavenly realm as a perversely "hellish" one.[21] The "beyond" to which Gerald gains access is "obscene," not because he tortures the rabbit, but because its "fear of death" scream acts as an erotic turn-on. Dismemberment of the animal body is the clue to a transcendence that destroys the habitual meanings ascribed to ritual acts. As if to confirm the connection between sacred sacrifice and sexual stimulation, Bismarck suddenly "burst[s] into life" again, his body returned from the dead, rushing round in circles as if it were "obeying some unknown incantation"—an urgent participator in an imaginary sacrificial rite in which he is the chosen victim.

The alternative function of sacrifice—to make man's "humanity manifest" by immolating an animal (Bataille 1990, 25)—is reserved for the vignette's conclusion, where Gerald and Gudrun evasively comment on the scene they have witnessed. In making their species ascendancy quite clear to each other, they claim membership in an exclusive club called the "human." In response to Gudrun's assertion that Bismarck is "decidedly mad," Gerald subtly redraws the species fault line: as opposed, Gerald implies, to the cool rationality that marks human behavior, madness is the very essence of rabbithood ("That's what it is to be a rabbit"). In turn, Gudrun's rapturous affirmation—"God be praised we aren't rabbits"—at once confirms the species abyss Gerald is avouching, while implicitly challenging the gender distinction it entails: though rabbits may be an inferior species, Gudrun (as female) is not inferior to the male, as a humanist carnophallogocentric culture assumes. Thus, her response to Gerald's terse interpolation—"Not rabbits?"—takes the form of a "strong, slow, almost man-like" assertion that makes him feel as if "she had hit him across the face": "All that, and more," Gudrun replies—the "more," in my reading, implying that when it comes to inflicting pain to intensify sexual pleasure, her capacity is even greater than his (D. H. Lawrence 1987c, 238–43).

III.

"Rabbit" is the last vignette where the species issue takes center stage as a prime determinant of how the protagonists conceive of themselves and of one another. From this point on, its role is largely submerged beneath other more pressing discourses—sexual, gender, aesthetic—that dominate the remaining chapters, though species questions frequently operate "from below" to complicate the uneasy distribution of vital forces these discourses represent. The enigma of the human relationship to its own animality still exerts a subliminal pressure, a disturbing power to destabilize attempts to assert a human autonomy, free from carnal vicissitudes. While Birkin and Ursula (as good biocentrists) progressively incorporate the nonhuman other as essential to their constitution as humans, Gerald and Gudrun (androcentrically) repudiate it through a violent repression that reifies and desensualizes the flesh: thus, Gudrun's longed-for "beyond" is the "navel of eternal snow" in the Austrian Alps, while Gerald's ultimate "beyond" is the "hollow basin of snow" into which he falls down and dies (D. H. Lawrence

1987c, 410, 474). We can trace Birkin and Ursula's enraptured embrace of the human animal body first of all.

In the episode "Excurse," for example, Birkin and Ursula climax their lovemaking by retreating to a dark, silent forest, signaling topographically their proximity to feral nonhuman being: their chosen territory is also that of untamed woodland creatures. Before their retreat, however, and through their discovery of a strange new site—"the darkest, deepest, strangest life-source of the human body"—they celebrate embodiment itself as the mode of erotic fulfillment. The anal site they discover in the Saracen's Head is also the same site Freud locates as a critical turning point in evolutionary history, when, through "organic repression," man separated himself off from his animal past: civilization, Freud asserts, is the "organic defense of the new form of life achieved with man's erect gait against his earlier animal existence" (Freud 1957, 12:296) There is a major paradox here: the same site that, for Freud, marked a crucial advance into civilization, for Birkin and Ursula marks their radical retreat from it. Put differently, this is precisely the secret site a Western humanist culture represses as its mode of securing ascendancy over animal being. Thus, Birkin and Ursula's break is not with their own animal past—on the contrary, they desire to incorporate it—but with a traditional Enlightenment ethos that tries to repress it. In a sequence of hospitable gestures toward such claims ("wander about for a bit"), they imagine dispensing with clothes—thus reneging on all those symbolic signs of the human, those Lacanian supplements for a libidinal lack that dissolves in their access to the plenum of animal being (D. H. Lawrence 1987c, 312–16)

Sherwood Forest is the locus where Birkin's biocentric manifesto at last finds its erotic realization. Caught up in a network of larger cosmic dependencies, the lovers embrace the nonhuman other as part of themselves—"the body of mysterious night upon the body of mysterious night, the night masculine and feminine"—accessible to all creatures who possess bodily being. In the process the logic of sacrifice is subtly undone. Because the "vital, sensual reality" to which the lovers access "can never be transmuted into mind content," it can never be used as a sacrificial offering to cultural ideals that would seek to eradicate it. Unlike Gerald and Gudrun's the lovers' bodies are not the vehicles of a culture of sacrifice that would eliminate erotic *jouissance* to prove the sovereignty of the human. In a supreme creaturely gesture Birkin and Ursula "hid[e] away" the "magnificence of the night"—that "inheritance of a universe of dark reality," which is also their primal inheritance from their animal past. To recall it would inevitably return it to memory, and to the sphere of the culturally human that they feel they have overcome. In all of this, however, Lawrence is not asserting an identity of human and nonhuman being, but a participation in the same root energies that fuel the cosmic flow of desire (320).

That the anal site is a crucial fault line, both for Freud and for Lawrence from their different perspectives, is highlighted by its dominance in the last, climactic love engagement between Birkin and Ursula. The sexual is still the arena where fixing the species caesura in its proper place is at its most problematic. In their final encounter in the Gasthaus in the Alps, the lovers literally put into practice those "mystically-physically satisfying" rites (314), which the metaphorics of the Sherwood Forest description masked and occluded. As the ultimate site of acceptance of their animal past, the anal marks the critical cultural threshold that splits off human from animal sex—the locus at which old humanist markers like "beastly" or "debasing" lose their discriminatory force. While it appears that Birkin has fully accepted the evolutionary continuum with animal being, Ursula as yet has not: the vignette stages her final working-through toward acceptance.

As they dance together, Birkin moves toward her with a "subtle, animal, indifferent approach"—with a "mocking brutishness" that at once "fascinates" and "repels" her. These descriptive markers already lay out the erotic parameters within which the scene is played out. Eliding the sex-act description, Ursula's retrospective responses take the form of a "conversion" rhetoric, running the gamut from an initial anthropocentric "shame" at Birkin's licentious behavior to a biocentric affirmation of all sexual acts that lift cultural repression and that strengthen the link with the animal past. Compelled by a humanist moral opprobrium that stigmatizes such acts as "bestial," "degrading," and "shameful," she revaluates each term in turn, embracing a biodiversity that, in "go[ing] the whole round of experience," restores anal eroticism to its proper place in the sexual pantheon. Indeed, her renunciation of shame has something of a Nietzschean ardor and exultation—her protest against what Nietzsche calls that "sickly . . . moralizing by means of which the animal 'man' finally learns to feel ashamed of all his instincts" (1996, 48). Linked to her new sense of "freedom," shame is the cultural stigma that brands humans as animals, though animals exemplify the freedom from anal repression and shame ("She was free, when . . . no dark shameful things were denied her"). In becoming the human-animal beings that they are, Birkin and Ursula shatter the last sexual barrier that separates human from nonhuman being (D. H. Lawrence 1987c, 412–13).

IV.

The fate of their doppelgängers (Gerald and Gudrun) pursues a parallel but reversed trajectory, where near-identical metaphors are employed to create opposite effects. While Birkin and Ursula embrace their dark "inheritance" from the evolutionary past, Gerald and Gudrun eliminate it in their quest for a transcendence that leaves the body behind. Subsuming the erotic into the death drive, a sacrificial sadism, earlier directed toward animals, is now unleashed on each of them. Gudrun's erotic initiation—her first fantasized encounter with Gerald—starts, not with a "real" engagement, however, but with a historical scenario that combines sacrifice, sadism, and death in one spectacular showpiece. As she recalls "the abandonments of Roman license," including the sacrificial slaughter of both humans and animals in a public arena, Gudrun's "heart gr[o]w[s] hot." The kind of traditional speciesism that permits killing nonhuman but not human beings is temporarily suspended, as the legal is transformed into "license." Gudrun's imagined "licentiousness" may at first sight be difficult to distinguish from the "bestial" unrestraint of Ursula we have already explored: both vignettes share the same rhetoric of a "brutal" and unbridled release. The difference, however, is encapsulated in the end effect: while Ursula's "different reality" turns on a vivid new world opened up, Gudrun's "final reality" is already "distinct and perfect," closed off from further development (D. H. Lawrence 1987c, 187, 413). As the already too well "known," too realized, Gudrun "shut[s] . . . off" the animal body that Ursula embraces as the hitherto "unknown" part of herself.

In Gerald and Gudrun's love encounters, species discourse plays a subliminal role, marked mainly by its latencies and by the libidinal lack that its eclipse implies. An insistent drive toward transcendence that dematerializes the body takes precedence over those somatic propulsions that simultaneously excite it. Thus, Gudrun's first kissing of Gerald (under the dark bridge where colliers habitually kissed their sweethearts) already etherealizes the body; its "palpable real otherness" (320) dissolved into a kind of substanceless wraith. Gudrun's caress is not of the material flesh but of a phantasmal object of her own creation—a "living radio-active body" that precipitates her "transcendent fear of the thing [Gerald] was." This "delicate" movement of her fingers "over the mould of his face" coimplicates the aesthetic (Gudrun is a sculptor) with the psychical in a way that dissolves its threatening corporeality through the same touch that is meant to arouse it. In the context of his discussion of an Enlightenment, rational culture (of which Gerald and Gudrun are classic representatives), Slavoj Žižek speaks of the "desubstantialization [of the subject] which opens up the empty space . . . which fantasies are projected, where monsters appear" (2001, 136)—the same "empty space" Gerald embodies, later filled by the "bronze" monster who, "clos[ing] over [Gudrun] like steel," virtually rapes her (D. H. Lawrence 1987c, 402). In species discourse terms, her "strain[ing] of [Gerald] into her knowledge" betrays the same drive toward transcendence—toward securing a dematerialized abstract identity that excludes animal being. More "knowledge" of Gerald, as it were, serves to distance her even further from the menacing animality she uses her art to transcend. Thus, her touch is essentially defensive, resistant—a medium for channeling a purely ideational content that fortifies her ultimate power over him. If the aesthetic is the realm that most effectively "erects a barrier between species" (Wolfe 2003a, 176), subtly closing off the instinctual, then Gudrun's rapturous aesthetic appreciation—"You are so *beautiful*"—completes that distancing that, like the artwork itself, splits the body off from its instinctual roots. In the end, purged of their animal residues, both erotic bodies are freed through a psychical transcendence that presages the "death" the text already anticipates (D. H. Lawrence 1987c, 330–32).

Gerald and Gudrun's consummation of their relationship once again plays on eliding the animal body, though this time the techniques of exclusion are different. Locked into an oedipal cage, desire itself is constrained within a Freudian paradigm that confines both lovers to single-role identities: Gudrun is the unsatisfied mother, and Gerald the insatiable child. Here the elision of the nonhuman is achieved paradoxically through a lack in the human—that "specific prematurity of birth" (Derrida 2003, 124) that dooms man to a prolonged dependence on parental role figures from which animals are naturally free. Such infantile dependency, in effect, conditions the sexual roles Gerald and Gudrun assume toward each other. In confining desire to unidirectional satisfactions, the erotic is subordinated to the infantile drive that frenetically feeds off the maternal one. Because from the Deleuzean perspective, oedipal desires are a "disfigured image by means of which repression catches desire in a trap" (Deleuze and Guattari 1984, 116),[22] Gerald and Gudrun's lovemaking imposes a radical disfigurement on the erotic body itself. Shorn of its camouflaging rhetoric, Gudrun gives Gerald a bath ("He . . . sink[s] to rest in the bath of her living strength"), breast-feeds him ("[l]ike a child at the breast, he cleaved intensely to her"), and then quietly puts him to sleep. Put differently, Gerald's frenzied identification with the maternal (his father has just died) blocks off erotic desire just as effectively as Gudrun's exclusive role as mother blocks off hers. In this sense Gudrun is the sacrificial victim of a cruelly restrictive oedipal regime that insists on the satisfaction of needs that are not her own, and that give her no pleasure.

As Gerald soundly sleeps, Gudrun's subsequent destruction "into perfect consciousness" obeys the sacrificial law of at-one-ment that negates bodily needs to satisfy the dream of transcendence—in her case, that "violent active superconsciousness" which demands a rehearsal of her whole oedipal history: "her childhood, her girlhood . . . her lovers, her acquaintances, everybody." With this blocking of that "inhuman" desire the oedipal regime represses, two balked streams of erotic libido flow unrecognized past each other (D. H. Lawrence 1987c, 344–46).

While Gerald and Gudrun's first Alpine encounters reinforce the same repressively oedipal frame, it reverses its dynamics, projecting Gerald as the "superhumanly" masterful father who violates his "helplessly" vulnerable child. In this process the erotic animal body transmutes into a mechanized one—the nonhuman "bronze" monster who, "like steel," closes over his chosen nymphet, who in turn has no defenses against him. The animal body itself is the sacrificial victim of a sexual exchange in which the sacred offering is to the god of the machine who, in using it, tears it apart. Though the balance of power continually shifts within the relationship, its baseline is the petrification of animal energies that fuels Gerald and Gudrun's desire to annihilate each other. Locked within a sadistic oedipal regime, Gerald's mechanized body and Gudrun's glacialized one are functions of a submerged species discourse—that lost animal vitality, the missing link between nature and culture—that at once asserts and conceals what is lacking in all these encounters (401–2).

Intercalated between these scenes of oedipal self-destruction in action and Gerald's final transcendence in death, the Loerke figure makes his appearance, and, with him, a singular, highly significant vignette that puts on display, not another "live" animal, but one raised up and subsumed into the condition of art. Here the aesthetic and the sacrificial reinforce one another, at once elevating and downgrading the animal body. Underwritten by a powerful species discourse that refines and finesses its arguments, the bronze statuette of the stallion provokes a highly charged discussion of modernist art. Of the four participants, Loerke and Gudrun are artistic initiates who proclaim the absolute autonomy of the artwork, Ursula is the naïve anthropomorphist who confuses art with reality, and Gerald, the casual outsider, is uninvolved in such "esoteric" affairs. Already, throughout the text, both Loerke and Gudrun are located on the wrong side of the species divide. Identified with "inferior" creatures on the Lawrentian scale—mice, bats, magpies, fleas, rabbits—Loerke, like them, lacks the life-assertive, animal vigor and courage that fuel the creation of art. Gudrun's minimalist art—her "tiny" animal sculptures—in turn shrink rather than enhance animal power, locating her at the farthest possible distance from it (like looking "through the wrong end of the opera glasses," as Hermione cruelly observes [39]).

The discussion itself has its baseline in a submerged species hierarchy, designed to secure an autonomous human identity through its re-creation in art. Occupying the highest niche, art is the elitist cultural means of overcoming the animal being in the human. Sadomasochistic subjection—the sacrificial putting down of the flesh—is at once the critical issue and what sparks the quarrel from which Gerald largely excludes himself. Loerke, we hear, beats his girl-model into submission to get her to pose. The statuette in turn configures repression itself in a state of symbolic crisis: curbed, checked, restrained—"rigid with pent up power . . . its flanks . . . pressed back"—the stallion stands at the threshold of an unleashing of energy that never occurs. Exalting the cultural over the natural, the aesthetic posits cruel repression as the catalyst for the creation of art, insinuating a Cartesian mind/body split that desubstantializes the flesh, fueling its re-creation as formalized image or figure. In its divorce of the aesthetic from the animalistic, art is Homo sapiens's mode of access to an identity that proves he or she is no longer an animal.

The bronze statuette already harks back to an earlier "real-life" vignette. There, an all-powerful male figure (Gerald) sits astride a terrified Arab mare: here, by contrast, a terrified young naked girl sits sideways on a powerfully inhibited stallion. The fierce disciplining of vulnerable flesh links the vignettes together—the former through Gerald's violent suppression of the animal body, the latter through the girl's "fearful" sense of exposure ("naked on the naked flank of the horse") at precisely the moment of access to a full human identity ("a maiden passing towards cruel womanhood"). Loerke's subsequent confession that he had to slap the girl hard and "ma[k]e her cry" binds the pregnable human and nonhuman bodies together—one bloodily sacrificed to ensure male transcendence, the other cruelly disciplined to ensure the transcendence of art.

To boost their elitist status as artistic initiates, Loerke and Gudrun put the maximum distance between themselves and the animals they use in their art to create symbolic meaning for humans. The absolute autonomy of the artwork —"*I* and my art have *nothing* to do with each other. My art stands in another world, I am in this world," as Gudrun succinctly puts it—mirrors the divorce of the aesthetic from an animality that would draw it back into the corporeal world it claims to transcend. Art, as the two artists perceive it, secures an elitist artistic identity in a manner no other form of sacrificial practice achieves. Thus Gudrun, as Gerald perceives her, has already attained to a self-engendered autonomy ("closed round upon herself, self-complete, without desire" [445]), while Loerke visibly grows in aristocratic stature as he secures his artistic credentials ("he seemed to grow more uppish and lordly"). Proclaiming their unique status as artists, both become more (human) species–assertive, as perfected beings without dependence on anything other than art creation itself. Insofar as the art/life caesura mirrors the human/animal one—"life doesn't *really* matter—it is one's art that is central," as Gudrun declares (448)—both already inhabit a rarified aestheticized universe, purging both the artistic persona and the artwork from the taint of instinctual being.

Yet in its relation to animal power, the bronze statuette violates the law of aesthetic autonomy, since it configures, not a radical break with, but an intimate continuum between, (Loerke's) "two different and distinct planes of existence" (nature and art) that should be kept absolutely separate. Put differently the young model's "shame and grief," as the narrator presents it, are the outcome of her subjection to the stallion's raw, instinctual animal energy that she neither understands nor controls, and that seems to violate her integrity as a virginal girl. In subtly deconstructing the "art-autonomy" theory through an artwork that exhibits the opposite in action, the artwork enacts its revenge on a theory that seeks to falsify the artistic practice that brought it into being.

But what of Gerald and Ursula, both of whom contribute their share to the quarrel's development? Gerald's disapproval of Ursula's hysterical protest against Loerke's "brutal" art portrayal has both a class and a species basis: his aristocratic dislike of public displays of emotion that should by rights be suppressed is linked to his sense that art may be the ultimate rite that separates man from his animal past—"the esotericism which gave man his last distinction." Unlike Loerke and Gudrun's elitism, which is aesthetic, Gerald's is essentially social. In turn, Ursula's anthropomorphic identification with the statuette is "maudlin" in exactly the manner Birkin earlier said he "detested" (139). While Ursula shares the same deep-rooted species prejudice as Loerke and Gudrun (animals are an "inferior creation" [143]), she nevertheless differs from them in two essentials: in her empathic susceptibility to creaturely pain (Gerald and Gudrun are of course highly sensitive too, but they exploit pain as a mode of erotic arousal), and in her lack of sophistication vis-à-vis art, which she views purely mimetically as a "picture" either of the art object or of the artist's psychology. Thus Loerke's "rage" at Ursula is because she sees in the statuette only his "stock stupid brutality"—exactly the condition he assumes his artwork transcends (428–34).[23]

As it moves ineluctably to its violent conclusion, Gerald and Gudrun's tortured (and torturing) relationship to the animal body manifests itself no longer through vivid animal vignettes (like the Arab mare and the rabbit episodes), but through an intensification of the link between sacrifice and transcendence. Sacrificial sublimation fuels the destructive drive that will set them free from the body itself—their dream of discarnate states, at once spectral and vaguely psychotic. While Gerald aspires to a kind of formless state or location—an "unrealized heavens . . . the unfinished bliss of his own yearning"—Gudrun dreams of becoming a "pure spirit," the consummation of her earlier dream of at-oneness with the "timeless, frozen centre of the All" in the Austrian Alps (446, 410). Fleshly immolation thus underwrites their mutual desire for destruction—the annihilation of corporeal being. Indeed, it is precisely Bataille's "excitement of sacrifice"—its "sacred horror" (Stoekl 1990, 21) —that incites Gerald's "voluptuous" fantasy of "kill[ing]" off Gudrun in the snow: "strangling" her would at once ensure his ultimate possession ("he would have had her finally and for ever") and his release from the "torture" of her sexual presence (D. H. Lawrence 1987c, 460). The event itself, when it occurs, combines a "frenzied" erotic excitement with the sense of its sacrificial acceptance by a well-pleased and appeased deity ("a god-given gratification") (471–72). Thus it comes as no surprise that, just before his death, Gerald encounters the archetypal Western image of sacrificial immolation—"a half-buried crucifix"—displaying the body tortured to death to propitiate an omnipotent god. Fantasizing the possibility of becoming the sacrificial victim of the "Lord Jesus" himself, who is no longer savior but executioner, Gerald raises his hands in anticipation of the deathblow descending. In the end Gerald is sacrificed to the petrified snow body that, in snapping the spirit/flesh link, returns him to the passive animality he repudiated in life ("as he fell something broke in his soul, and immediately he went to sleep") (473–74).

The final pages of *Women in Love* ("Exeunt") are strewn with dead bodies—a rabbit ("frozen like a board on the snow"), a stallion ("a dead mass of maleness"), and, as a catalyst for these remembered images, Gerald's "cold, mute, material" body, curled up on a slab. This harrowing cross-species inventory foregrounds the harsh corporeal destiny, shared by humans and nonhumans alike. Dissolving the anthropocentric hubris that locates man at the top, the long perspectives of Birkin's meditation shrink the species hierarchy itself to the status of a local delusion, cultivated by man to ensure his ascendancy. Because "man is not the criterion," "new species ar[i]se," "more lovely" than man, and with creative possibilities far beyond his imagining. A narrow anthropocentrism, Birkin suggests, must give way to a broad biocentrism—the commonality of life shared by all sentient beings. In Birkin's terms this involves having "one's pulse beating direct from the mystery" in precisely the same manner as the nonhuman creation. More theological than Darwinian in its orientation, the meditation deconstructs the foundations upon which man separates himself off from animal being. Only at the point where "[h]uman and inhuman" cease to matter does Homo sapiens at last realize its full human potential (477–80).

Notes

1. In three excellent essays, Carrie Rohman engages the question of the animal presence in man in the early modernist novel, and in D. H. Lawrence's *The Plumed Serpent.* See Rohman 2003, 2005, 2007. For illuminating essays on related topics, see also Cary Wolfe's "Aficionados and Friend Killers: Rearticulating Race and Gender via Species in Hemingway" 2003a, 122–68, and Feldman 2006.

2. Throughout this essay my use of the term "animal body" includes nonhuman and human varieties.

3. In relation to language Gillian Beer neatly sums up the connection: "Language is anthropomorphic by its nature and anthropocentric in its assumptions" (1983, 50).

4. An excised passage from *The Rainbow* contains Lawrence's meditation on the vital need to incorporate the nonhuman in order to become fully human. It takes the form of Ursula's visionary insight, as she gazes into the microscope in the college laboratory: "I am all of these beasts [tigers and apes]. . . . Within my body at this moment is the whole sequence of creation, from the start up to this moment. And every pulse of the sequence still beats in me. And at times, I am scarcely more than the amoeba. And at times I am a marsh beast, a clammy lizard. And at times I am a jungle beast with a cat's cry and a cat's lust. . . . But none of these do contradict that I am. For none of these *shall* contradict that I am I. For I am I, pushing into the unknown" (D. H. Lawrence 1989c, 656).

5. In *Beasts of the Modern Imagination* Margot Norris draws together a small group of thinkers, writers, and artists who create, not *like* an animal, but "*as* the animal . . . with their animality speaking" (1985, 1). This "biocentric tradition" spans the era between Darwin and Lawrence, and died out after the Second World War. Tim Gadd, however, maintains that "the tradition did not exactly die out, but gradually reemerged and transformed, becoming a salient characteristic of popular culture" (2005, 258).

6. See especially Freud's speculations about how man's assumption of an erect posture and the depreciation of his sense of smell threatened not only his anal eroticism with "organic repression," but "the whole of his sexuality" (1957, 12:296).

7. See Girard 1977, and Georges Bataille's "Hegel, Death and Sacrifice" (1990, 9–28). In his classic essay, "From Restricted to General Economy: A Hegelianism without Reserve," Jacques Derrida explores the connection between sacrifice, death, and destruction, and the privileged sacrificial moment when man "raises [himself] above life" by overcoming his fear of death (1978, 251–77).

8. For fascinating reflections on pack animals in general, including the wolf, see Deleuze and Guattari 1987, 264–68.

9. As Mark Feldman puts it, the zoo with its physics of caging "shows the animal marginalized and re-presented as educational spectacle, amusement, or token of empire" (2006, 178).

10. For an illuminating analysis of the "gaze" in this particular vignette, see Ingersoll (1994, 90–94).

11. The distinction between human "response" and animal "reaction" goes back to Descartes, who argued that while animals have sensations (they can react), these are not "sensations in the full sense of the word as they are with humans, because they are not accompanied by propositional thoughts" (Smith 2005, 232).

12. Jeremy Bentham famously based the value of sentient life itself on its ability to feel pleasure or pain: "[T]he capacity for suffering, rather than the capacity for abstract reasoning or language, is the proper basis for a being's inclusion in moral calculations" (Steiner 2005, 163). "[T]he question is not, Can [animals] *reason?* nor Can they *talk?* but, Can they *suffer?*" (Bentham 1948, 310–11).

13. Carol Adams, for example, offers an abundance of examples showing how "[l]anguage fuses women's and animals' inferior status in a patriarchal culture" (2004, 81–84).

14. Not only do the animals speak to Zarathustra: they also teach him the doctrine of the eternal recurrence, and of the advent of the Superman (Nietzsche 1978, 232–38).

15. For the opposite point of view that plays down Lawrence's anthropomorphizing, and that foregrounds the "uncanny fires" of the cats' eyes that "look beyond or through the human beings," see Parker (2004, 230).

16. For Deleuze and Guattari's account of "Oedipalized animal[s]," see Deleuze and Guattari 1987, 269–70. Cary Wolfe depicts them as those "*humanized animals* . . . that we exempt from the sacrificial regime by endowing them with ostensibly human features" (2003, 101). Mino's second appearance (D. H. Lawrence 1987c, 299–301) extends the oedipal regime to include Hermione who (as bossy mama) tries in vain to exert her "will to power" over him.

17. For Lawrence's subsequent revisions of the term "will to power," see (among a host of less interesting examples) D. H. Lawrence 1988a; 297, 1979, 164–65; and 1981a, 489.

18. As a good humanist, Jacques Lacan, as Derrida shows, constrains animals to the presymbolic stage of development, keeping them "prisoner within the specularity of the imaginary." Indeed, the passage from imaginary to symbolic is "determined as a passage from animal to human order" (Derrida 2003, 130–34).

19. Gudrun's "palpitating" body resonates with echoes of the first "palpitating" body in *Women in Love*—that of the Arab mare, in Gudrun's fantasy, brought "under control" between Gerald's "clench[ed]" thighs (D. H. Lawrence 1987c, 113).

20. Deleuze and Guattari quote from a Lawrence letter to John Middleton Murry (D. H. Lawrence 1993b, 294) to distinguish between a "sen-

timental or domestic relation" (oedipal) to an animal, and those "unheard-of becomings," which Lawrence writes of in his "Tortoise" poems. "But the objection is raised against Lawrence: 'Your tortoises aren't real!' And he answers: Possibly, but my becoming is, my becoming is real, even and especially if you have no way of judging it, because you're just little house dogs" (Deleuze and Guattari 1987, 269–70). Gudrun's desire to subjugate the Highland cattle to her will is clearly a wrong kind of "becoming animal."

21. The note explaining the term "ether" in the Cambridge Edition suggests that it is "the medium supposed to fill the upper regions of space, as air fills the lower regions" (D. H. Lawrence 1987c, 559).

22. In *Anti-Oedipus* Deleuze and Guattari fantasize the nature of Lawrence's protest against the oedipal trap: "Oedipus is not a state of desire and the drives, it is an *idea*, nothing but an idea that repression inspires in us concerning desire" (1984, 115). In this sense Gerald and Gudrun's *idea* of each other is caught in an oedipal trap of the same kind.

23. See Jeff Wallace's interesting analysis of the vignette, especially in relation to Ursula's anthropomorphism (2005, 133–34).

Modernism's Fourth Dimension in *Aaron's Rod*: Einstein, Picasso, and Lawrence

Kumiko Hoshi

EINSTEIN, PICASSO, AND LAWRENCE—AT FIRST SIGHT, THERE may seem no significant connection among these three, except that roughly speaking they were contemporaries; their fields of achievements as well as nationalities were entirely different. Albert Einstein—born in 1879 in Ulm, Germany—introduced the special theory of relativity in 1905 and the general theory of relativity in 1915, and caused a great paradigm shift in the history of science. Pablo Picasso—born in 1881, in Málaga, Spain—painted *Les Demoiselles d'Avignon* in 1907, a picture regarded as the most significant work in the development of the modern art movement, cubism. D. H. Lawrence—born in 1885 in Nottingham, England—published *Women in Love* in 1920, a novel that helped him to establish his status as one of the greatest modernist writers. Closer examination, however, will lead us to recognize that they indeed had much more in common. They opened the new "windows" in their respective fields, and more importantly, what is seen through these "windows" is one and the same: that is, a new vision of the world that is based on the concept of relativity.

With regard to Einstein and Picasso, Arthur I. Miller has explored close similarities in their personal and working lives in *Einstein, Picasso*. Miller states: "Relativity and *Les Demoiselles* represent the responses of two people—Einstein and Picasso, although geographically and culturally separated—to the dramatic changes sweeping across Europe like a tidal wave" (2001, 2). To these "dramatic changes sweeping across Europe" Lawrence also responded.

The connection between Lawrence and Picasso has received little attention from critics.[1] And yet, it is evident that Lawrence was greatly interested in Picasso's pictures. Lawrence's first reference to Picasso could be found in *Women in Love*, where he changed the name of the artist from "Pisarro" to "Picasso" when he was revising the typescript in November 1916 (1987c, 560). Therefore, Lawrence surely had known Picasso's pictures by then. Later in his life, Lawrence made brief comments on Picasso, most of which seem to suggest a negative view toward the artist. For instance, in "Pictures on the Walls," an essay written in 1929, Lawrence states: "[I]f I had some Picassos I should want to keep them about six months . . . then, probably, I should be through with them" (2004d, 260). In comparison with "at least a year or two" for "a Renoir nude" and "all my life" for "the Titian 'Adam and Eve,' " "six months" for Picasso's paintings is much shorter (611). In "The Real Thing," which Lawrence wrote in 1930, the works of Picasso are considered as things for which men and women in the younger generation have "counterfeit love" (2004f, 201). In spite of these unfavorable comments on Picasso, the fact that Lawrence had maintained his interest in Picasso's pictures should shed a light on the more significant connection between these two modernists.

In contrast, as Michael Whitworth and Bruce Clarke have noted (Whitworth 2004f, 124; Clarke 2001, 213), Lawrence made a quick and enthusiastic response to Einstein's theories of relativity. In 1921, Lawrence read Einstein's *Relativity: The Special and General Theory* in English translation. He had asked Koteliansky to send a copy of Einstein's *Relativity* and later wrote to him: "I like [Einstein] for taking out the pin which fixed down our fluttering little physical universe" (1987a, 37). His enthusiastic response to Einstein is articulated in *Fantasia of the Unconscious* (1922): "We are all very pleased with Mr Einstein for knocking that external axis out of the universe. The universe isn't a spinning wheel. It is a cloud of bees flying and veering round. Thank goodness for that, for we were getting drunk on the spinning wheel" (2004a, 72). In *Kangaroo* (1923), written right after he read Einstein's *Relativity,* Lawrence shows his enthusiasm for Einstein more clearly. Here he refers to Einstein's theories of relativity themselves as "fashionable" "at the moment" (1994, 109). In addition, he uses some of the well-known clichés regarding relativity, like "everything is relative" (280) and "All things are relative, and have their sacredness in their true relation to all other things" (328).

Lawrence's interest in Einstein's theories of relativity seemed never to diminish in Lawrence's lifetime. His last collection of poetry, *Pansies* (1929), includes the poem entitled "Relativity":

> I like relativity and quantum theories
> Because I don't understand them
> and they make me feel as if space shifted
> about like a swan that can't settle,
> refusing to sit still and be measured;
> and as if the atom were an impulsive thing
> always changing its mind.
>
> (1972, 524)

This short, witty poem is thought-provoking partly because it shows Lawrence's predilection for Einstein's theories of relativity, and partly because the first two lines of the poem, "I like relativity and quantum theories / Because I don't understand them," show the most common response among Lawrence's contemporaries to the theories of relativity. There is an interesting anecdote regarding what Charlie Chaplin said to Einstein when they first met in 1931: "They cheer me because they all understand me, and they cheer you because no one understands you" (qtd. in A. I. Miller 2001, 235).

In fact, Einstein's special and general theories of relativity had a great impact on his contemporaries, and not only those who were specialists in physics, but also artists, writers, and philosophers. What these theories achieved was first and foremost a subversion of the traditional paradigm of the universe as explained by Newton's idea of absolute space, and secondly the presentation of an alternative vision of the space-time continuum in which everything was relative. This new vision of the universe influenced, as Peter Childs has shown, modernist writers such as Marcel

Proust, James Joyce, and Virginia Woolf; the Russian philosopher Mikhail Bakhtin; and cubist painters such as Pablo Picasso and Georges Braque.[2]

At the same time, however, there are those who question the direct influence of Einstein's theories of relativity on these contemporaries. Linda Dalrymple Henderson firmly denies the influence of Einstein's theories of relativity on the cubists: "The cubists were not influenced by Einstein's relativizing of simultaneity" (1983, 89). Rather than Einstein's theories, she points out the influence of the notion of the fourth dimension on the cubists. Henderson also states that Proust, Joyce, and Woolf—those who, according to Childs, were under the influence of Einstein's theories of relativity—in fact explored the concept of the fourth dimension in their novels.

Although Einstein used the term "four-dimensional" in his special theory of relativity published in 1905, the idea of the fourth dimension did not originate with him.[3] The fourth dimension was, as Henderson says, "initially formulated in [the] 1820s" as non-euclidean geometry (11). At the outset, the fourth dimension was considered to be the element of time, added to the conventional three elements of height, length, and width. H. G. Wells was one of the earliest writers to be drawn to the concept of time as the fourth dimension, writing such science fiction as *The Time Machine* (1895). From then up to the beginning of the twentieth century, the fourth dimension gradually developed into a much wider concept, signifying a new vision of the world. Henderson explains: "A variety of connotations were gradually added to the geometrical meaning of 'the fourth dimension,' so that by 1900 the term had philosophical, mystical, and pseudoscientific implications along with its alternative interpretation as time" (11). This ambiguous and complicated concept of the fourth dimension attracted other artists, such as the cubists and Marcel Duchamp, who became known for engaging themselves in portraying the spatial aspect of the fourth dimension in the plastic arts.

It is also important to note that technologies invented in the same period, such as the Kodak camera (1888), the X-ray (1895), and the cinematograph (1895), acted as a stimulus to this aspiration among artists and intellectuals. For example, as Childs writes, "[T]he Kodak camera had made it possible . . . to give a lifelike representation of any chosen object," and made artists need "to assert an alternative, nonrepresentational approach that differed from that of the camera" (2000, 108). The X-ray, according to Henderson, revealed "previously invisible forms," suggesting "a new, more fluid relationship of those forms to the space around them" (2003, 135). As Henderson also points out, the cinematographs of Étienne-Jules Marey succeeded in representing "a type of invisible reality . . . a reality in flux" (2005, 7). In other words, all these technologies made a crucial contribution to the work of the contemporary artists mentioned above.

What these circumstances make clear is that from the late nineteenth to the early twentieth century the cultural climate aspired to a dynamic, relative vision of the space-time world that was very different from the old, static, and fixed vision of the world. This aspiration for a new vision of the world was shared by a number of artists and intellectuals of the time and gradually molded the international, interdisciplinary movement known as modernism. In this sense, a modernist was in essence what Lawrence called a "thought-adventurer" (D. H. Lawrence 1994, 279; 1988c, 197).

Lawrence was in the midst of this cultural climate, exploring the new vision of the world as a "thought-adventurer." It is true that Lawrence was strongly attracted by the new vision of the space-time continuum presented in Einstein's theories of relativity. However, what Lawrence found in Einstein's theories seems to be a theoretical framework to revitalize his own concept of living relationships in the world. Mark Kinkead-Weekes states clearly: "[Lawrence] is pleased to find, in Einstein's 'popular exposition' of his theory of relativity . . . that the new theory subverts the idea of a universe governed by a unitary system of scientific laws, and substitutes instead the idea that cosmic forces can only be known in relation to one another. This seemed to reinforce . . . his belief that life was always a matter of *relationship*—between opposite impulses within the self, and between selves, none paramount, all 'purely relative to one another,' in an essentially creative pluralism" (1996, 659). While *Kangaroo* is the first novel in which Lawrence consciously presented the concept of relativity, those written before *Kangaroo,* such as *Women in Love* (1920), *The Lost Girl* (1920), and *Aaron's Rod* (1922), are works in which Lawrence, though unconsciously, struggled to represent the concept of relativity. This essay aims to show how Lawrence contributed to the modernist movement by opening a new "window" to the spatial fourth dimension in *Aaron's Rod.*

Aaron's Rod is one of the works in which Lawrence most successfully presents the vision of this new dynamic and relative world, the examination of which was also attracting the attention of artists. Lawrence completed this novel right before he read Einstein's *Relativity* and showed a keen interest in the theories of relativity in *Fantasia of the Unconscious.* The letters to Robert Mountsier and Curtis Brown, both dated June 1, 1921 (D. H. Lawrence 1984, 730, 731), show that Lawrence had finished *Aaron's Rod* by the end of May. Three days later, on June 4, he asked Koteliansky to send a copy of Einstein's *Relativity* (1987a, 23), and on June 16, he wrote his impression about it (37), which has been quoted earlier. This timing comes to have a special significance when Lawrence's process of writing is taken into consideration. As Lawrence himself admitted, he was inclined to create his works on the basis of "philosophy" or a "metaphysic," even though he was unaware of its true nature at the stage of writing. In *Fantasia of the Unconscious,* Lawrence states:

> [I]t seems to me that even art is utterly dependent on philosophy: or if you prefer it, on a metaphysic. The metaphysic or philosophy may not be anywhere very accurately stated, and may be quite unconscious in the artist, yet it is a metaphysic that governs men at the time, and is by all men more or less comprehended, and lived. Men live and see according to some gradually developing and gradually withering vision. This vision exists also as a dynamic idea or metaphysic—exists first as such. Then it is unfolded into life and art. (2004a, 65)

The passage above endorses the notion that while writing *Aaron's Rod* Lawrence was indeed "living and seeing" according to the "metaphysic" of relativity that was "gradually developing" within himself. He himself was perhaps even "quite unconscious" of this fact.

The "metaphysic" of relativity in *Aaron's Rod* is represented through the idea of the fourth dimension, particularly with a focus on its spatial aspect. The fourth dimension in Lawrence's works has been examined by Richard O. Young. Paying special attention to the influence of P. D. Ouspensky's *Tertium Organum: A Key to the Enigmas of the World,* which Lawrence read in 1924, Young interprets Lawrence's concept of the fourth dimension as "the vast and timeless space" that "we are able to . . . perceive" "in moments of illumination" (1980, 31). Indeed, as Virginia Hyde argues (2004, 113–14, 123–27), the mythical interpretation of Young is not entirely irrelevant, especially in view of Lawrence's later works. Yet, even if Lawrence was strongly drawn to the mythical aspect of the fourth dimension expounded in *Tertium Organum,* it is important not to miss other features of Lawrence's concept of the fourth dimension, such as its spatial aspect. As Bruce Clarke says, "Lawrence's implicitly fourth-dimensional metaphors are consistently *spatial* in construction" (2001, 216). Especially in *Aaron's Rod,* which Ronald Granofsky calls Lawrence's "most spatially oriented work" (2000, 29), what should be noted is the spatial aspect of the fourth dimension, rather than the mythical one.

Aaron's Rod embodies the spatial fourth dimension through Aaron's continuous and quick movement. Aaron Sisson, a checkweighman in a mining company, deserts his wife and children, and sets out on a journey. The reason for his action is never explained in the text; on the contrary, when he is asked about his reason, Aaron answers on two separate occasions that he has no particular reason. First, when he is asked by Josephine Ford: "Will you tell me why you left your wife and children?—Didn't you love them?" (D. H. Lawrence 1988a, 65), he answers "For no particular reason" (66). The second occasion is at Sir William Franks's house. When Sir William asks Aaron the reason, he says, "There were no grounds. . . . No, there weren't. I just left them" (145). In spite of Aaron's being so explicit, very few critics have taken his words at face value. Instead, most have criticized the novel, saying that Aaron's desertion of his family is not sufficiently explained.[4] Some critics such as Paul G. Baker and William R. Barr, however, focus on *how* Aaron acts instead of *why,* asserting that there is a "picaresque" aspect in this work. Baker states: "Lawrence has presented us with a vast collage of persons and events, all thematically interconnected and, within his assimilation of the picaresque-*bildungsroman,* a part of Aaron's continuing 'education' or growing awareness of himself" (166). Following the example of Baker and Barr, we would do well to pay special attention to Aaron's movement itself. Then the form of the novel, though paradoxically, reveals itself. It is the spatial fourth dimension, rather than the picaresque.

The depiction of the spatial fourth dimension in *Aaron's Rod* performs three functions in the development of the novel. First, Aaron's quick movement reveals his changing relationship with the world around him. Second, Aaron's movement produces multiple perspectives for him, resulting in the destruction of the absolute three-dimensional space that he had accepted up to then. Some similarities to these first two points can be found in the paintings of the cubists and the early Marcel Duchamp, who attempted to present the spatial fourth dimension in their paintings. As Bruce Clarke suggests, Lawrence might have realized the idea of the spatial fourth dimension portrayed in Picasso's paintings. Clarke states: "[H]is sudden invocations of van Gogh and Cézanne [in "Art and Morality" and "Morality and the Novel"] may indicate Lawrence's renewed awareness that an aesthetic discourse on the spatial fourth dimension had also flourished in important theoretical discussions of postimpressionist, cubist, and futurist art" (2001, 215). In fact, Lawrence writes in "Art and Morality": "Design, in art, is a recognition of the relation between various things, various elements in the creative flux. . . . You recognise it, in the fourth dimension" (1985a, 167). The keen interest shared by Picasso and Lawrence in the idea of the spatial fourth dimension can be made clear by focusing on Paul Cézanne, an artist toward whom both took sympathetic attitudes.

The last of the three functions that the idea of the spatial fourth dimension performs in *Aaron's Rod* is related to Lawrence's reference to H. G. Wells's *The Invisible Man* (1897). As has often been said, what inspired Wells to write this novel was the new spatial vision produced by the X-ray. The visual image of the Invisible Man in *Aaron's Rod* enables Lawrence to highlight the existence of the spatial fourth dimension, in which the relationship between the self and the surrounding universe is invisible and unstable.

Aaron is characterized as what Lawrence called "a thought-adventurer, an emotion-adventurer, and a discoverer of himself and of the outer universe" (D. H. Lawrence 1994, 279). What is important for Aaron's "thought-adventure" (D. H. Lawrence 1994, 279) is his movement; his actual journey helps him to gain a new vision of the world. Aaron is clearly presented as a person in motion, and the movement begins from his first appearance in the story. "[Aaron] strode over a stile, *crossed* two fields, strode another stile, and was in the long road of colliers' dwellings. Just across was his own house: he had built it himself. He *went through* the little gate, up past the side of the house to the back. There he hung a moment, glancing down the dark, wintry garden. . . . Aaron rummaged in his shed at the bottom of the garden, and found a spade and a box that was suitable. Then he *came out* to his neat, bare, wintry garden" (1988a, 5–6; my emphasis).

As shown in this passage, Aaron moves from one place to another. He enters a specific area, spends some time there, and then leaves. This pattern is repeated throughout his travels. After leaving the Royal Oak, he moves to Shottle House in the Midlands, then to London, and leaving England for Italy, he visits Novara, Milan, and on the last leg of his journey, Florence. Aaron keeps on moving as if he is following Rawdon Lilly's words: "One is a fool to be lachrymose. The thing to do is to get a move on" (102). Moreover, moving is described as Aaron's "own inward destiny" (179).

What is characteristic about Aaron's movement is his quickness; he constantly moves quickly as though he were trying to escape from his sense of confinement.[5] A good example of Aaron's speed of movement can be found in the scene in which Aaron leaves the Royal Oak, a local pub, where he feels the landlady to be almost suffocating him.

This scene is important because it becomes a turning point in Aaron's life; here he deserts his family and starts on his endless journey.

> [Aaron] should take the road home. But the devil was in it, if he could take a stride in the homeward direction. There seemed a wall in front of him. He *veered.* But neither could he take a stride in the opposite direction. So he was destined to *veer round, like some sort of weather-cock,* there in the middle of the dark road outside the "Royal Oak." But as he turned, he caught sight of a third exit. Almost opposite was the mouth of Shottle Lane. . . . He *veered* towards the off-chance of this opening . . . and plunged away into the dark lane, walking slowly, on firm legs. (25; my emphasis)

What is noteworthy here is the motion of "veering round" "like some sort of weather-cock" and that this rapid movement and constant changing of direction results in his finding "a third exit." Interestingly Aaron's motion in the passage above reminds us of Marcel Duchamp's *Nude Descending a Staircase, No. 2* (1912), which also gives us a sense of moving and relativity. Like the kind of graphic art that Duchamp produced, the passage enables us to see Aaron spinning around on multiple legs, in plural directions, as though several actions in time were telescoped into a single static image—as though to "picture" the time dimension in visible form.

It is important to specify two direct influences on this work of Duchamp: cubism and cinematography. While working on this painting, Duchamp was in contact with the so-called Puteaux circle of Gleizes and Metzinger, who were fascinated by the paintings of Picasso and Braque and were working with the idea of the fourth dimension. Picasso's *Les Demoiselles d'Avignon,* an epoch-making cubist painting, was an outcome of his conscious attempt to materialize four-dimensional space on a two-dimensional canvas. The fourth dimension in this work was represented as "distortion" produced by employing multiple perspectives, which Picasso learned from Cézanne's paintings. Cézanne looked at objects from various points of view and incorporated them into one picture. In fact, according to Erle Loran, "several eye levels" can be recognized in Cézanne's paintings. Taking Cézanne's *Still Life with Fruit Basket* (1880–90) as an example, Loran remarks: "The first eye level . . . takes in, roughly, the front plane of the fruit basket, the sugar bowl, and the small pitcher. . . . The second eye level, much higher . . . looks down at the opening of the ginger jar and the top of the basket, as well as other objects, including the table top" (1946, 76). Loran asserts that this device results in "distortion" creating "a greater sense of three-dimensionality" (76). Although Loran does not go much beyond the conventional concept of three dimensions, this "greater sense of three-dimensionality" can be paraphrased as the spatial fourth dimension. László Moholy-Nagy clearly states: "Distortion can then be understood . . . as a space-time synonym" (1947, 118). Picasso and other cubists radically transformed this "distortion" into, in Moholy-Nagy's words, "vision in motion" (118). It is this "vision in motion" that Duchamp seems to represent most efficiently in *Nude Descending a Staircase, No. 2.*

The other vital influence on Duchamp's *Nude* was cinematography, especially sequential photos taken by Étienne-Jules Marey and Eadweard Muybridge in the 1880s. Robert Hughes explains that "[b]y giving the successive positions of a figure on one plate, these images introduced time into space" (1991, 44). In other words, Marey and Muybridge succeeded in visualizing "vision in motion" in the form of sequential photos. The influence of these sequential photos can be found in other modernist works, such as Giacomo Balla's *Dynamism of a Dog on a Leash* (1912), as well as in Duchamp's *Nude Descending a Staircase, No. 2.*

The same kind of "vision in motion" seems to be represented through Aaron's speed of movement in *Aaron's Rod.* In addition to the scene in which Aaron is spinning like a weathercock, he also moves rapidly in Sir William Franks's house in Novara. At first, in the luxurious, comfortable household, Aaron becomes rather inactive, which is very much out of character. He spends most of the time looking leisurely at furniture inside the house or gazing out of the window. It seems that the comfort of Sir William's affluent household deprives Aaron of his usual speed of movement. However, Aaron soon overcomes this inertia and starts to move quickly again. Feeling that he has "trespassed" (D. H.

Lawrence 1988a, 149), he dashes out of the house. Symbolically, in this scene, Aaron is compared to "a bird dashing out of a trap where it has been caught: that warm and luxurious house" (150). Once he gets outside, he recovers his usual quickness; he moves in and out with great energy, which is expressed in such kinetic words as "dash" and "run."

Significantly, for Lawrence, the word "quick" means more than "rapid"; it also means "living," which is one of the original meanings of the word (*OED*, A.I.1). The concept that "living" means to have a quickly changing relationship with circumstance is a very important part of Lawrence's vision of the world. He regards that which is relative to be alive and that which is absolute to be dead. In the essays written around 1925, he repeatedly asserts the importance of the relative as well as the rejection of the absolute. "We should ask for no absolutes, or absolute. Once and for all and forever, let us have done with the ugly imperialism of any absolute. There is no absolute good, there is nothing absolutely right. All things flow and change, and even change is not absolute" (1985f, 196).

Lawrence believes that the novel ought to be the epitome of such a world: "In the novel, everything is relative to everything else, if that novel is art at all" (1985d, 179). He also says in a different essay: "[T]he novel is a perfect medium for revealing to us the changing rainbow of our living relationships" (1985c, 175). Furthermore, with regard to the characters in a novel, he writes: "The man in the novel must be 'quick' . . . it means he must have a quick relatedness to all the other things in the novel" (1985d, 183). The dynamic motion of Aaron indeed gives us the impression that he is having "a quick relatedness to all the other things."

The special nature of Aaron's "quick" and "living" movement becomes much clearer when compared with Sigmund's movement in *The Trespasser* (1912). There are some similarities between *The Trespasser* and *Aaron's Rod* in their plots, settings, and characterization. For example, both Sigmund and Aaron leave their families and go traveling. They are both musicians, though the instruments they play are different. What should be particularly noted is the similarity between the scene in which Sigmund gets bewildered and finally kills himself, and the scene quoted above, where

Aaron, unable to decide which direction to go, keeps veering. They are both in a cul-de-sac, though Sigmund is in one in a psychological sense while Aaron is in one in the actual situation. In *The Trespasser,* Sigmund, who has returned from a five-day trip with Helena, cannot move; he is paralyzed by an acute headache and pains in his body. He is in a dilemma because he can neither "break with Helena and return to a degrading life at home" nor "leave his children and go to Helena." Sigmund is compared to "a man tangled up in a rope." Being deprived of free movement both physically and mentally, he is driven to a negative and tragic conclusion; thinking that "there remained only one door which he could open in this prison corridor of life," he commits suicide (D. H. Lawrence 1982, 202). While Aaron's speed of movement enables him to go on living, Sigmund's inertia leads him to his death. It is thus obvious that Lawrence intends to show in a positive manner how Aaron, unlike Sigmund, achieves a constantly changing, living relationship with his surrounding universe.

Another feature of the spatial fourth dimension represented in *Aaron's Rod* is related to Aaron's way of looking at things, a way that has something in common with Cézanne's way of looking at objects. By moving and changing his physical position constantly, Aaron sees things from various angles. In *Aaron's Rod* there are quite a few scenes where Aaron views things from above. For instance, in London, Aaron looks down from the box seat at "the disheveled theatre" (D. H. Lawrence 1988a, 54), and in Novara, he looks down from the top of Sir William's garden in the city (150). In Milan, he views from the balcony of the hotel "the packed black shoulders of the mob" in procession with a red flag (183), and in Florence, from Argyle's balcony, he sees "innumerable black figures" passing across the piazza (232). Aaron's upward and inward gazes, in addition to downward ones, are also described in the novel.

These multiple perspectives gained through Aaron's changing position contribute to rendering the absolute perspective relative. For instance, when he climbs up to the top of Sir William's garden, Aaron first realizes that the Alps surround the city. As shown by his later confession to Sir William—"I never expected the mountains" (155), his change of position brings him a new perspective. From this viewpoint, the city of Novara looks "beautiful" to Aaron. However, when he returns to a lower level, he notices "the littleness and the momentaneousness of the Italians in the street" of the same city (151). Thus, by changing his viewpoints, Aaron comes to see "[m]any worlds, not one world" (152).

It is noteworthy that this way of looking at the world can also be observed in *The Lost Girl,* a novel written right before *Aaron's Rod.* When Alvina Houghton visits Throttle-Ha'penny, the small mining field of coal managed by her father, she has a peculiar experience that changes her conventional ways of looking at her native town. Going down to the working place underneath, she has a strange feeling as if the collier working there were "not human: a creature of the subterranean world, melted out like a bat, fluid" and as if she herself were "melting out also, to become a mere vocal ghost, a presence in the thick atmosphere." Then, "up on the earth again," she blinks "at the world in amazement," thinking: "What a pretty, luminous place it was, carved in substantial luminosity. What a strange and lovely place, bubbling iridescent-golden on the surface of the underground" (1981b, 47). After spending some time in the utter darkness of the underground, Alvina seems to be dazzled by brightness on the surface. What she experiences here, however, is not merely dazzlement; she indeed gains another perspective on her native town. As a result, despite her awareness of the "poverty, dowdiness, obscurity, and nothingness" of Woodhouse (48), she comes to the decision to stay at home for the time. Most importantly, this experience causes her to change her own idea of sexuality: "At the back of her mind somewhere was the fixed idea, the fixed intention of finding love, a man. But as yet, at this period, the idea was in abeyance, it did not act" (49). The idea of "finding love, a man" here means marriage, which was considered to be natural for women during the Victorian period. Alvina has "been bred to think of herself as a delicate, tender, chaste creature with unselfish inclinations and a pure, 'high' mind" (34). However, the experience in Throttle-Ha'penny helps Alvina deconstruct this conventional idea deeply rooted in her inner self.

Aaron has a similar experience that changes the view he holds of himself in a radical way. After moving energetically around in Novara, Aaron returns to Sir William's house and reflects on his relationship with his wife, Lottie. This reflection brings him not only to a truth about their relationship but also to a new realization of himself. Aaron becomes aware that "he [has] a horror of [the female will]" (1988a, 158), that "he [has] never intended to yield himself fully to [Lottie] or to anything," and that "this [has] been the root cause of his strife with Lottie" (162–63). Then suddenly he seems "to have dropped his mask on the floor, and broken it." Being "invisible and undefined," he feels "like Wells' *Invisible Man*" (163–64).

The representation of selfhood in this scene seems to reflect Lawrence's own view of the self. In the very famous letter to Edward Garnett, Lawrence articulated that *The Rainbow* was written with the aim of representing the nature of woman. He compares "what the woman feels" to "diamond" while "what the woman is" to "coal," asserting that his "theme" is the latter (1981a, 183). In fact, near the end of *The Rainbow,* Lawrence actually describes how Ursula perceives the true nature of the self by presenting the "shells" and "kernel" of acorns as metaphors (1989c, 456). The "shells" represent Ursula's easily recognizable self-identity, such as her family background and past experiences, while the "kernel" implies the invisible quality of the self. The relationship between the "shells" and "kernel" seems to be similar to that between the "mask" and the "Invisible Man" in *Aaron's Rod.* Significantly, in both scenes the latter categorization—"kernel" and the "Invisible Man"—is considered to be the more real. As Ursula discards her superficial identities and feels "free," Aaron, like Wells's "Invisible Man," continues to move, seeking for a sense of fulfillment, freed from the constraint of any self-identity.

However, the difference between these two scenes is more significant than their similarity. Through a description of Aaron's situation, Lawrence explores the relationship between the self and the surrounding universe. In *Aaron's Rod,* by referring to Wells's *The Invisible Man,* Lawrence not only considers the invisible quality of the self, but also the invisible space-time world surrounding the self. Interestingly, although known for science fiction such as *The Time Machine,* in which he treated the fourth dimension as time, Wells wrote this particular novel in response to the concept of the spatial fourth dimension, visualized by the X-ray. The X-ray, discovered by Wilhelm Conrad Röntgen in 1895, offered "a model of the clairvoyant vision a higher spatial dimension would make possible" (Henderson 2003, 136). In fact, in *The Invisible Man,* the main character, Griffin drinks a potion "involving four dimensions" "and painfully turns invisible" (Wells 1924, 120). Obviously, Lawrence had this particular scene in mind when he wrote, "The old Aaron Sisson was as if painfully transmuted, as the Invisible Man when he underwent his transmutations" (1988a, 163–64). In addition, the visual image created here is the one provoked by the idea of the spatial fourth dimension; Aaron is indeed described as "invisible and undefined" (163). Lawrence's reference to Wells's *The Invisible Man* reveals his awareness of the spatial fourth dimension. Thus, *Aaron's Rod* depicts how Aaron's actual journey moves him toward a new perception of reality, the reality that can be called the spatial fourth dimension.

Importantly, what Lawrence sees in the light of relativity in this novel is not only the relationship between humans and the universe surrounding them; he also adapts the principle of relativity to his idea of human relationships. Lawrence expresses this idea as "a theory of human relativity" in *Fantasia of the Unconscious.* Right after acclaiming Einstein's new vision of the universe, Lawrence shifts his focus to human relationships. "We won't be pinned down, either. We have no one law that governs us. For me there is only one law: I am I. And that isn't a law, it's just a remark. *One is one, but one is not all alone. . . .* I am I, but also you are you, and we are in sad need of *a theory of human relativity.* We need it much more than the universe does" (2004a, 72; my emphasis)

The part that "[o]ne is one, but one is not all alone" in the passage above seems to account for Lawrence's characterization of Aaron; in short, Aaron cannot be alone, however desperately he needs to be. Although this essay cannot allow much space to discuss this issue, it is significant to point out the fact that Aaron's relationships with Rawdon Lilly and women reveal the "theory of human relativity." In the novel Lilly can be regarded as a theorist asserting aloneness for human existence, and Aaron as a practitioner of Lilly's theory.[6] However, Lilly's theory and Aaron's practice are portrayed as not always compatible. Aaron's experience with women in the novel most clearly reveals the split between theory and actual experience regarding human aloneness. Aaron seems to start his journey in search for his own aloneness, but in the course of his journey he is driven into relationships with women: first, with Josephine Ford, and then the Marchesa del Torre. The nature of these relationships follows the same pattern as the relationship between him and Lilly. Aaron and Lilly have ambivalent feelings toward each other; like "brothers," they have not only "an uncanny understanding" but also "a profound hostility" (1988a, 106). Aaron feels attraction as well as repulsion toward Lilly, oscillating between the two opposite feelings.

This experience of Aaron reminds us of Lawrence's own words in his ". . . Love Was Once a Little Boy." In this essay, Lawrence states: "Love itself is a relationship, which changes as all things change. . . . Hate is not the opposite of love. The real opposite of love is individuality" (1988e, 331). In other words, to take a balance between the two opposite desires of "love" and "individuality" is difficult, or rather impossible, because the more one loves the other, the less one can secure one's integrity; in reverse, the more one secures one's integrity, the less one can love the other. This is what Lawrence calls "a perpetual paradox" (331). In *Aaron's Rod,* Aaron feels his "individuality" being threatened by women as well as by Lilly, and wants to escape from them to preserve his "integrity." Nevertheless, he cannot bear to be alone, and seeks for "love" unwittingly. It seems as if Aaron cannot escape from this "perpetual paradox" between "love" and "individuality" even after the story ends. *Aaron's Rod* is, like most of Lawrence's novels, open in the end.[7] At the ending of the novel, Aaron asks Lilly, "And whom shall I submit to?" and Lilly answers, "Your soul will tell you" (1988a, 299). Concerning the issue of whether Aaron is to submit to Lilly, critics' views have been clearly divided. John Worthen states that "it ends with the mystical submission of one man to another" (1979, 132), whereas Virginia Hyde argues that "Aaron apparently remains uncommitted, still speaking 'rather sarcastically' to Lilly near the book's end" (1987, 475). A focus on Aaron's ambivalent feelings and attitudes toward Lilly allows us to conclude that Aaron will never submit to Lilly or anybody else.

Thus, the concept of relativity in *Aaron's Rod* is represented through "a theory of human relativity" as well as the spatial fourth dimension. Lawrence's representations of the spatial fourth dimension, as has been discussed above, show quite a few affinities with those of other modernists such as the cubists, Duchamp, and Wells. Furthermore, when special attention is paid to the importance of a change of perspective, which has been observed in both Lawrence's *Aaron's Rod* and Picasso's *Les Demoiselles d'Avignon*, it will lead us to Einstein's proposition that a view of anything varies according to one's point of view. The new vision of the relative world that Lawrence tries to present in this novel happens to correspond to the vision Einstein scientifically demonstrates in his theories of relativity, or the one Picasso artistically portrays in his paintings. These three modernists were in the same intellectual climate, and opened their "windows" to a new vision of the universe, in which the concept of relativity played a significant role. Through Lawrence's own "window" in particular, even the relationship between humans could be seen on the principle of relativity. This way of looking at Lawrence's attempt in *Aaron's Rod* will provide insights into a new perspective on his position as a modernist.

Notes

1. Izumi Wicks has observed some similarities between Lawrence's *Women in Love* and Picasso's *Les Demoiselles d'Avignon* in terms of artistic form (collage) and motifs (African sculpture) (Wicks 2003, 65–96).

2. As examples of contemporaries who were influenced by Einstein's theories of relativity, Peter Childs cites Marcel Proust, James Joyce, and Virginia Woolf in literature, the Russian philosopher Mikhail Bakhtin

(who coined the term "chronotope" for his literary theory), and the artists who employed the technique of montage and collage (Childs 2000, 66–67).

3. For instance, Albert Einstein writes in "The Special Theory of Relativity": "The four-dimensional mode of consideration of the 'world' is natural on the theory of relativity, since according to this theory time is robbed of its independence" (1961, 62).

4. For instance, Eliseo Vivas denounces *Aaron's Rod* as "the worst of [Lawrence's] novels" because of "its utter lack of form" and "its failure to elucidate an important point in which the reader is legitimately interested, the grounds on which Aaron leaves his wife and children" (1964, 21–23). Graham Hough also refers to its "structural lapses" (1956, 95). R. P. Draper calls it "the most formless and disconnected of Lawrence's novels" (1970, 92). H. M. Daleski insists that "Lawrence is now no longer concerned with form in the novel" (1965, 211), while Frank Kermode examines "notions, expressed with virtually complete indifference to the form of the novel" (1973, 80).

5. Ronald Granofsky (2000) has fully discussed Aaron's sense of confinement.

6. As for the relationship between Aaron and Lilly, various views have been presented. F. R. Leavis considers Aaron to be "an alter ego [of Lilly]" (1994, 43) and Lilly to be the "direct presence of Lawrence himself" (39). G. M. Hyde considers them to be "one split hero" (1990, 92). Granofsky views Lilly "as a writer" and Aaron as the "fictional character" of Lilly's scenario (2003, 104–5).

7. With regard to this open-ended conclusion of *Aaron's Rod,* critics have offered various views. Paul G. Baker says it is "a puzzle which Lawrence deliberately leaves unsolved" (1983, 180), while Steven Vine uses the expression "mystical inconclusiveness" (1995, xxxiv).

Crossing Europe: Political Frontiers in Lawrence's *The Lost Girl*

Theresa Mae Thompson

> But who is going to put you in the history books? These border troubles are of no significance. In a while they will pass and the frontier will go to sleep for another twenty years.
>
> —J. M. Coetzee, *Waiting for the Barbarians*

> Let the darkness turn violet with rich dawn.
> Let the darkness be warmed, warmed through to a ruddy violet,
> incipient purpling towards summer in the world of the heart of man.
>
> —D. H. Lawrence, "Craving for Spring"

IN NOVEMBER 1919, ONLY A YEAR AFTER THE ARMISTICE BROUGHT the Great War to an end, D. H. Lawrence traveled by train from England to France and on into Italy, where he would write *The Lost Girl*. In a letter to Rosalind Baynes of November 17, he wrote the following about his journey across the European frontiers: "It is all perfectly easy—only *slow slow—slow*. No bother at frontiers—only rather a crush . . ." (1984, 415). Lawrence sought the sunlight of Italy; perhaps he hoped to lighten as well the oppressive darkness left by the Great War. Italy offered sunlight, but dark clouds of fascism were gathering within its borders. Lawrence's train journey serves as an accidental metaphor for the ideological frontiers he himself would cross to write *The Lost Girl*.

The Lost Girl ostensibly depicts the life of Alvina Houghton, a "nice" middle-class English girl who can make a "suitable" marriage with a "nice" English boy if she does not lose her way: but she does. Yet her fall and redemption parody both "new woman" and romance heroines rather than emulating them. The parody of Alvina as a lost girl opens up a unique frontier for Lawrence to explore: the budding "science" of eugenics and the perceived threat—at the close of World War I—of the imminent degeneration of the human race. In many ways, Alvina embodies the "new woman" stereotype: she fails to marry young and becomes educated as a nurse, only to find herself dissatisfied with what that life offers. She returns home, and again fails to marry. Her story then parallels stereotypical romance stories about good-but-fallen heroines. Alvina, in trying to rescue her father's failing fortunes, is seduced by the "wrong" man: Ciccio, a "dark," vagabond Italian dancer with the Natcha-Kee-Tawara dance troupe, soils her virginity with no promise of marriage. Through a combination of both new woman and romance heroine plots, when the affair with Ciccio ends Alvina gets a chance to restore her respectability: as a career woman and a wife. She returns to natal nursing, and a respectable doctor offers to marry her. Alvina's path, however, only parodies these solutions, rejecting the expected outcome of redemption and respectability. Ciccio returns to her. To marry Ciccio, she abandons England for Italy, and so becomes "lost" to romance and new woman plots. *The Lost Girl* may be Lawrence's least experimental in form, but it arguably represents a unique crossing of traditional narrative frontiers. But to what purpose?

Human genetics demarcated the most significant scientific frontier of the twentieth century. At the beginning of the century, no one understood the mechanisms of genetic inheritance, yet by its end, scientists would have mapped the human genome. Eugenics, the study of how to improve the human race, at the end of the nineteenth century—when much of *The Lost Girl* is set—relied more on social and national prejudices than on biological evidence, as Henry Boies makes clear in his book *Prisoners and Paupers* (1893): "[C]riminals and paupers, both, are degenerate; the imperfect, knotty, knurly, worm-eaten, half-rotten fruit of their race. . . . Here is the gangrened member of the body politic; the question is not how it came to be so, but what shall be done to stop the spread of the poison, and save the life of the patient" (qtd. in Carlson 2001, 89).

After World War I, fears regarding both "paupers" and the degeneration of the "body politic" grew into fears about the degeneration of Western civilization. After the Great War, as Griffin's study on fascism clarifies, the conflation of eugenic fears of biological degeneration with nationalism became a motivating force for the proliferation of fascist ideologies across Europe: "Extensive study of the primary sources of Fascism and of other fascisms convinced me that at the core of its mentality was the *idée fixe* of devoting and, if necessary, sacrificing individual existence to the struggle against the forces of degeneration which had seemingly brought the nation low, and of helping relaunch it towards greatness and glory" (Griffin 1995, 3).

Postwar fears of a near-apocalyptic degeneration of the human race and civilization's "body politic" also darken Alvina's potential to bear the fruit of a better future in *The Lost Girl*. Alvina's sexual alliance with Ciccio rejects the idea of individual sacrifice to restore the "greatness and glory" of any nation. *The Lost Girl* offers instead a different possibility for apocalypse, one that would come only if people sacrificed the "life force" to promote political agendas.

Kinkead-Weekes asserts that the "Lawrence of 1918" begins sharply to differentiate himself from the Lawrence of *The Rainbow* and *Women in Love* (1996, 484). Virginia Hyde argues, in her examination of Alvina as a Persephone figure, that after the war, "the 'times' have not improved [for Lawrence] but worsened . . . ; in fact, he openly regards history as a degenerative process—even an apocalyptic one—in which only the most radical reversal can allow either communal or individual revitalization. For the individual, the change means such a profound shift of priorities that it can come only in extremis" (1994, 105). Lawrence's altered vision and his fears about history as degeneration reflect in many respects an altered understanding of the mechanics of nationalism developing during and after World War I. I will not rehash here the argument that Lawrence was protofascist, or that he sympathized with any of the many fascist factions of the times. As he would write in 1923, just a few years after he published *The Lost Girl*, "Fascism won't hold against the lust for anarchy which is at the bottom of the Fascisti themselves" (1995, 248). That fascist "lust for anarchy," however, does help clarify the apocalyptic warning Lawrence gives in *The Lost Girl*.

The Lost Girl enters into fascist and antifascist debates about postwar reconstruction and its relationship to the "science" of eugenics—a relationship both antifascist and fascist adherents in general accepted.[1] Lawrence, as Peter Fjagesund argues, felt that as catastrophic as World War I was, it "did not bring the apocalyptic finality necessary for the millennium to begin, and Lawrence's frustration and impatience forced him to look elsewhere for alternative solutions" (1991, 88). To recognize Lawrence's changed vision after World War I and his desire for "alternative" solutions to bring about the millennium enables a different perception of Lawrence's transformation of "The Insurrection of Miss Houghton" into *The Lost Girl*.[2] It enables a more comprehensive context for his parody of romance and new woman heroines. Lawrence's insistence on "Mixed Marriage"—his working title for *The Lost Girl*—as "a perfect selling novel" (D. H. Lawrence 1984, 439) comes to signify an "alternative solution" to fascism and to the life-crushing forces of English morality.

The Lost Girl's superficially conservative romance plot about a woman falling into immorality parodies much eugenics propaganda of the day that exhorted women to make "good" sexual alliances, based not on class inheritance but on biological inheritance.[3] The parody creates both a threat and a promise about possible future degeneration. *The Lost Girl* pretends to adhere to romance and new woman plotlines—a disguise that remains quite effective. But the parody of these genres reveals how the novel has transgressed their conservative borders to explore a radically different frontier. *The Lost Girl*, when read as parody, announces itself as a politically apocalyptic work. As Derrida writes,

> Nothing is less conservative than the apocalyptic genre. And as it is an apocalyptic, apocryphal, masked, coded *genre*, it can use

> the detour to mislead another vigilance, that of censorship. We know that apocalyptic writings increased the moment State censorship was very strong in the Roman Empire, and precisely to catch the censorship unawares. Now this possibility can be extended to all censorships, and not only to the political, and in politics to the official . . . well, then we would perhaps think that apocalyptic discourse can also get round censorship thanks to its genre and its cryptic ruses. By its very tone, the mixing of voices, genres, and codes, apocalyptic discourse can also, in dislocating [*détraquant*] destinations, dismantle the dominant contract or concordat. (1993, 159–60, my emphasis)

But *what* dominant contract does the apocalyptic tone of *The Lost Girl* mean to "dismantle"? I argue here that Lawrence's love story attempts to dismantle more than just the puritanical moral contract that denies the life force—although it does dismantle that as well. The novel struggles to deconstruct the many political agendas to which that moral contract had long been inextricably linked.

Lawrence told Edward Garnett in 1913 that he saw the text then as "a sort of answer to the *want* of today: to the real, deep want of the English people, not to just what they fancy they want. And gradually I shall get my hold on them" (qtd. in Worthen 1995, xxii). Lawrence later anticipated that the book would "get round censorship." In a letter to Koteliansky in April 1920, Lawrence claims the novel "is as proper as proper need be" (D. H. Lawrence 1984, 500). If seen as a straightforward attempt to write a romance about a new woman, then yes, the novel is "proper" and should "get round censorship." As parody, however, it is anything but proper.

In this post-Holocaust world, eugenics conjures up images of Hitler's gas chambers and human bodies stacked like cordwood. It represents for many the end result of the misapplication of human evolutionary science to contemporary political agendas. Certainly eugenics did not have such connotations before World War II. The term literally means "good birth." Eugenics advocates hoped to reproduce the "best" humans "scientifically." Darwin's cousin Francis Galton first coined the term "eugenics" in 1883. Galton also attached Darwin's theory of evolution to growing fears in England of social degeneration, offering eugenics as scientific support for many social reforms regarding the "unfit" during and after World War I.[4]

Biological degeneracy was connected to social behaviors many years before Galton came onto the scene. Immoral behavior was thought to cause an individual to degenerate and then to breed true to type: "Long before Francis Galton introduced the term eugenics, there was a growing concern during the 18th and 19th centuries that degeneracy was a major problem. The degeneracy might be physiological (caused by masturbation, occupational exposure, or alcoholism), or economic (in which the pauper lacked the ability to rise out of poverty). . . . Masturbation was the first type of degeneracy associated with a physiological mechanism. The loss of semen or the ejaculatory shocks to the nervous system were believed to cause physical and mental illness" (Carlson 2001, 23).

The definition for the "unfit" degenerate shifted throughout the nineteenth century, but the connection to individual morals remained intact. As Carlson's extensive study of eugenics, *The Unfit*, makes clear, by World War I "the idea of degeneracy led to the belief that three social classes—tramps, paupers, and criminals—were the products of generations of neglect and abuse and that two types of defective individuals—the feeble-minded and the insane—could appear as degenerate offshoots from any social class in society" (51–52).

The time period for *The Lost Girl*—pre–World War I—coincides with a shift in eugenic debates involving morality. During the late nineteenth century, "the plea for a new and 'higher' morality had become commonplace. . . . [Many] writers saw Victorian values as an enervating force in British society and proclaimed unfettered [female] sexuality as a constructive force that would arrest national degeneration and effeteness" (Robb 1996, 590). By the turn of the century, those debates came to connect the "new woman" to declining birthrates among the English middle and upper classes. The beginning of *The Lost Girl* points to that degenerative process within the mechanical rigidity of Victorian England's rigid class structures: "A well-established society is Woodhouse . . ." (1981b, 1). That late-Victorian, "well-established" Woodhouse society suffers from "one chronic and dreary malady: that of the odd women. Why, in the name of all prosperity, should every class but the lowest in such a society hang overburdened with Dead Sea fruit of odd women, unmarried, unmarriageable women, called old maids?" In focusing on the "Dead Sea fruit" women of "every class but the lowest," Lawrence echoes eugenic debates about "the fertility of the lower classes" and the sterility of the upper classes (Carlson 90).

The extensive and pervasive interest in eugenics debates among liberals and conservatives, and a growing popular interest in fascist ideas about controlling the health of the national "body," creates in *The Lost Girl* a distinct code for understanding Alvina Houghton's crossing of the new frontiers being created for class, race, and nation.

The years immediately before, during, and following the Great War saw liberals and conservatives alike trying to use the "science" of eugenics to formulate public policies regarding birth control, marriage laws, the sterilization of "defectives," abortion laws, and—most notably for Lawrence—censorship laws. The morality of liberated women became the central focus of much public discussion about eugenics. If women were free to choose, many argued, they would choose the best and the brightest, regardless of social class or wealth. Lawrence mocks the "scientific" morality of eugenists throughout *The Lost Girl.* A scandal develops in Woodhouse when Alvina Houghton becomes friends with Mr. May, the man her father hires to run his theater, The Endeavor. The only "erection" Mr. May shares with Alvina is The Endeavor: "But it was all purely verbal, descriptive. He made no physical advances" (D. H. Lawrence 1981b, 104). Significantly Mr. May's estranged wife is both a Fabian and a eugenist. As Mr. May tells Alvina: "I didn't know such people existed. And her friends! Oh the dreadful friends she had—these Fabians! Oh, their eugenics. They wanted to examine my private morals, for eugenic reasons.—Oh, you can't imagine such a state! Worse than the Spanish Inquisition—And I stood it for three years" (103).

In this sexless friendship, in Mr. May's pronounced effeminacy, and in his estranged wife's eugenics-based moral inquiries, Lawrence mocks many long-term and often contradictory debates of the 1890s concerning eugenics, socialism, and feminism. Alfred Russel Wallace, a "distinguished naturalist," argued in 1890 that "in a truly equitable, socialist society where women were economically independent, intellectually active, and full participants in public life, they would meet a much wider range of able men from whom to select their husbands" (Soloway 1995, 130). Quite a few antisocialist feminists agreed with Wallace. Unfortunately Alvina finds no such pool of prospective mates in Woodhouse after she returns from school. Mr. May soon becomes her only option, but he is married already and desires only "the angel-mother in woman. Oh!—that he worshipped" (D. H. Lawrence 1981b, 104).

Soloway's study of eugenics points out that "[t]he growing militancy of the suffrage movement after 1905, coupled with the racial anxieties aggravated by the differential decline in the birthrate, greatly stimulated defensive arguments about the consequences of female emancipation" (1995, 124). Lawrence's letters from Italy in 1919—as he was writing *The Lost Girl*—indicate, Worthen argues, that he "was not writing a continuation to an unfinished book, but actually starting again" (Worthen 1995, xxvii). He did not finish "The Insurrection" manuscript or lengthen "Elsa Culverwell," although they share commonalities with *The Lost Girl.* Lawrence in this new vision of the story focused more on the idea of a mixed marriage. Lawrence wrote to Thomas Seltzer that he felt the novel "should be more popular" than his other novels and less likely to be censored. Lawrence's claim that this would be a more popular novel seems likely; the story of Alvina had become connected for Lawrence to the public debates about degeneracy, morality, and women's emancipation. The time was perfect for a novel about a "new woman" who makes a sexual choice without regard for class proscriptions. The issue of crossing racial boundaries added to the possibility.

The focus on an educated, middle-class heroine who becomes involved in a mixed marriage might have allowed the text to support—however peripherally—the increasing numbers of international debates after the war regarding English racial degeneration (Stone 2002, 1–7). The groundwork had been laid for a broad interest in mixed marriage among many different eugenic groups both in Britain and America. Negative eugenic policies (sterilization, institutionalization, or complete eradication of unfit populations) won popular support in the United States as early as 1907 when "Indiana passed the first compulsory sterilization law for the unfit" (Carlson 2001, 211). Britain, relying on Galton's own view that "the brightest, healthiest, and most talented males and females in Great Britain had a moral duty to have more children" (265), was more inclined to institute positive eugenic policies to encourage reproduction in "fit" populations and discourage reproduction among the "unfit." The *New Age: An Independent Socialist Review of Politics, Literature, and Art*—in which Lawrence occasionally published—produced an article about the efficacy of positive eugenics policies almost weekly between 1909 and 1918.[5]

Negative or positive, any determination of public policy centered inevitably on how to define the "unfit," and race became conjoined to such arguments rather peripherally through poverty. At the beginning of the twentieth century "there was common consensus that the unfit were the products of environments that brought about a hereditary degeneracy" (Carlson 2001, 52). According to Henry Boies in *Prisoners and Paupers,* poverty was the environment most likely to create hereditary degeneracy. Boies identifies three levels of the lowest class: First were the mentally, morally, physically disabled: the "cripples, deformed, deaf, blind, imbecile, weak minded, diseased, insane, or criminal" defectives (qtd. in Carlson 2001, 88). Second, as Carlson phrases it, were "beggars, vagrants, tramps, idlers, and criminals who preyed on others in preference to working. . . . Only the third class . . . deserved charity or the efforts of public good will. These included the victims of adversity, old age, sickness and accident who were forced into poverty. . . ." (Carlson 2001, 88).

Most eugenics groups equated pauperism with degeneracy: "In the 1890s . . . the word 'pauper' had taken on the image of a fixed degenerate class" (89). In emphasizing that "fit" women of the middle classes become barren fruit left unplucked on the vine, so to speak, while those of "social problem groups" increase the members of the lowest class, *The Lost Girl* gestures toward a population problem of near-Malthusian proportions.[6]

Blithely having raised the fear that the affluent classes might cease to reproduce, leaving the English race's future in the hands of "beggars, vagrants, tramps" and other unfit groups, the narrative subtly undermines this fear almost immediately: "However it be, it is a tragedy. Or perhaps it is not" (D. H. Lawrence 1981b, 2). From this point on, the text constructs Alvina's search for the eugenically "right" mate around a central contention of most eugenic debates regarding the declining birthrate among middle and upper class families: "[T]he *Fertility of Marriage Census*, the National Birth-Rate Commission, the Fabian Society study of *The Decline in the Birth-Rate*, and the Eugenics Laboratory *Report on the English Birth Rate* all confirmed that the unrelenting if socially differentiated fall in fertility since the 1870s had nothing to do with depleted fecundity but was the direct result of the 'artificial limitation' of conception" (Soloway 1995, 57).

The fortunes and numbers of the middle-class Houghton family, which "had always been well-to-do," had declined over the generations (D. H. Lawrence 1981b, 2). Like many distinguished Victorian families whose members were "putative repositories of the favorable genetic traits," the Houghton family did not pass on "their superior, heritable qualities to a sufficient number of progeny" (Soloway 1995, 35). James Houghton—Alvina's father—is an only son; he is effete; he "had a taste for elegant conversation and elegant literature and elegant Christianity" (D. H. Lawrence 1981b, 2). James Houghton does not succeed in trade, although he comes from excellent tradespeople stock. Indeed, his standards for "quality" cloth to market in his shop create fear among his customers rather than commerce: "The inhabitants of Woodhouse were afraid lest James Houghton should impose his standards upon them" (5). Houghton marries a woman of good social background—the daughter of a squire—which should ensure a solid next generation of Houghtons. Class superiority, like James Houghton's fashionable cloth, does not sell well in Woodhouse. The marriage produces only Alvina, who, for much of the novel, appears to be just another "Dead Sea fruit."

Alvina's personality parodies fears about a growing degeneracy among upper-class families of England. *The Lost Girl* implies again and again that Alvina is not quite mentally sound; there is in her something profoundly not bound by the "superior" qualities of Englishness one might expect from a woman of her social breeding. She is potentially not just a barren fruit, but an unfit fruit that should remain unplucked for the health of future generations. Again and again the narrative hints at Alvina's inherited mental instability. Her father's "supercilious tone" comes out in Alvina as "mad bursts of hilarious jeering" (21). Her eyes have "an odd, derisive look . . . that scare[s] away the young men." Her "odd recklessness" affects her marriage options among the men of her own class more than her education. Of course, this is part of Lawrence's point. Where can Alvina find someone suitable to marry, someone able to make her fecund rather than sterile, and who could transform such a woman into a suitable vessel for the next generation?

Alvina dates and almost marries an Australian doctor, raising yet another eugenic issue: "Eugenicists were . . . troubled by the exodus of able, healthy, energetic men whose departure to the colonies at a time when the birthrate was no longer on the rise threatened to deplete the mother country of its best stock" (Soloway 1995, 60). Conversations with Graham bring out a "curious bronze-like resonance" in Alvina's voice "that acted straight on the nerves of her hearers: unpleasantly on most English nerves, but like fire on the different susceptibilities of the young man—the darkie, as people called him" (D. H. Lawrence 1981b, 23). Graham likes the laugh. Her madness, if such it is, attracts someone who might deplete England of its women and not be quite fit for reproduction. In her temporary engagement to Graham, Alvina, as Lawrence writes in a letter to McKenzie in May 1920, in part "moves towards reunion with the dark half of humanity" (qtd. in Worthen 1995, xxxi).

Alvina's education as a maternity nurse parodies arguments concerning the effect education might have on both degeneration and the declining birthrate in the middle and upper classes. The issue of education as a way to improve working-class intelligence was often debated in the *New Age*. On August 29, 1918, for example, an anonymous contributor argued that the "criterion of education would tend to become the increase of intelligence" among the working classes if that education was not controlled by the ruling class ("A Reformer's Notebook: Education" 289). This contributor simply continues the argument Herbert Spencer (the progenitor of social Darwinism) made against the social restrictions placed on women. Spencer "believed that the alleged inferiority of women arose from inequality of education and opportunity" (Carlson 2001, 120).

Alvina's education appears to make her unmarriageable. She rejects Albert Witham—a successful man of business—because she could not "get over the feeling that one was looking at him through the glass wall of an aquarium: that most horrifying of all boundaries between two worlds" (D. H. Lawrence 1981b, 63). The unfitness of the homosexual enters the passion equation when James Houghton buys The Endeavor—a show and cinema house—and hires Mr. May as his manager. Mr. May's attraction to Alvina emphasizes her apparent ability to attract the "right" man for procreation and the improvement of the race: Mr. May, an Englishman, "had spent his boyhood in a German school" (133) and then many years in America, developing "American deference" and American manners (101). Their friendship makes "Woodhouse [buzz] with scandal. . . . It could not believe that he was only so fond of Alvina because she was like a sister to him, poor, lonely, harassed soul that he was: a pure sister who really hadn't any body" (113). However, Mr. May is "unsuitable." Notably, "well-established" Woodhouse buzzes with scandal not because Mr. May is, as Miss Pinnegar says, "So unmanly! . . . In his dress, in his way, in everything—so unmanly," but because his married status will not allow him to marry Alvina (104).

Mr. May is probably not a character Lawrence wants us to admire. When Mr. May plays the role of Kishwégin in place of Madame Rochard, the text clearly mocks his effeminacy (133). Yet Lawrence gives to Mr. May many attributes that he himself had, such as a dislike of cinema and a preference for live shows (115). And Mr. May's distaste for Fabians prying into his morals reflects Lawrence's own experiences with and feelings about morality and censorship.

The parody of eugenics-based politics regarding morality becomes central to the events at Houghton's theater, The Endeavor—particularly those in chapter 7, "Natcha-Kee-Tawara." Alvina's association with The Endeavor emphasizes that her education has done nothing to improve her ability to attract eugenically "sound" men. She is lost to those debates long before she meets Ciccio, the Italian member of the "vagabond" Apache dance troupe, the Natcha-Kee-Tawara. Alvina becomes increasingly "vulgarized" by association with different traveling performers at The Endeavor: "[S]he liked being déclassée. She liked feeling an outsider" (117). She laughs that "the Woodhouse youths recognised her, and looked on her as one of the inferior entertainers. She was off the map: and she liked it" (118). Alvina's sexual interests put her "off the map": "The usual rather American-looking, clean-shaven, slightly pasty young man [leaves] Alvina quite cold," but the entirely tattooed "Jap" entrances her (119).

When Alvina becomes involved with the Natcha-Kee-Tawara performers, the text truly deconstructs accepted eugenist beliefs that women's education would help them see the "tramp" as unfit. Education as a maternity nurse showed Alvina "the human social beast in its abjection and its degradation" (33). Her experiences as a nurse support the position of some advocates of free love, like Ellen Key, who "argued that passion was nature's way of selecting the most evolutionarily fit. . . . No one could possibly fall in love with the eugenically unsound, although one might be induced to marry them for economic reasons" (Robb 1996, 593). Alvina's subsequent romantic involvement with Ciccio—a member of the most "eugenically unsound" class—allies Lawrence with this side of the eugenic debate.

The Natcha-Kee-Tawara's status as vagabonds and as performers increases their membership in the "dangerous classes" (Carlson 2001, 62). The Natcha-Kee-Tawara troupe performs a Red Indian show at The Endeavor that, as Kinkead-Weekes says, draws heavily on James Fenimore Cooper's fictional depiction of colonial encounters with natives: "[Lawrence] had seen the encounter of the 'white' with the 'Indian' . . . as actually Cooper's search within himself, to discover and be reconciled with the deeper and darker part of him that his civilisation had almost destroyed" (1996, 575). As Kinkead-Weekes argues, Lawrence uses the relationship between Alvina and Ciccio "both to show the unattractive and life-denying nature of the differing rinds that protect and conceal their darker and more fruitful selves; but also to show how the force that pulls them together cracks those open, to reveal a dark beauty hidden, almost lost, within the pale English girl and the seedy foreigner" (575). Yet Lawrence, like many American eugenicists, felt ambivalent about real Indians, though for a different reason, perhaps. "Such ambivalency," Wayne Templeton argues, "arises naturally from Lawrence's primitivist attitudes towards Indians, whom he romanticizes as Noble Savages without a history, and thus always available idealistically" (1996, 19). The ambiguous space of the Natcha-Kee-Tawara "Indians" becomes less ambiguous in the context of eugenic debates underpinning those "rinds" of "pale" Alvina's Englishness and Ciccio's "seedy" darkness.

U.S. negative eugenics policies nearly eradicated its Amerindian populations after 1880. What more suitable space than that created by the Indian could Lawrence find to construct a vision for apocalypse than in the conflated space of the Amerindian and the vagabond? As he would later do in *The Plumed Serpent,* Lawrence uses what he saw as the Indian's null-historical space to erase the rind of "life-denying" civilization, in all its new eugenic guises, and to attempt a return to a more "natural" progression for human evolution (Kinkead-Weekes 1996, 575).

The Natcha-Kee-Tawara performers embody a major frontier for Lawrence to explore and deconstruct. The performers see themselves as separate from the well-established centers, those of Woodhouse and the rest of England. As a troupe, according to Madame Rochard—who dances as the Indian maiden Kishwe—they are members of "but one nation, the Red Indian, and but one tribe, the tribe of Kishwe" (D. H. Lawrence 1981b, 151). Unfortunately, Kishwégin's tent on this frontier—like any Old West frontier fort—is influenced by the various "races" of its members. The dancers come from, as Madame Rochard points out, "three races": Max is German Swiss, Louis is French Swiss, Geoffrey and Madame Rochard are French, and Ciccio is Italian (122). And in Kishwégin's tent racial prejudices flare. Max mutters that Ciccio is part of "ein schmutziges italienisches Volk"—a filthy Italian race (124). Ciccio responds like the lowest of criminals when he knifes Max for calling him "[a] dirty Eyetalian" (150). Of course, the violence in Kishwégin's tent reflects the national and racial biases brewing across Europe in 1920. Such events, however, link Ciccio ever more closely to fears by eugenists about degeneracy among the lowest classes.

The advent of World War I comes toward the end of *The Lost Girl.* Alvina wonders how war will "affect the Natcha-Kee-Tawaras" (262). The advent of war delineates most clearly the way nationalism restricts the human desire. Throughout the novel, Alvina's views of Ciccio continuously shift, and each shift reveals common English ideas about race, class, intelligence, and degeneration. Alvina variously sees Ciccio as "rather common looking"; again and again she sees his smile as "bashful and stupid" (127). Alvina, however, prefers Ciccio's commonness, his seeming stupidity, and his darkness to that of the working-class English, who at one point she compares to "a gang of grey baboons" (137). Madame Rochard tells her that Ciccio's last name, Marasco, means the type of badness that "sends life down—down—instead of lifting it up," but Alvina rejects eugenic notions about human evolution and degeneration (183). She says: "Why should things always go up? Why should life always go up?" When at last Alvina marries Ciccio, she compares herself to "the woman with the negro husband, down in Lumley" (215). Alvina acts in spite of her own upbringing and education, not because of them.

Alvina rejects the restrictive moral codes that restrict sex to the marriage bed and the marriage bed to those of equal social rank. Alvina lets Ciccio take her virginity without any demand for marital stability or children. Alvina in this transgression of morals recognizes Ciccio's power and beauty: "If only she could, for one second, have seen him ugly, he would not have killed her and made her his slave as he did. But the spell was on her, of his darkness and unfathomed handsomeness" (202). After Ciccio makes love to her, "she didn't care a bit, really, about her own downfall" (234). Yet when men come to investigate her relationship to the Natcha-Kee-Tawara—possibly in connection with white slave traffic—Alvina runs away with barely a backward glance to resume her profession as a maternity nurse, which "suited her best" (252).

Like many Lawrence heroines, Alvina's return to nursing represents her resistance to the loss of her own will. However, she struggles even more against the loss of her status as a white, middle-class, educated English woman. In this flight back to the independence of nursing, the text relies heavily on coded references to racial purity: "So clean, she felt, so thankful! Her skin seemed caressed and live with cleanliness and whiteness, luminous she felt. It was so different from being with the Natchas." Again Lawrence parodies the ideas of eugenics about what the educated woman will do if not restricted by family or social pressures. As one writer in the *Englishwoman* claimed in 1909, "[T]he woman of 'a higher type' remained unmarried . . . because of her race-conscious obligation to wait for 'a higher type of mate' " (qtd. in Soloway 1995, 124).

As a maternity nurse, Alvina meets yet another man who might qualify as a "higher type of mate." Dr. Mitchell rose from poverty to a professional position of power and authority. He desperately wants to marry Alvina. Again the text mocks the idea that Dr. Mitchell might be a superior man and so more suitable for Alvina. The doctor's temperament is bad; Mitchell is "furious for weeks" after a drunken laborer implies Mitchell does not work hard enough to need more than "rice pudding" to sustain him (D. H. Lawrence 1981b, 256). The narrative reveals that Mitchell is like a man who "must assert he is a gentleman" and in doing so only "shows himself a clown" (257). Mitchell further demonstrates his weakness when he violently pushes Alvina because she does not wish to marry him. After his violence, unlike Ciccio after his own moments of violence, Mitchell grovels at Alvina's feet, begging, "Love me! Love me! Love me!" (268). This "right" man is in Alvina's estimation nothing more than "a hysterical child" (270). She agrees to marry him because she finds it "pleasant to be respected" and part of the "revered caste of medicine-men" (273). However, she knows that she could never actually marry him.

So Alvina abandons a perfect genetic match when Ciccio returns. And she forever ends the possibility of an "honourable engagement" according to class morals or eugenic thought when she marries Ciccio.

This decision does not free Alvina from the debates concerning possible degeneration and the middle-class woman's reproductive responsibilities. Alvina's thoughts and experiences circle around fears of possible degeneration from the moment she leaves Dr. Mitchell for Ciccio. The word "atavism" haunts her as she prepares for her wedding (288). The word "atavism" should haunt Alvina: Ciccio exhibits many physical characteristics associated with atavism. Atavism—the belief that ancestral traits return in future generations—was a code word for many "perverse" sexual practices that led to extremes of criminal behavior. Most Europeans and Americans believed, up until the publication of the *Kinsey Report,* that "the mental effects of masturbation were atavistic, imposing behavior like that of 'lower animals,' including a slouching posture and absence of eye contact" (Carlson 2001, 29). Cesare Lombroso, the late nineteenth-century biologist who "began classifying the personalities and behavior of soldiers he observed and treated" as an army surgeon, conflated the violent criminal with the atavist "who reproduces in his person the ferocious instincts of primitive humanity" (Carlson 2001, 43). Before she leaves England, Alvina believes that "she had come down in marrying Ciccio. She had lost caste" (D. H. Lawrence 1981b, 289).

Lawrence's parody of eugenic beliefs about atavism increases after the marriage. Ciccio and Alvina return to his home in Italy where she meets Ciccio's uncle Giovanni. Ciccio's uncle Pancrascio tells Alvina "he is not quite sensible" (307), and Giovanni "has a slightly imbecile face" (312). Again the text rejects ideas about class inheritance when Alvina recognizes in Ciccio "a certain wistful nobility which . . . put him beyond all class inferiority" (293). Alvina then receives a letter from Dr. Mitchell venomously thanking her for saving him from "the disgust and shame" of marrying a woman who would carry on "with a dirty Italian organ-grinder" (328). Because Mitchell's opinion of Ciccio can not be taken as a serious medical assessment, the text forces a reexamination of the possibility of the marriage for reproductive purposes.

The text, however, resists the promise this mixed marriage offers, and any promise of its bearing even a worm-eaten fruit. From the rubble the text has made of eugenic debates, Lawrence constructs a "mid-air ending"—which, as Worthen notes, was quite deliberate (D. H. Lawrence 1981b, 397). War with all its chaotic power provides the final code emphasizing the nature of the apocalypse Lawrence's text predicts. England's entrance into the Great War provides Alvina with the chance to leave Dr. Mitchell for Ciccio (265). War even helps Alvina find Ciccio again (272). However, the war in Europe breaks apart the tent of Kishwégin, as its male members abandon that frontier outpost to fight for their original homelands (282). And when Italy joins the war, it restricts any guarantee of future regeneration from the marriage of Ciccio and Alvina.

When Italy declares war on Austria, Ciccio is called up for military service. Alvina begs him to promise he will return to her and that they will go to America. However, his promise comes as if from a man already doomed: "And still he sat there unmoving, like a corpse" (339). Alvina's marriage to Ciccio and her eventual pregnancy occur within this restrictive space that war constructs. The future of the union with the dark half of humanity becomes unstable. Yes, war helps them to marry. Yes, the marriage promises "fruit." However, neither of these promises of a fruitful future offers more than a small space of possibility against the growing conflicts war creates. Effie, the pregnant patient Alvina is nursing when Ciccio returns to her, states the apocalyptic theme laced throughout the text: "But I hate life. It's nothing but a mass of forces. I am intelligent. Life isn't intelligent" (282). Alvina argues, "[I]f you have to be torn to pieces by forces, well, you have. Other forces will put you together again." But what forces will put the world together again after World War I?

The Lost Girl opens briefly a small space for deconstructing the fascist drive for biological and national regeneration. The novel ends in the uncertainties of 1915, yet it was written during the postwar year 1920. The novel parodies eugenic fears about the sterility and degeneration of the upper- and middle-class English before the war. We can conceptualize in this fear-filled, uncertain ending that the

Great War, the war to end all war, has left a significant legacy. As Alvina's Italian language teacher, Bussolo, says—oddly anticipating the opening line from Yeats's "Sailing to Byzantium"—"No, this country is a country for old men. It is only for old men" (334). Can any life thrive either in Italy or England? The text offers only Alvina's unborn child, a child created from the union between a lost, slightly mad English girl and a slightly atavistic Italian peasant with an imbecile uncle. It is indeed an ending where the end remains shrouded in darkness.

Notes

1. Throughout this essay, I use "fascism" to refer to a wide range of generic phenomena. This is in accordance with Griffin's definitions: "I capitalize Mussolini's Fascism . . . and use lower-case 'fascism' to refer to the generic phenomenon. . . . Moreover, [fascism] is identified with a whole range of forces which crush any genuine human creativity of word or deed . . ." (1995, 1).

2. As Worthen says in his introduction to *The Lost Girl*, there are many links between "Elsa Culverwell," "The Insurrection of Miss Houghton," and *The Lost Girl* (Lawrence 1981b, xix–xxi). But the final version bears little resemblance to these earlier works beyond the names of characters and the town where Alvina grows up.

3. See, for example, the article by Alice Vickery Drysdale (writing as Eugenia Newmarch) in the *Englishwoman* 28 (1910): 36–38, where she argues that "the new woman would be instinctively attracted to the best sort of man and would choose him for her husband rather than the dullard or wastrel who had nothing but wealth or family connections to recommend him" (qtd. in Soloway 1995, 130). See also Marie Stopes's popular romance *Married Love* (1918).

4. According to Carlson, "Galton introduced the term eugenics in 1883 in *Inquiry into Human Faculty and Its Development* (Macmillan) pp. 24–25, but it was not until the first decade of the 20th century that societies with the word eugenics in their names appeared" (2001, 14).

5. See, for example, the May 5, 1910, supplement in which *New Age* editor Patrick Geddes writes his "thanks to that veteran of the social sciences, Sir Francis Galton, for the cordial letter of encouragement he has sent from his sick-room. And pending the personal paper we may still hope to elicit from him, when health and strength return to *his* hale and veteran frame, let us meantime point to himself, in personality and in achievement, as affording one of the best answers to these oft-asked and not easily so briefly answered questions, 'What *is* a Sociologist?' " (qtd. in Carlson 2001, 277)

6. "Malthus suggested 'moral restraint' through the process of delayed marriage, especially among the poor, with a heavy emphasis on moral virtues, to make them aware of their duty not to procreate beyond the means of subsistence. . . . He did not feel it nccessary to enact a law forbidding foolish marriages because the laws of nature will punish those who enter them" (Carlson 2001, 103).

Male Sexuality on the Frontier in D. H. Lawrence's *Kangaroo*

Nancy L. Paxton

"It takes more than manliness to make a man."
—D. H. Lawrence, *Kangaroo*

WHEN D. H. LAWRENCE ARRIVED IN AUSTRALIA IN 1922, HE defined himself, as Judith Ruderman reminds us, as "a man without a country"; he had, by this time in his life, taken many bold steps to become a man no longer "firmly moored in his class, nation, or gender" (Ruderman 2003, 50). Lawrence frequently used gendered terms to describe the tantalizing appeal of crossing the border between the old world and the new, proclaiming, in *Fantasia of the Unconscious,* for example: "You've got to know you're a man, and being a man means you must go on alone, ahead of the woman, to break a way through the old world into the new" (2004a, 218).[1] *Kangaroo* presents Lawrence's first sustained attempt to respond to this call. He begins by describing Richard Lovatt Somers's realization that the old world was "done for" and his imperative desire to go to "the newest country, to young Australia" (1994, 13), a desire impelled by many of the same impulses that induced the Lawrences to make a similar journey. Nonetheless, from nearly the first page of this oddly uneven novel, Lawrence draws attention to Somers's English ideas about maleness, friendship, sexual desire, marriage, power, class politics, and violence, as he describes his protagonist's increasingly more disorienting confrontations with Australian men who embody alternative ideas about male identity.

By selecting Australia as the scene for this "romance," Lawrence chose a cultural location that offered him more latitude to explore the sexual themes that so challenged his agents, editors, reviewers, and readers of his earlier works. As Michael Bell has noted, one of the advantages of the exotic "primitivism" of *Kangaroo* is that it allowed Lawrence to write more freely about male gender identity and sexual desire in a "democratic" society that was distant and relatively unfamiliar to most of his English and American readers (Bell 2004, 133). Lawrence composed *Kangaroo* with astonishing speed, incorporating his first impressions of his visits to Sydney and Wollongong as well as his fourteen-week stay in Thirroul.[2] Lawrence's "thought-adventure" demonstrates that even in a settler society of the British Empire like Australia where the English language and culture were widely shared, "maleness" was nonetheless nationally defined and culturally mediated. Jack Callcott, the first Australian character that Somers meets in the novel, embodies many of the nationally specific ideas about male identity and "mateship" that Kay Shaffer and others have identified as central to emergent definitions of Australian national identity in the 1920s.[3]

Lawrence complicates what might otherwise be a simple comparison of English and Australian concepts of maleness in this novel, however, by including Ben Cooley, whose charismatic leadership, "Jehovah-like" paternalism, Jewish mysticism, national pride, authoritarian politics, and frankly homosexual orientation unsettle the polarized ideas of maleness otherwise dramatized in Somers's relationship with Jack Callcott. Moreover, while Richard Lovatt Somers clearly plays the part of the transgressive artist in this novel and envisions himself as the enemy of convention, he remains unable to find a "window to the sun" (D. H. Lawrence 2005a, 109). Instead, *Kangaroo* ponders what happens when an artist leaves his own culture and is paralyzed by gender melancholy and despair.

In *Kangaroo,* Lawrence invites readers to consider how the return of the repressed determines Richard Lovatt Somers's understanding and performance of maleness and its relation to sexual desire, by including four life-changing dreams. Somers's experiences in Australia ultimately force him to relive the earlier wartime traumas that motivated his bitter decision to become "a man without a people, without a land" (1994, 259). Although the autobiographical dimensions of the long retrospective chapter in *Kangaroo* entitled "Nightmare" have long been recognized,[4] it is less frequently acknowledged that this novel also tests the rigid gender prescriptions that Lawrence asserted in *Psychoanalysis and the Unconscious* and in his more polemical and defensive *Fantasia of the Unconscious.* Though the paint was barely dry on the "under-side of the umbrella" described by these essays, Lawrence nonetheless allowed himself to challenge the "stability" of the sex/gender absolutes he posited by describing life on the Australian frontier in *Kangaroo* and in his next novel, which he cowrote with Molly Skinner, *The Boy in the Bush.* In the latter, Lawrence moves his protagonist, Jack Grant, into the emptiness of the outback of Western Australia where he is free to discard all the restraints—sexual and otherwise—that were central to English male identity in the early twentieth century. In *Kangaroo,* Lawrence focuses on the "terror of chaos" provoked by Richard Lovatt Somers's recognition of the power of the "dark gods"; the dark passage charted by this novel allowed Lawrence subsequently to imagine new ways to open "a window on the sun," as Virginia Hyde suggests in her introduction to the present volume.

Many scholars have, of course, invoked Freudian psychology to account for the "leadership" turn in Lawrence's fiction in this remarkably restless period of his career. Fiona Becket, for example, reads Lawrence's mature novels as exhibiting a nostalgia for the maternal that "necessarily embraces taboo, fetish, and loss" (1997–98, 265). Scott Brewster has invoked Julia Kristeva's trope of the "inescapable boomerang" in *Black Sun* in order to trace the "structure and experience of abjection" in Somers's life in Australia (S. Brewster 1997–98, 217–18). Because Freudian or neo-Freudian models of nostalgia and abjection presume a return to the maternal and typically reinstall essentialist notions of gender, they prevent us from recognizing how radically Lawrence questioned male sex/gender identity in

Kangaroo. By considering Lawrence's "thought-adventure" in light of Judith Butler's recent analysis of gender melancholy, I hope not only to reveal the audacity of Lawrence's exploration of the physical and psychological frontiers defining maleness in this novel but also to illustrate how Somers's crisis of identity exposes the instability at the center of heterosexual identity itself and in the symbolic order it authorizes.

In *The Psychic Life of Power, Bodies that Matter,* and other works, Judith Butler argues that melancholy is central to the formation of heterosexual identity because "gender is acquired at least in part through the repudiation of homosexual attachments" (1997, 136). In arguing that heterosexuals experience a period of what she calls "gender melancholy" as part of their developmental maturation, Butler invokes Freud's revisions in 1923 to his famous essay, "Mourning and Melancholy." Drawing on Freud's contrast between those who identify what they have lost and those who are overcome by melancholy because they do not recognize the object of their grief, Butler concludes that "if we accept the notion that heterosexuality naturalizes itself by insisting on the radical otherness of homosexuality, then heterosexual identity is purchased through a melancholic incorporation of the love that it disavows: the man who insists upon the coherence of his heterosexuality will claim that he never loved another man, and hence never lost another man" (139). One of the strengths of Butler's model of the formation of sex/gender identity is that while it employs Freudian terminology it also critiques gender essentialism and makes room for historical and geographical variables.

Moreover, by considering *Kangaroo* in a theoretical context that links sexual and psychological development with economic models as well as with historical and geographical specifics, we can gain a better understanding of Lawrence's "leadership" turn and trace some of the unrecognized causes of the misogynistic rage that finds persistent expression in *Women in Love* and subsequent texts. Twentieth-century consumer capitalism intensified the sex/gender conflicts that male modernist writers faced, and, as Greg Forter observes, "inasmuch as the creative origin is felt to be feminine and maternal, to be incarnated as a man is to assume a disjunctive relation between one's gendered self and its creative source" (2003, 154). Demonstrating the implications of Judith Butler's theory of gender melancholy through his innovative reading of F. Scott Fitzgerald's *The Great Gatsby,* Forter argues that Jay Gatsby embodies an earlier model of American maleness on a collision course with the hard new idea of manhood represented by Tom Buchanan. Showing how Fitzgerald's novel "marshals its melancholy for conservative class and gender purposes," Forter demonstrates how "melancholic rage" provides the "aesthetic means by which Fitzgerald transforms an incipient critique of modern capitalism and misogyny into a resigned capitulation to them" (164, 143). Anticipating Fitzgerald's *The Great Gatsby* by two years, Lawrence presents a similar exploration of divergent definitions of manhood under democratic capitalism and in *Kangaroo* explores the psychological links between gender, sexuality, national identity, politics, and violence. By thus considering how repressed mourning and melancholy shadow *Kangaroo,* I hope to shed new light on Lawrence's often contradictory ideas about gender, sexuality, politics, and nationalism in his fiction and essays of the 1920s.

Gender Identity in Lawrence's Australian Romance

When Lawrence arrived in Perth in 1922, Australian national identity had recently been tested in the terrible bloodbath of the Great War. In *Women and the Bush,* Kay Schaffer identifies the fiction of Henry Lawson and other writers of the 1890s as providing the textual foundation for an Australian national identity that valorized a "rough-and-ready" mateship and explicitly rejected class-bound English ideas about what defined a gentleman. Lawrence may have first heard of Lawson from Edward Garnett, who wrote an admiring review of one of Lawson's stories, "The Drover's Wife" (Schaffer 1988, 40, 128). Schaffer goes on to identify the qualities defining national identity for Australian men by contrasting them with those of English men; allowing for some latitude in the term "religion," her lists apply in every detail to the polarized contrasts that Lawrence draws between Jack Callcott and Richard Lovatt Somers:

Typical Australian	*Other*
Practical	Theoretical
Rough-and-ready manners	Polished manners
Natural/common man	Affected/civilized man
Improviser/original	Planner/derivative
"Near enough" standards	Exacting standards
Laid-back	Hardworking
Skeptical of:	Believer in:
Religion	Religion
Intellectual/cultural pursuits	Intellectual/cultural pursuits
Egalitarian	Master/elitist
Fiercely independent	Officious authority
A mate	An individual
Swears/gambles/drinks	Controls swearing/gambling/drinking
Freedom	Containment

Indeed, when Jack Callcott first sees Somers on the streets of Sydney, he not only displays a political paranoia by wondering if Somers is a "Bolshy," he also recognizes how the "strange foreign-looking little man" (D. H. Lawrence 1994, 1) challenges specific Australian ideas of maleness. Upon better acquaintance, Jack realizes that Somers is English, but he also notes that he is paradoxically "a gentleman and not a gentleman" (38). For his part, as soon as Somers begins to feel the effects of being "immersed in real democracy" (21) for the first time, he regards Jack as an intelligent but unreflective man "with a vast empty desert at the centre of him" (40), thus reasserting his own unexamined sense of national and class superiority, as well as an "Englishman's instinct for authority" (22), as Lawrence's narrator puts it.

At the same time, Jack Callcott's ideas about maleness and "mateship" also demonstrate the pressure that the modern, postwar culture exerted on earlier Australian ideas about masculinity. Jack tells Somers, for example, that he does not want to have any children (88), suggesting a dramatic shift in postwar attitudes about maleness and paternity, not to mention the greater availability of birth control in urban centers like Sydney. Callcott likewise tacitly recognizes Australian women's political enfranchisement in 1902, sixteen years before women won the vote in the United States or England, by acknowledging their *ostensible* right to participate in the secret political movement that he is helping Kangaroo to organize. Callcott tests Somers's commitment to male solidarity, for example, when he argues for an all-male organization, asking him, "'We're not having the women in, if we can help it. Don't believe in it, do you?'"—a premise with which Somers readily agrees, "'Not in real politics I don't'" (92). While Jack expects unquestioning allegiance from his male mates, he apparently does not demand marital fidelity from his wife or himself, as is evident when he later suggests to Harriett Somers that they "swap" partners.

In describing Somers's relationship with Jack Callcott and later with Ben Cooley, Lawrence recognizes that "mateship" began to take on new significance in the 1920s as male and female homosexuality became more visible in England, the United States, and Australia.[5] While Lawrence provides no overt explanation for Somers's ambivalent response to Callcott's invitations to "talk together as man to man" (33), he dramatizes the psychological "chaos" that is precipitated when Jack flings "his arm round his shoulder and presses him close" (53). Somers instinctively recoils from Jack, though he is mystified by his own resistance (53). His ambivalence about "mixing and mating" with Jack is later illuminated by his dream about a woman with a "face swollen and puffy and almost mad or imbecile" who berates him bitterly with betraying her love, an image Somers at first associates with Bertha Mason from *Jane Eyre*. When he recognizes, however, that the dream woman was "so awfully like his mother, risen from the dead" (97), he begins to feel a deepening "horror."[6] Rereading his dream, Somers then realizes that it also suggests that his wife was somehow "departing from this life" (97), thus exposing his guilt for shutting her out of the "impersonal business of male activity." At this point, Somers is not ready to recognize how his intensifying friendship with Jack Callcott and Ben Cooley might jeopardize his marriage, or, indeed, prompt a refusal to participate in the heterosexual regime altogether, though Lawrence's readers might.

Instead, Somers wonders why he rejects Jack's invitation to greater intimacy when he "all his life had this craving for an absolute friend, a David to his Jonathan, a Pylades to his Orestes: a blood-brother. All his life he had secretly grieved over this friendlessness. And now at last, when it really offered . . . he didn't want it" (107). The pattern of melancholy, ambivalence, and rage that Somers displays is typical, as Judith Butler has shown, of subjects caught between mourning and melancholy. Since the Freudian "prohibition on incest presupposes the prohibition on homosexuality" and presumes the "heterosexualization of desire," social restraints on homosexuality, Butler argues, must be repeatedly reinforced (1997, 135). Cut loose from nationally defined and psychologically engrained definitions of maleness that reinforce normative heterosexual identity and desire, Somers panics when he begins to glimpse the chaos of a world beyond the neat gender polarities of English heterosexual normativity.

Somers remains in the dark about the political implications of Jack's ideas of mateship, male loyalty, and violence until much later in the novel when the riot in Canberra Hall exposes the covert fascism and ruthless violence that underpins *Kangaroo*'s benevolent rhetoric. When Ben Cooley is shot during the riot and Callcott and his mates retaliate by beating several Labour supporters to death, Jack is utterly unrepentant, telling Somers he feels like a "perfect angel" and regards killing a man to be as natural as—and more satisfying than—"lying with a woman" (D. H. Lawrence 1994, 319). Jack's example suggests an equation between violence and manliness, especially common among the returned Australian soldiers who survived World War I. In this way, Lawrence intuits how, to borrow Greg Forter's terms, "structural melancholy is yoked to conservative politics through the channeling of melancholic rage toward the socially vulnerable" (2003, 143), a dynamic clearly at work in the riot as well as in Jack's misogynistic remarks.

National Identity and Cosmopolitan Desires

If Richard Lovatt Somers's relationship with Jack Callcott exposes the political consequences that arise when Australian "mateship" is linked to protofascist goals, his relation with Kangaroo raises a series of more personal questions about power, sexual desire, and same-sex love. Lawrence excised several of his descriptions of Somers' relationship with Ben Cooley, and these censored passages illustrate how "even our deepest personal experiences are socially constructed, mediated by visions and values that are 'political' in nature, that refer outward to the world beyond the individual" (Mohanty 1997, 207). In their first meeting, Somers recognizes how national identity is literally inscribed on Kangaroo's body when he notices that his "long and lean and pendulous" face and heavy thighs recall Australia's totem animal. At the same time, Lawrence also indicates that Ben Cooley's identity as an Australian is counterbalanced by his more cosmopolitan affiliations as a Jew, as Judith Ruderman has shown.[7] In their first interview, Somers deduces Cooley's Jewish heritage when he observes his beautiful, benevolent smile and feels the power of his "pure Jehovah-like kindliness" (D. H. Lawrence 1994, 110), an impression reinforced, as the narrator unfortunately explains, by Cooley's work as a lawyer, which allows him to exercise his "ancient, unscrupulous shrewdness" (110). Lawrence's initial description of Cooley thus suggests his sense of "kinship with that paradigmatic modern, the wandering Jew" and humanizes, to some extent, his otherwise distressingly anti-Semitic portrait of Kangaroo (Ruderman 2003, 62).

Lawrence further complicates Ben Cooley's portrait by inviting readers to consider him in the context of Jewish mystical traditions that call into question Somers's ideas about maleness. As Charles Burack has shown, Lawrence knew that in the *Zohar* and other kabbalistic texts, "strength" is associated with the feminine and "loving kindness" with the masculine (Burack 55). Thus, if we read Lawrence's references to Cooley's "loving kindness" in this context, we will recognize that he is not necessarily defining him as "feminine." Likewise, Kangaroo's repeated appreciation for Somers's "beauty" does not necessarily indicate that he sees the younger man as effeminate, since beauty is associated with the masculine in this spiritual tradition.

Cooley's embodiment of and reference to these mystical Jewish gender scripts confuse Somers during their first interview, but he is nonetheless attracted by Cooley's paternalistic "ideal of Law" and by his conservative program of social reform, which would legitimize a single male authoritarian leader who supposedly fulfills ordinary male citizens' emotional needs for order in the public and private realm. After flattering Somers by praising his essays on democracy, Cooley expounds on his similarly antidemocratic views of education, arguing that "in sixty percent of the people it is useless" (D. H. Lawrence 1994, 112). Cooley "marshals" gender melancholy in support of conservative authoritarian social policy, noting that he wants to teach his "people what it is truly to be a man, and a woman" (112). Kangaroo's desire to impose a single idea of manhood and womanhood on Australians can also be read as a symptom of the "melancholy produced through the compulsory production of heterosexuality," which finds expression, according to Judith Butler, in a desire to impose "rigid forms of gender and sexual identification" upon heterosexuals and homosexuals alike (1997, 143–44). When Cooley asserts, "'Man again needs a father—not a friend or a brother sufferer, a suffering Savior. Man needs a quiet, gentle father who uses his authority in the name of living life, and who is absolutely stern against anti-life'" (D. H. Lawrence 1994, 111), Somers is "thrilled" by his rhetoric. It is Cooley's assertion of the primacy of the father—not the mother—that prompts Somers to silently declare to his "astonished self": "'Why the man is like a god, I love him'" (112).

Male Leadership and Sexual Politics

Somers's unfolding relationship with Kangaroo demonstrates why gender roles are central to national identity and why, as Judith Butler argues, the state depends upon the "psychic idealization" of gender roles in defining citizenship not only to ensure reproduction but also to make the "power of the state invisible—and effective—as the ideality of conscience" (1997, 191). Cooley's ambiguous sex/gender identification attracts and challenges Somers not only politically and spiritually but also psychologically and sexually. In fact, throughout the second half of this novel Lawrence dramatizes the "anarchy" that erupts in Somers's personal life when he begins to recognize and respond to male same-sex desire.[8] To be sure, the representation of homosexual desire remained an "unspeakable" subject in most English-language fiction throughout the 1920s, as Lawrence knew from painful personal experience. One sign of this continuing taboo can be seen in Robert Mountsier's request that Lawrence tone down the descriptions of the erotic attraction between Kangaroo and Somers, though Lawrence strategically resisted this request, with Thomas Seltzer's help.[9] But anyone who has seen the holograph of *Kangaroo* cannot help but be impressed by the lack of ambivalence suggested by Lawrence's penmanship and by the straightforward approach he takes in describing the homoerotic aspects of Cooley's relationship with Somers.[10] While Lawrence later cut several long passages that explore this forbidden territory, he retained numerous passages that emphasize Cooley's homoerotic attraction to the younger Somers prompted by his small size, his physical beauty, his literary sensitivities, and his passionate interest in questions of male power. The passages that survive Lawrence's self-censoring allow readers to see parallels between Somers's conflicted sexual identity and what Butler later calls "gender melancholy," as well as, perhaps, Lawrence's efforts to "discipline" his own unresolved homosexual desires, as Howard Booth has argued.

Moreover, Ben Cooley's gender performance and sexual provocation throughout *Kangaroo* precipitates *"chaos"* in Somers's marriage and prompts his futile efforts to impose more orthodox and rigid gender roles upon himself and his wife. In their second meeting when he invites Somers and Harriett to join him for lunch in his quarters, Cooley summarizes his unconventional sexual history. He initially displays his courtly side by giving Harriett a bunch of violets and telling her she is " 'a remarkably beautiful person' " (D. H. Lawrence 1994, 118), but when she asks him if he had ever been married, he replies with biting irony that he has been "married" several times: "'First to Benny Cooley—then to immortal verse—after that to the law—once to a haughty lady—and now I'm wedded to my ideals. This time it is final. I don't take another wife'" (119). When Harriett probes further, Cooley's response indicates the same psychological process that Greg Forter identifies in *The Great Gatsby*, suggesting how an individual male citizen's "effeminaphobia" can be converted into "full-fledged misogyny" (Forter 2003, 153). After teasingly telling Harriett she is "'a dangerous ogre, a Medusa with her hair under her hat'" (D. H. Lawrence 1994, 119), he turns deadly serious when he cautions her not to imitate the "cold" modern women who paralyze men like stinging "white ants" (123). Cooley terminates their discussion by turning his back on Harriett, and when she protests his rudeness, asking why he has turned "'the wrong end'" to her, he responds with, "'How do you know it is the wrong end of me?'" (123).

Cooley's admonishments about female dominance and aggression seem to intimidate Harriett Somers, since she uncharacteristically accepts his claim on her husband, but this episode also underlines the role of civil and religious law in regulating marriage and gender arrangements. Frustrated by Somers's frequently expressed desire "for some living fellowship with other men" (107) and browbeaten into acquiescing to his involvement with Kangaroo's secret organization, Harriett responds by performing an inverted version of the "homosocial" bonding ritual that Christopher Lane has identified as central to British imperial culture.[11] In a letter addressed to "'Kaiser Kangaroo,'" she assumes the patriarchal prerogative when she hands over her husband to Cooley, saying "'You have my sympathy—and my Lovatt'" (124). Lawrence's narrator underlines these cross-gendered parallels with traditional Christian marriage ceremonies by noting that Harriett felt as if "she had signed the marriage register" (124) when she seals the envelope containing her letter. Kangaroo likewise echoes the language of a good divorce lawyer in his reply when he thanks Harriett for her "'deed of gift to Lovatt'" and informs her that "'no court of law in New South Wales'" will support her if she makes any further "'claims'" on her husband (123).

Somers's subsequent response to Kangaroo's sexual and political seduction, however, shows that he remains in the paralyzing grip of "melancholy" as Freud described it in "Mourning and Melancholy." Freud notes that mourning is prompted not only by "the loss of a loved person" but may also reflect "the loss of some abstraction which has taken the place of one, such as one's country, liberty, an ideal and so on" (Freud 1957, 14:244). Furthermore, Freud's description of the melancholic subject who experiences "a profoundly painful dejection, cessation of interest in the outside world, loss of the capacity to love, inhibition of all activity, and a lowering of the self-regarding feelings to a degree that finds utterance in self-reproaches and self-revilings, and culminates in a delusional expectation of punishment" (245) fits nearly all of Somers's symptoms. After this meeting, Somers felt that he "had no feelings and speech had gone out of him," and he distances himself from his wife, thinking he wanted to be "alone like a single fish" (D. H. Lawrence 1994, 125). Yet, unable to tolerate this feeling that "everything had suddenly become unreal to him" for long (125), Somers visits Kangaroo a third time, and this episode illustrates Lawrence's notion that "hate is not the opposite of love. The real opposite of love is individuality" (Bell 2004, 9).

In this third meeting, Somers is still unable to find a "window to the sun"; on the contrary, he remains mesmerized by the powerful appeal of the "dark gods that enter from below" (D. H. Lawrence 1994, 134). Alone with Cooley for the first time, Somers initially tries to keep his distance with his defensive, and notorious, criticism of Australians for being "'hollow'" and "'having no insides'" (131). When Cooley defends his countrymen's "'generosity'" and critiques Somers's "'old-world carping'" and "'damp, European spirit'" (131–32), Somers's overwrought emotional response suggests an escalating gender panic. Feeling overcome and "rather stupefied than convinced" by Kangaroo's angry counterarguments, Somers suddenly sees him as "huge and beautiful like some god that sways and seems clumsy, and then suddenly flashes with all the agility of thunder and lightning" (132). In this moment, Somers realizes that he "*did* wish he would get up again and carry him quite away" (132), a desire the narrator confirms when he notes that "if Kangaroo had got up at that moment Somers would have given him heart and soul and body, for the asking, and damn all consequences. He longed for it" (132). The holograph draft of this episode shows little evidence of Lawrence's reputed ambivalence; there is not a single word change in the paragraph describing Somers's desire to surrender.[12]

In the published version of this episode, however, Somers's more "puritanical" side reasserts itself a few paragraphs later when he hears something frightening and "obscene" in Cooley's subsequent assertion of the power of love: "'I trust myself entirely to the fire of love. . . . Where I don't love, I use only my will and my wits'" (133). The rest of this interview is heavily edited, with several long paragraphs excised. In the published version, Kangaroo, having missed his cue to make a more physical move, invites Somers to acknowledge the creative potential of "love," while Somers provocatively counters by asserting his desire to worship the "'dark gods that enter from below'" (134). Admitting that heterosexual "'love has somehow become like cardboard to me,'" Somers provokes Kangaroo to say, "'I am going to exorcise that demon, and release your beautiful Andromeda soul'" (136). But when Somers taunts him, "'Try,'" and Kangaroo jumps to his feet as if he would "smother him in violent warmth," Somers resists by saying coldly that Cooley's "'love seems somehow a bondage and the spirit seems like something that belongs to the will alone'" (136). Having provoked this revelation about the relation between love and power, Somers leaves Kangaroo with his heart feeling "queer and cave-like and devoid of emotion" (137).

That evening Richard and Harriett Somers stay with Jack and Victoria Callcott in Sydney, and Jack tries to guarantee Richard's loyalty to Kangaroo—as well as his secrecy about their protofascist society—by enacting the ultimate gesture of homosocial bonding when he observes that he has been flirting with his pretty young wife. Telling Harriett, "'We'd better make a swap of it'" (149), he then leaves Somers and Victoria alone together, as if to indicate that he has accepted him as a trusted "mate" by tacitly granting him permission to have sex with his wife. Victoria promptly approaches Somers "like a maiden just ready for love," but he unaccountably rejects her even though he felt "his limbs full of desire, like a power" (142). Afterward, Somers wonders why he has refused Victoria's invitation to experience one of the "great moments of the gods, from the major moment with Hera to the swift short moments of Io or Leda or Ganymede" (143), but his regret seems directed less by his refusal to have sex with Victoria than his wish to repeat Ganymede's sexual encounters with Zeus. That night Somers has the second of his disturbing dreams, this time about being overpowered, blindfolded, held from behind, and robbed by a "rough sort of Australian" man (144). This dream, like the previous one, reveals the psychological origins of Somers's fear as well as the unacknowledged losses that he can neither recognize nor mourn.

National Identity and Revolutionary Politics

After his third meeting with Kangaroo, Somers's melancholy deepens and his conflicts with Harriett sharpen. Before he meets Kangaroo a fourth time, Somers discusses Australian Labour politics with Jaz Trewella and Willie Struthers. These conversations show that Lawrence had a more subtle, if incomplete, understanding of the divisions separating the various fractious groups on the Left and Right in Australia after the Great War. As Stuart Macintyre explains, the Labour Party gained dominance in Australian party politics more quickly than anywhere else in the British Empire, winning large majorities in both houses in the general election of 1910. But when Billy Hughes, Australia's second Labour prime minister, broke with his party over his support for mandatory conscription during the Great War, he provoked a crisis that splintered the Labour Party, since the majority of Australian voters in national referendums twice refused to support conscription. After the general elections of 1917, Hughes, who by then headed the breakaway Nationalist Party, was returned as prime minister and served until December 1922. Hughes's defection "shifted Labour's center of gravity to the left" (Macintyre 1998, 47), and the ensuing "struggle between the pragmatists and the radicals" on the Left continued throughout the 1920s.

Somers's conversations with Willie Struthers revive his working-class loyalties as well as his sympathies for other imperial subjects on the Celtic fringe. Yet Somers retains a specifically English perspective on Labour politics when he tells Struthers, for example, "'You'll never get labour, or any of the socialists, to make a revolution. They just won't act. Only the anarchists might—and they're too few'" (D. H. Lawrence 1994, 195). Struthers replies by insisting on Australian exceptionalism, arguing for a "revolution by degrees" (196) and asserting the need to establish "[s]olidarity" among male workers against the "washed middle classes" (196). While Somers then declares that he "'loves the working people'" and recognizes their capacity "'for great generous love for one another'" (201), he remains skeptical about Struthers's program for a revolution and subsequently rejects his invitation to serve as the editor of his workingman's paper. Although Somers's private reluctance to join Struthers also expresses Lawrence's emerging reservations about a Whitmanesque "love of comrades," the structure of the novel suggests that Somers's concerns are determined at least as much by his gender melancholia. He silently refutes Struthers's championing of mateship when he concludes, for example, "Since man has been trying absolutely to love women, and women to love man, the human species has almost wrecked itself. If now we start a still further campaign of men loving and absolutely trusting each other, comrades or mates, heaven knows the horror we are laying up" (198).

In their next meeting, Kangaroo immediately notices that Somers has shifted his political allegiance, when he urges him to defer his planned takeover as leader of Australia until after the nationalization of "all industries and resources" and the "confiscation of property above a certain amount" have been accomplished, arguing that the ensuing social "chaos" would provide a better opportunity for Kangaroo to act as savior and establish the "benevolent fatherly autocracy" that he has in mind (207).[13] But, later in the interview, when Somers is forced to confront the sexual implications of Kangaroo's alternative definition of "men loving and absolutely trusting each other," his "horror" compels him to reject Cooley's personal advances as well as his fascist program. Confronted with evidence that Somers plans to defect, Kangaroo calls him a "'perverse child'" (208). He then catches the "slight body of the lesser man against his own big breast" (208), and squeezes him so that "he could hardly breathe" (208), acting out Somers's earlier wish that he would "get up again and carry him quite away" (132). Yet the embrace that Somers once desired now threatens something even more fundamental, when Kangaroo tells him, "'Don't thwart me. . . . Don't—or I shall have to break all connection with you, and I love you so'" (208). Immediately afterward, in one of the longest passages cut from the holograph, Kangaroo tenderly tells Somers, "'You have the most lovable eyes I have ever known, and your voice can be the most lovable voice in the world. I have never loved a man as I love you,'" to which Somers replies, "'You are the most lovable man in the world, by far: and the most loving. Your love is wonderful. You almost convert me'" (430). In the published version, however, Somers, still clasped to the "warm passionate body of Kangaroo," simply thinks angrily, "'Damn his love. He wants to *force* me'" (208).

This fourth interview ends with Kangaroo's warning to Somers not to try to "damage" him politically or personally with any blackmailing "talk," and he advises Somers to leave Australia immediately (210). Somers responds by seeing Cooley as "a Great Thing, a horror" (211), evoking Conrad's similarly homoerotic story set on another imperial frontier. This exchange and its aftereffects dramatize the melancholic's "delusional expectation of punishment" that Freud describes. That night Somers experiences a "volcanic" upheaval from his "unconscious" in the form of the nightmare that vividly recalls his wartime experiences in England, and later in the retrospective chapter Lawrence universalizes Somers's experience by noting that 1915 to 1919 was the period "when the world lost its real manhood" (213).

Nightmares and New Definitions of Masculinity

By inserting this long retrospective account of Somers's traumatic experiences during the Great War, Lawrence asks his readers to consider a deeply troubling question: whether any man "who has really consciously lived through this can believe again absolutely in democracy" (D. H. Lawrence 1994, 220). Characterizing the second winter of the Great War, 1915–16, as the time when the "integrity of London collapsed, and the genuine debasement began" (220), Lawrence protests against the civil liberties that were sacrificed during wartime and excoriates the petty English bureaucrats and "stay at home bullies who governed the country," harassing political dissenters, war resisters, and conscientious objectors (212).[14]

Somers's memories of his life in Cornwall also parallel Lawrence's wartime experiences when he was "turned out of his house," was forbidden to return to Cornwall, and "treated like a criminal" by being forced to report to the police wherever he went (257). In retrospect, Somers is able to identity the day when he was summoned for the "torture" of a physical examination for military service as the central trauma of these years. Jeered by the petty "insolent . . . stay at home military who had all the authority in England" (257), stripped naked and obliged to let the doctors "handle his private parts," Somers confronts his fear of "any sort of physical compulsion" (241). Somers's nightmare thus helps readers understand why he rejects Kangaroo's politics and practice of "love." At the same time, it is important to note that Somers's last highly sexualized encounter with Kangaroo prompts this sudden involuntary rush of memories that point to a more obvious loss: his bitter decision to leave England, making him a man "without a people, without a land" (259).

Given his vehement objections to Freudian notions of the "unconscious" in *Fantasia,* it is perhaps surprising that Lawrence echoes Freud's vocabulary in defending his inclusion of this long "nightmare" in *Kangaroo.* As the narrator explains, Somers suddenly "realized that all the time, since the year 1918 . . . deep in his unconsciousness had lain the accumulation of black fury and fear, like frenzied lava quiescent in his soul. And now it had burst up: the fear, then the acute remembrance" (260). While the two chapters that follow the eruption of these memories have been recently read as expressing Lawrence's sudden adoption of "surrealist" techniques or his anticipation of a postmodernist perspective,[15] one can just as easily read them as representing Somers's nervous breakdown as he attempts to reconcile the personal and political revolutions he has experienced. In an effort to explain Somers's apparent emotional paralysis, Lawrence's narrator acknowledges, "[W]hen it comes to the deepest things, men are as entirely irrational as women" (261). By the end of the "Bits" chapter, Somers acknowledges that Kangaroo was the real "queen bee" of the new "beatitudes" that he is struggling to write. Somers cannot answer his own persistent question, "'Why am I so beastly to Kangaroo? . . . I am a detestable little brat to them all around'" (282), but Freud and Butler argue that such self-depreciation and fear of punishment are typical of the melancholic subject.

Moreover, Somers, like Lawrence himself, cannot escape a self-definition as a writer that forces him to recognize what Forter calls the "disjunctive relation" between his gendered self and his "creative source." Determined to face "the beginning and end, the alpha and the omega, the one absolute: the man alone by himself, alone with his own soul, alone with his eyes on the darkness which is the dark god of life" (D. H. Lawrence 1994, 281), Somers ironically imagines himself in feminine terms. Directed by his dreams and nightmares, he recognizes that he is "alone like a pythoness on her tripod, like the oracle alone above the fissure into the unknown" (281). In other words, at this point in the novel, the only way that Richard can imagine himself as a "transgressive artist," able to slit the "Absolute Umbrella" and open a "window to the sun" (109), is by imagining his artistic self as female, but this same gender identification makes him feel vulnerable to Kangaroo's sexual advances.

Somers is not able to cut himself free from his ambivalent attraction to Kangaroo until the man lies on his deathbed. Though Somers has, in the meantime, recognized the murderous side of Kangaroo's politics, revealed during the riot at Canberra House, and has decided that he wants nothing more to do with his protofascist movement, he comes twice more, at Cooley's request, to see the dying man in the hospital. After their first conversation, Somers feels angry and "tormented," and he worries, "'Was it just fear that made him hold back from admitting his love for the other man?'" (327). Judith Butler's analysis of gender melancholy provides a gloss for Somers's dilemma, since, as she explains, "a loss in the world that cannot be declared enrages, generates ambivalence, and becomes the loss 'in' the ego that is nameless and diffuse and that prompts public rituals of self-beratement" (Butler 1997, 185).

In their final meeting, when Kangaroo, looking "like a dead man," weakly commands, "'Say you love me, Lovatt'" (D. H. Lawrence 1994, 336), Somers still cannot repeat the words, though he now recognizes the feelings of "grief, torture, shame" that "seethed low down in him" (335). When Jack Callcott, who has witnessed this exchange, chastises Somers for not being willing to "'speak two words out of pity for a man in his state'" (338), he recognizes the national ideas of maleness that divide them. He scoffs, "'I suppose chaps from the Old Country are more careful of what they say—might give themselves away or something of that'" (338). In response, Somers tries rather childishly to absolve himself of guilt over his unsympathetic withdrawal, thinking, self-righteously, "'I don't love him—I dislike him. He can die. He must die.—And I don't like Jack either'" (347). His comments, nonetheless, reveal the melancholic anomie that Freud and Butler describe, when he concludes: "'I love nobody and I like nobody, and there's the end of it, as far as I'm concerned'" (347). In this way, Somers reveals that he has purchased "the coherence of his heterosexuality" by claiming he "never loved another man" (Butler 1997, 139).

In the original holograph, Somers's meditation is extended to allow him to locate the ultimate object of his mourning. Pondering why he cannot feel love for Kangaroo, Somers realizes, "He didn't love anybody, not even Harriett," and thinks back to his earliest memories. Recalling that "when he was a boy among the colliers, the men didn't 'love' their wives," Somers hears the voice of his mother, addressing his father as "'our master'" (Lawrence 1994, 470). The sequence of Somers's memories thus demonstrates how thoroughly he is stuck between mourning for his mother and a melancholic refusal to acknowledge the effects of his lost connection with his father.

Bringing the Revolution Home

In the end, readers must decide why Lawrence designs a plot for *Kangaroo* that concludes with Somers's rather unconvincing reconciliation with Harriett and his departure from Australia, a country he suddenly insists he "loves like a man wants a woman" (D. H. Lawrence 1994, 347). One explanation for Somers's transformation can be found in the two models of revolution that Cooley and Struthers describe and in the political and psychological reasons offered for Somers's rejection of both. Lawrence describes the litter of consumption in the tin cans and wastepaper that deface the Australian landscape, but he does not evoke, in his narrative or his metaphors, the industrial factories where Australian workers labored. Moreover, by casting Ben Cooley as a lawyer rather than, for instance, a mine owner, Lawrence indicates that the revolution he has in mind is more about the economy of desire than about political economy. At the same time, by setting *Kangaroo* in Australia, Lawrence more easily ignores the "feminized mass-market commodity capitalism" that is vilified in other modernist texts like T. S. Eliot's *The Waste Land* or F. Scott Fitzgerald's *The Great Gatsby*.

Indeed, Somers's talks with Struthers show that he, like Kangaroo, envisions a revolution in homosocial terms, for both men imagine political revolutions that will keep marriage and orthodox gender roles intact. While both leaders apparently assume that Australian women will continue to produce children and take primary responsibility for caring for the family, the novel questions their visions. Victoria Callcott, the only Australian woman allowed to say more than a few words in this text, identifies herself, to borrow Liz Conor's terms, as a "spectacular" woman who takes a thoroughly modern view of her sexuality, with "none of that feminine rapacity which is so hateful in the Old World" (D. H. Lawrence 1994, 33). Marriage means something different to Victoria than to her "Old World" counterparts; as the narrator observes, "The Callcotts had come to no agreement, verbally, as to their marriage. They had not thought it out. They were Australians, of strongly, subtly-developed desire for freedom, with considerable indifference to old formulae and the conventions based thereon" (34). Indeed, Victoria's willing participation in the wife-swapping that Jack tries to stage-manage suggests that the social rituals and the male "honor" that they celebrate apparently function differently Down Under. But if Victoria Callcott is typical of Australian women in her refusal of marital chastity and motherhood, there is reason to doubt that Kangaroo's or Struthers's revolution will be able to reproduce itself. In other words, both leaders try to erase the consequences of a political revolution that had already occurred in Australia when white women were enfranchised in 1902.

In the end, Somers returns to his wife who, in contrast to Victoria, is ostensibly aligned with "Old World" values, but overly biographical readings that identify Harriett as simply a stand-in for Frieda Lawrence have prevented readers from noticing the implications of the sharp political criticism she offers not only of the political plans of Jack Callcott and Ben Cooley but also those endorsed by Jaz Trewella and Willie Struthers. Perhaps because of her more upper-class and less-parochial life experiences, Harriett is more secure in her sex/gender identity than Somers is, but she has already accepted a more "modern" cosmopolitan identification as a sexually liberated woman and sees herself as the transnational subject that Somers struggles to become. Throughout the text, Harriett displays her political acumen as well as her resentment of the sexist exclusions of the men who are planning these revolutions. She explodes, for example, " 'What is all their revolution bosh to me! There have been revolutions enough, in my opinion, each one more foolish than the last' " (162).

In fact, *Kangaroo* shows that Somers fails entirely to convince Harriett to accept his conservative program of reform in their own marriage so that he may act as "lord and master" with Harriett assigned to the obligingly subservient role. Indeed, Harriett reminds Somers of his limited economic power as a writer in a modern consumer economy when she scoffs, "'Him, a lord and master! Why he was not really lord of his own bread and butter, next year they might both be starving. And he was not even master of himself, with his ungovernable furies and his uncritical intimacies with people'" (175). At the same time, the ending of the novel shows that Harriett is also trapped by the political and economic constraints that she faces as the wife of a man without a country. When Jack learns that Somers has broken with Kangaroo and plans to leave Australia, he visits the couple at their home. He invites Harriett to remain behind, without Somers, saying, "'You stop here. We'll look after you'" (288). Embarrassed, Harriett acknowledges that as a wife without skills or money, she is economically dependent upon Somers, "'Oh, he wouldn't give me any money, and I haven't a *sou* of my own'" (288). Jack then says, "'You wouldn't be short of money'" (288). Harriett protests, saying she could not live on "charity," but he counters that it would not be "charity" but "appreciation," suggesting, perhaps, a more sophisticated sexual arrangement as an alternative to living on the dole. Harriett is enraged by Jack's sally, but his remark acknowledges the economic realities that prompted the majority of Australian women in the 1920s, including Callcott's wife, to remain in marriages rather than take up the life of completely independent women.[16]

Jack Callcott's subsequent exchanges with Somers reveal the psychological links between Somers's fears of persecution and his gender melancholy, suggesting how, as Judith Butler argues, the "critical agency of the melancholic is at once a social and psychic instrument" (Butler 1997, 191), an agency that Lawrence clearly exercises in the insufferably didactic passages that disrupt the narrative as well as in his representation of the "return of the repressed" that chastens Somers. When Somers tells Jack that he is leaving Australia because he does not believe in "'revolutions—and public love and benevolence and feeling righteous,'" that he doesn't believe in being one of "'the Saviours of Australia'" (D. H. Lawrence 1994, 290), he begins to feel some of the same fear of chaos that he felt in Kangaroo's presence. Jack hotly replies, "'We don't pretend to be saviours. We want to do our best for Australia, it being our own country'" (290). In a passage cut from the final text, Somers responds by lapsing into satirical self-beratement that clearly reveals his conflicted gender identity. He tells Jack: "'I'm a nasty little know-all from the old country, and a cad and a wash-out and a let-down. And you are real sporting Aussies and he-men. And I'm a diddling she-man. All right. We'll agree on it'" (Lawrence 1994, 462). Warned by his dreams, Somers rejects Jack's politics and rhetoric by which "civilians can be mobilized to kill or be killed in peace-time" in service to an authoritarian theocracy like the one that Kangaroo envisioned.

With no one else to turn to, Somers tries to revive the "vital connection" he once had in his marriage with Harriett, though his final wordless and rather implausible reconciliation with his wife seems, in this context, more like a nostalgic, psychological defense than an expression of authentic desire. After reexperiencing his wartime nightmare and the breakdown that follows it, Somers begins to repeat Harriett's criticism of his failures, for this feminine voice is really a voice he values, one that is "entombed" within, the voice that allows him to write such distinctive prophecy and poetry. In the final chapter that Lawrence rewrote after he and Frieda arrived in Taos, New Mexico, Lawrence adds one more dream sequence to the final pages of the novel. Somers dreams he is walking in Paris in the shadow of a cathedral and recognizes that he has been standing in "the gulf between" shadow and light (D. H. Lawrence 1994, 346). After this dream he is able to appreciate the landscape of the "new world" of Australia more fully than ever before, though the bush, as he apprehends it, is depopulated and best appreciated at nightfall. The narrator asserts that Harriett and Somers have suddenly reversed their views of Australia, and she now feels a "mad loathing" of the country while he feels nostalgic regret for leaving, but this reversal is not very convincing.

Lawrence signals Richard's and Harriett's reconciliation as a heterosexual couple by staging a mock-marriage ceremony when they go out into the bush on Wattle Day and gather "fluffy gold wattle-bloom" that seemed to be the gifts of angels (355), but their reconciliation is premised less on a renewal of sexual passion than on their mutual recognition of the brevity of human life. Though Somers realizes he is saying farewell not only to Australia but also to "Britain and the great Empire," his valediction hardly indicates a resolution of the psychological ambivalence of melancholia that Butler and Freud describe. Still unable to find a "window to the sun," Richard contemplates the next stage of his life journey across a "cold, dark, and inhospitable" ocean (361).

If the "Nightmare" chapter in *Kangaroo* allowed Lawrence to revisit the scenes of "mourning" that he acknowledged, recalling his loss of his mother, his lost faith in the enduring values of British liberal democracy, and his rejection, finally, of a life in the most democratic country in the British Empire, the text as a whole also offers a testament to the losses that he did not mourn, including his repudiation of homosexual desire, the diminishment of the heterosexual intensity of his relationship with Frieda Lawrence, and his alienation from his elderly father at home in England. Kangaroo's death apparently released Somers from his agonized ambivalence about his homoerotic desire, allowing Lawrence to restore a semblance of heterosexual "romance" to this text, but Somers's persistent rage and nostalgic desire to reproduce the terms of his parents' damaged and subordinated marriage hardly provides a hopeful vision of the future of his marriage to Harriett. Significantly, Somers refuses to attend Kangaroo's funeral or engage in any other rituals of "mourning" to recognize what he has sacrificed in rejecting Kangaroo's love and erotic appeals. Lawrence's uneasy and ambivalent ending for *Kangaroo* thus reveals not only Somers's continuing battle with gender melancholia but also his ambivalence about Kangaroo's fascist revolution and Lawrence's own messianic drive to resurrect more orthodox marriage and gender arrangements based on phallic idolatry.

Kangaroo does, nonetheless, demonstrate Lawrence's sad rejection of many values associated with English maleness, even as it reinforces others that seemed psychically necessary to him at the time. In Australia, as far away as possible from the Old World, Lawrence glimpsed alternatives to English notions of political and sexual "freedom," though he could not evade the Freudian psychology he tried to revise.

In a letter written in October 1922, shortly after his arrival in the United States, he admits, "One uses words to cover up a crying inside one. . . . England seems full of graves to me" (D. H. Lawrence 1987a, 327). *Kangaroo,* seen from this perspective, remains shadowed by "gender melancholy" and by the losses that Lawrence did not recognize, perhaps most notably the father he did not see or communicate with for five years after he left England. His final meeting with Arthur John Lawrence was probably during his visit to Eastwood in 1924; Lawrence's father died nine months later on September 10, 1924 (Ellis 1989, 153).

Finally, we can better understand Lawrence's objections to Freud's oedipal theory as expressed in *Psychoanalysis and the Unconscious* and *Fantasia of the Unconscious* by recognizing in them Lawrence's effort to find a window to the sun in order to see beyond scientific paradigms that assumed and "normalized" heterosexuality. Written in the shadow of these texts, *Kangaroo* itself exposes Lawrence's continuing struggle with the psychoanalytic ideas about repression and the "unconscious," as well as with Freudian psychology more broadly, which paradoxically promised liberation and fulfillment while imposing an intellectualized psychological conformity that was, and still is, restricted by narrowly defined concepts of maleness and femaleness, as well as by the heterosexual romance that this utterly modern discourse normalizes.

Notes

1. Becket 1997–98, Becket 2001, S. Brewster 1997–98, and Ruderman 1984 have been particularly helpful in assessing Lawrence's various responses to psychoanalytic writing.

2. Davis 1988 presents a comprehensive discussion of Lawrence's life in Thirroul. Ellis 1998 and 1989 reassess Robert Darroch's controversial claim that Lawrence met the organizer of a secret army during one of his visits to Sydney. See also Bruce Steele's introduction to D. H. Lawrence 1994, xix–lvi.

3. Recent essays in Bennett and Strauss 1998 by Robert Dixon (66–88), Richard Nile (130–46), and Adrian Caesar (147–65), for example, confirm Schaffer's analysis.

4. See Kinkead-Weekes 1996, 332, 467–71; Wussow 1998, 44–49; and Delany 1978, 373–77.

5. For influential discussions of the new visibility of gay and lesbian sexuality in the 1920s, see, for example, D'Emilio and Freeman 1988; and Conor 2004.

6. Butler offers a persuasive argument about how mourning for the mother is a symptom of gender melancholy in Butler 1997, 167–98.

7. See Ruderman 2003 and 1991.

8. Robert Darroch, has, of course, famously warned that outsiders often mistake Australian mateship for "latent homosexuality" (1981, 55). While his caution may apply to Jack Callcott, I argue that the text clearly identifies Ben Cooley as a homosexual man.

9. Gertzman and Squires (1999) recently recovered the correspondence between Lawrence, Seltzer, and Mountsier in 1922–23.

10. I consulted Steele's editing.

11. Lane 1995, incorporates Eve Sedgwick's influential analysis of "homosocial" relations in his reading of colonial fiction; see also Paxton 1999, 109–36.

12. I am indebted to Booth 2002, and to Ellis 1998, 39–54; both question the notoriously overstated reading in Meyers 1977 of the biographical support for Lawrence's representation of homosexuality in *Kangaroo*.

13. Davis argues that Somers's meeting with Struthers revives his "loyalty to class" (1988, 82).

14. See Wussow 1998, 44–49, for an account of the effects of DORA regulations on him.

15. See, for example, Radford 2002.

16. Macintyre notes that in 1907 the standards for wages in Australia were "premised on the male breadwinner," and women unsuccessfully contested the dual wage standard for the next sixty years (1998, 151).

Keeping His Flag Flying: Censorship and Lawrence's Poetry

Christopher Pollnitz

> Do you imagine I would haul down my flag to such an extent in front of the public, for all the Jixes in Christendom?
>
> —D. H. Lawrence, *Letters*

IN THE QUOTATION ADAPTED FOR THE TITLE, WRITING TO A PUBlisher who wanted to change his poetry, Lawrence likens his capacity to attract controversy to a self-identifying "flag" (1993b, 249)—a banner that made him recognizable to a minority public and to himself, a standard which became inseparable from his sense of mission as a writer. The later Lawrence set out to assault his readers' and even his own sensibilities; he rode into battle under a banner of disturbing class proprieties and offending standards of acceptability. In this respect, he repeatedly crossed frontiers, an image I address later in this essay.

I am not primarily concerned, as Chuck Stone and Jay Gertzman have been, with censorship as a constitutional or human rights issue, or with the legal history of censorship. My limited perspective comes from editing Lawrence's *Poems* for the Cambridge University Press edition of his works. My editorial task is to discover poems or passages censored or bowdlerized—chiefly by publishers, acting out of fear of prosecution under Obscenity Acts—and to restore, where possible, the text Lawrence intended. In assessing what censors have attempted to ban and publishers to bowdlerize, I shall nevertheless go beyond my editorial brief and ask what prompted Lawrence to persist in writing works that called down the censor's wrath. At times, he verged on the disingenuous—for instance, when claiming that he was unable rather than unwilling to expurgate the typescripts of *Lady Chatterley's Lover*, that he "got sort of colour-blind, and didn't know any more what was supposed to be proper and what not" (1991, 308). Elsewhere, he is more candid and the self-knowledge he displays is more acute: for example, when denouncing the English publisher who, he contended, wanted to make *Pansies* into a "bourgeois 'inoffensive'" collection of verse satires, "a nice null bourgeois book" (1993b, 242). It was this publisher to whom Lawrence addressed his "flag" comment.

Two preconceptions about censorship and Lawrence's poetry need dispelling. In October to November 1928, Lawrence received the reviews of *Lady Chatterley's Lover* that led to the novel's banning; he received from Morris Ernst a coauthored study of censorship, *To the Pure* . . . , and replied with his letter about the "censor-moron"; and he began composing his satirical poems, *Pansies*. The suggestive dovetailing of the three events highlights what would become a major concern in Lawrence's poetry and expository prose in 1929: an examination of the cause and effect of the pruning by censors of "living and growing human consciousness . . . in its newest, most sensitive activity" (1991, 613). In *To the Pure* . . . , Ernst and Seagle distinguished three forms of censorship—religious, political, and sexual—and they supposed that Lawrence's work attracted sexual censorship only.[1] The supposition has, until recent decades, been widely shared by the general public and by scholars of the period. Like his other writing, however, Lawrence's poetry underwent religious, political, *and* sexual censorship. A second assumption that even Lawrence scholars have fallen into is that his fiction alone bore the brunt of police raids, customs inspections, and postal seizures. While censors focused on the novels when issuing warrants or mounting prosecutions, Lawrence's publishers sought to improve their sales, and make their writer popular with a middle-class, middlebrow readership, by expurgating his short fiction, his nonfiction, and (just as relentlessly) his poetry.

Love Poems and Others is a first example. In 1911, Edward Garnett's expression of interest in Lawrence's short stories and poems was perhaps a ploy to poach the young author for the publishing firm of Duckworth. Since bringing out *The White Peacock,* William Heinemann had seemed indifferent to Lawrence, but Garnett's intervention reawakened Heinemann's interest in his young author. Lawrence, who had been copying out his verse for Garnett, embarrassedly asked his new mentor to forward the copies to the incoming poetry reader at Heinemann's (1979b, 317), who turned out to be Walter de la Mare. After Heinemann refused both *Sons and Lovers* and the volume of poems for several reasons—the principal appears to have been their "want of reticence" (D. H. Lawrence 1979b, 421 n. 4)—Duckworth went on to publish both *Love Poems and Others* and the novel in 1913. Lawrence was sure that his poems no less than his novel had "shocked [Heinemann's] modesty" (442).[2] The poems had shocked De la Mare, whose review of the Duckworth *Love Poems* verbally echoes Heinemann's complaint about *Sons and Lovers:* "[T]here are poems of sheer brutality, and passages almost without a vestige of restraint or reticence."[3] Lawrence had therefore had good reason to worry, after his poems were returned to Duckworth and Garnett, that the selection that Heinemann's poetry reader had made was unrepresentatively demure and "exquisite," "à la De la Mare —to convince the critics I was well brought up, so to speak" (D. H. Lawrence 1979b, 455). Not only Edward but his son, David Garnett, evidently enlarged De la Mare's selection of Lawrence's poems.[4] What Lawrence learnt from the publication of *Love Poems* was that publishers and their readers might misrepresent him as someone with polite, middle-class values. Thereafter, *he* would choose the poems for his volumes, then keep his eye on any alterations that his publishers proposed.

Duckworth raised no difficulties over Lawrence's second volume, *Amores.* Even though *Amores* includes "Last Words to Miriam," "Scent of Irises," and "The Hands of the Betrothed"—poems twenty-first-century readers may still find explicit, and cruel—Duckworth and Garnett were more comfortable with Lawrence's psychosexual realism than Heinemann and De la Mare had been.[5] Duckworth's relaxed attitude is surprising, given that, three months before Lawrence sent off the typescript of *Amores* (D. H. Lawrence

1981a, 521), a Bow Street magistrate had ordered all copies of *The Rainbow* destroyed. Not until terms for Lawrence's third volume of verse, *Look! We Have Come Through!*, had been agreed on did *The Rainbow*'s prosecution come back to haunt the poet. The "nice[,] old-flavoured" publishing firm of Chatto and Windus (D. H. Lawrence 1984, 144) demanded Lawrence omit two poems, bowdlerize three passages, and alter two titles.

In changing the titles "Eve's Mass" and "Candlemas" to "Birth Night" and "Valentine's Night," Lawrence was complying with a publisher's *religious* bowdlerizing of "poems of an amorous character" (145 n. 1). Because the 1912–13 *Tagebuch* of the *Look!* poems is lost, and no 1917 manuscript of *Look!* is extant, it can be tricky determining what Chatto and Windus objected to. Fortunately, Frieda Lawrence in *"Not I, But the Wind . . ."* preserved notebook versions of the poems that the publishers expurgated. The first, "Song of a Man Who Is Loved," begins and ends with the stanzas:

> Between her breasts is my home, between her breasts.
> Three sides set on me space and fear,
>   but the fourth side rests,
> Warm in a city of strength, between her breasts.
>
> . . . .
>
> And I hope to spend eternity
> With my face down—buried between her breasts
> And my still heart full of security
> And my still hands full of her breasts.
>
> (F. Lawrence 1935, 45)[6]

In their letter to Lawrence's agent, Chatto and Windus declared themselves averse to mention of "purely physical phenomena" (D. H. Lawrence 1984, 145 n. 1). The phenomena that offended them in the "Song" were a woman's breasts. If that complaint is "old-flavoured" enough to be straightforward, their objection to the second poem is more puzzling. "Meeting Among the Mountains" reached a wide audience through the popular anthology *Georgian Poetry, 1913–1915*, but its narrative is obscure without Frieda's gloss: the Austrian peasant whom the poet-speaker encounters had "accusing eyes" that reminded Lawrence of Frieda's first husband, Ernest Weekley.[7] A plausible explanation for Chatto and Windus's disquiet was that a friend or member of Weekley's family revealed the poem's association with a scandalous divorce. If so, fear of the law of libel rather than the law of obscenity underlay the firm's demand. Lawrence was not outraged by the omission of "Meeting Among the Mountains" as he was by "Song of a Man Who Is Loved." In 1928, he rewrote the "Song," drawing on the *Tagebuch* version, and reinserted it in the *Look!* sequence for *Collected Poems*. He opted not to do so with "Meeting Among the Mountains," although he had an equivalent text available in the *Tagebuch*.[8] When Vivian de Sola Pinto and Warren Roberts reinserted "Meeting Among the Mountains" in the *Look!* sequence for their *Complete Poems*, they countermanded Lawrence's final intention to omit the poem.[9]

If Lawrence ever lowered his flag before the censors, it was when preparing the volume *New Poems* for publication. With *The Rainbow* suppressed and *Women in Love* unpublishable, Lawrence saw his poetry as a way of keeping his name before the public and making a few pounds.[10] When approaching his agent, he sounds pathetically anxious to please:

> I am sending you MS. of a book of poems. I think there is nothing in it to offend anybody—tell me if you think there is: or if you think there is anything that would be better left out. . . . At first I had it in two little separate books, one called "In London," the other "Choir of Women." I can split it up again if you think publishers would rather have it that way. . . . But you will tell me what you think about these things, won't you. . . .
>
> Do write to those Literary Fund people. I am in a painful way about money, as usual: so if they will help, I shall have to be helped by them . . .
>
> Tell me if you have any suggestions for alterations in the poems. (1984, 255)

Long eager to have Lawrence on his list, Martin Secker snapped up the volume in manuscript. He pruned the poems to fit the sixty-four-page format necessitated by the end-of-war paper shortage, Lawrence disputing none of the cuts.[11] But is this the same author who, writing to his agent about Chatto and Windus, had mocked "the ways and taste of publishers" as "mysterious and beyond finding out" (145)?

The *New Poems* letter can be made out to be Lawrence's, if a sequence he put together after *The First "Women in Love"* is considered. Titled "All of Us" in typescript,[12] the sequence was based on the German archaeologist Heinrich Schäfer's collection of Egyptian folk songs.[13] Lawrence adapted the songs that the fellaheen laborers sang at Schäfer's excavation site, and remade the German translations into what he called the " 'war *literature*' [people] are looking for" (51). The sequence has never been published in full, its "too doubtful little pills" (234) scaring away publishers. "All of Us" is deeply *anti*war literature, but the pacifist bitterness of the sequence is hidden beneath layers of disguise and irony. Lawrence agreed with Lady Cynthia Asquith that the Allies' attempts to open an eastern front—by naval bombardment of the Dardanelles, garrisoning Salonika, and General Charles Townshend's foolhardy push toward Baghdad—served no purpose other than to "empty the future" (1981a, 414). In "All of Us," he changed the mostly Egyptian place-names in the folk songs to direct attention to military disasters like the invasion of Iraq—or of Mesopotamia, as it was then called. In 1918, he deployed similar strategies in some of the so-called *New Poems,* like "Reading a Letter." There, a girl sitting in a Croydon park is transported to Mesopotamia, and "stoops to see / The sandy desert beneath her, the dreary platoon" (1918, 50). Hence, there is a second agenda in Lawrence's letter to J. B. Pinker: if the author could get the "doubtful pills" of "All of Us" past the experienced agent, the ruse would surely succeed with a publisher. Lawrence was trying to avoid potential *political* censorship of his antiwar poems. His success was too complete: for all but ninety years, scarcely anyone has cared, or known how, to decode the velleities of *Bay, New Poems,* and "All of Us."[14] In the 1920s, Lawrence reverted to upsetting censors, and challenging readers, in more forthright style. As he remarked in 1925, "A book should be either a bandit or a rebel or a man in a crowd"—a laughing, or an angry, shin-kicking man, he went on to add (1989a, 201).

Written over three and a half years of travel, the animal portraits and still lifes of *Birds, Beasts and Flowers* resound with the extremist and nationalist politics of four continents, and are haunted by the search for a post-Christian religious clue. Lawrence hoped to pick up the clue eighty miles north of Santa Fe, where "Day has gone to dust on the sage-grey desert / Like a white Christus fallen to dust from a cross" (1923a, 190). Yet it was not primarily religious or political censorship to which *Birds, Beasts and Flowers* was subjected. Prosecutions, initiated by John Sumner of the New York Society for the Suppression of Vice and by Justice John Ford of the Clean Books League, drove the publisher Thomas Seltzer to ever more conservative bowdlerizing of sexual references in the poems. Sumner raided Seltzer's premises in July 1922, but the case against the three titles seized (including *Women in Love*) was dismissed by Magistrate George Simpson in September.[15] Then, after an unsuccessful attempt to have new legislation enacted, Justice Ford leagued with Sumner, and the two enlisted District Attorney Ferdinand Pecora to bring a Supreme Court prosecution against Seltzer.[16] On July 18, 1923 (Lacy 1976, 189), Seltzer was indicted by a grand jury for publishing "unclean" books; on July 19 (Ellis 1998, xix), Lawrence arrived in New York to correct the proofs for *Birds, Beasts and Flowers*.[17] With a friend and publisher facing criminal proceedings and a penal sentence, Lawrence was under moral pressure to expurgate his poems. Yet when the time came to correct proofs, Lawrence was not as cooperative as he had promised to be when sending Seltzer the composite manuscript-typescript for *Birds, Beasts and Flowers*, Roberts E47c:[18] "If you think there is anything needs modifying—you might in the 'Goat' poems,—let me know" (D. H. Lawrence 1987a, 378). Nor was Seltzer as open in his dealings as he professed he would be, given that Lawrence was an author "in whose work he thoroughly believed" (Worthen 1989, 17).

Three times Seltzer attempted to bowdlerize *Birds, Beasts and Flowers*. In sending the composite manuscript-typescript to Seltzer, Lawrence asked the publisher to have two "fair type-copies" prepared (D. H. Lawrence 1987a, 378). When one of these, Roberts E47d, was returned to him on March 14, 1923, Lawrence at once asked Seltzer to send the other type-copy, Roberts E47e, to London for Secker's edition (409). Though the description of Roberts E47e in the *Bibliography* as a "corrected carbon typescript" is not incorrect (Roberts and Poplawski 2001, 578), the light corrections are not authorial, but added by Lawrence's English publisher. Five weeks before receiving his type-copy in New Mexico (Roberts E47d), Lawrence had written to Seltzer of his plans to leave the Del Monte Ranch and move to Old Mexico. When the type-copy arrived on March 14, Lawrence opened it to discover that Seltzer had penciled marginal lines and queries against references in the poems to animal excretion and sexuality, and even plant reproduction. Thirty lines and passages in eleven poems were so marked. Already caught up in travel plans, Lawrence prioritized his move to Mexico. He jotted "OK" next to the marginal markings, corrected the type-copy in haste, and returned it to Seltzer. His American publisher erased the markings,[19] used the E47d type-copy (most of it at least) to set galley proofs, and prepared for the next phase of the bowdlerizing campaign.

When Lawrence arrived in New York in July, he complied with or was tricked into expurgating four poems. Take "Fig" as an example.[20] Seltzer had omitted the whole of "Fig" from the first proofs, Roberts E47f. Lawrence made a note in the galleys to show where the missing poem should be reinserted, found the type-copy version,[21] followed some marginal suggestions to bowdlerize, but also added creative changes of his own. Yet after Lawrence completed his alterations, Seltzer made still further deletions—for instance, of the two lines concluding this stanza:

> The Italians vulgarly say, it [the fig] stands
>   for the female part; the fig-fruit:
> The fissure, the yoni,
> The wonderful moist conductivity towards the centre.
>
> (D. H. Lawrence 1923a; cf. 1923b, 6)

Seltzer's pencil deletion of the two lines are distinguishable from Lawrence's ink revisions (in ink, he revised the second line to read "The break, the yoni").[22] Finally, after Lawrence handed Seltzer the sets of revised galley proofs and Seltzer made his deletions, the publisher also passed them on to one of his staff for a last phase of bowdlerizing—again kept secret from Lawrence. A handful of inane variants resulted. In Secker's version of "The American Eagle," for instance, the armorial bird is hailed as a "prosperity-gander" (D. H. Lawrence 1923a, 206), whereas in Seltzer's edition it is a desexed "prosperity-fowl" (D. H. Lawrence 1923b, 179).[23] Seltzer could not rely on Lawrence to make cuts that enfeebled his poems; Lawrence could not trust Seltzer to inform him of the cuts being made.

At the end of July, Lawrence had duplicate corrected proofs sent to England to help Secker correct his proofs, but Secker made, at most, selective use of the corrections from New York. He may have adopted some cuts—for instance, in "Cypresses"—but his policy was to ignore creative changes in the American proofs. "Elephant" is the record of a Ceylonese *Perahera* that Lawrence saw from ground level, and Edward, the Prince of Wales, from a "pagoda" erected above the procession. In the well-known conclusion, the persona thinks of the "three feathers," which the first Prince of Wales gained for his regalia after Crécy,[24] and wishes

> they had given the three feathers to me;
> That I had been he in the pavilion, as in a
> pepper-box aloft and alone
> To stand and hold feathers, three feathers
> above the world . . .
>
> (1923a, 175)

In the less well-known ending from the American edition, the persona wishes

> some dark-faced man could have taken
> the feathers three
> And fearless gone up the pavilion, in that pepper-box
> aloft and alone
> Held the three feathers out on the night, with a dark,
> fierce hand above the host. . . .
>
> (1923b, 144)

Secker's apathy toward Lawrence's revisions had an effect equivalent to political censorship. Because the text from the English edition was transmitted to the *Collected Poems* and *Complete Poems*, "Elephant" does not record Lawrence's shift, after spending time in Taos and Chapala, toward a postcolonial stance on the entitlements of indigenous peoples. It will in the Cambridge *Poems*.

That the banning of a novel preceded censoring of Lawrence's poetry is demonstrated by the volume *Pansies*. In January 1929, Lawrence sent two carbon type-copies of a first version of *Pansies* to his London agent at Curtis Brown's, Laurence Pollinger. The two copies were to be distributed to his London and New York publishers, but were intercepted by postal workers acting under instruction from "D" Division of the Home Office. This division had been given responsibility for coordinating British censorship while the genially puritanical Sir William Joynson-Hicks was home secretary and the forbiddingly puritanical Sir Archibald Bodkin was Director of Public Prosecutions (DPP). The ominous seizure of *Pansies* was conducted in the shadow of the ban that Joynson-Hicks, or "Jix," had laid on *Lady Chatterley's Lover*. *Pansies* would eventually see the light in two trade editions and a private edition (of which Charles Lahr was the effective publisher). Lawrence had developed this countercensorship strategy for *Pansies* when bringing out *Lady Chatterley*, privately published in Florence by Giuseppe Orioli. The state censors and the author based their strategies with regard to *Pansies* on what they learned, or believed they had learned, from *Lady Chatterley*. A month before the *Pansies* typescripts were reported seized, Lawrence had asked for six copies of *Lady Chatterley* to be addressed to Pollinger (D. H. Lawrence 1993b, 90). The officers from Scotland Yard, who announced to Pollinger, on January 19, 1929, that the six novel copies had been confiscated (146–47 n. 4), returned on January 23 to report the interception of the type-copies of *Pansies* (149 n. 1).[25]

In an article on the censorship and transmission of *Pansies*, I have discussed at length how Joynson-Hicks and the Home Office dealt with *Pansies*, and how Lawrence, despite the screening of his mail, coped with and outmaneuvered the British censors (Pollnitz 2005). Here I shall only pose questions not taken up in that article. Given that, in verse *pensées* like "My Naughty Book," "The Young and Their Moral Guardians," and "To Clarinda"—poems excluded from the trade editions—Lawrence satirized public reaction to and the banning of *Lady Chatterley,* did the Home Office seek to prevent publication of *Pansies* because it was thought obscene or because it attacked censorship? Given that the seizing of the *Pansies* type-copies did not prevent Lawrence from sharpening and expanding his volume of satires, what effect did the postal seizure of the typescripts have on public opinion? And given that Lawrence did, with Lahr's assistance, win the main battle when the unexpurgated private edition was published in London, what skirmishes did he have to fight to keep his flag flying "in front of the public" and "all the Jixes in Christendom" (D. H. Lawrence 1993b, 249)? The bid to censor *Pansies* divides into the interception of the type-copies and Martin Secker's bowdlerizing of the English trade edition.

Joynson-Hicks declared in the Commons, on February 28, 1929, that the "package" holding the *Pansies* type-copies had never been opened: sent via "open book post," the contents were, Jix maintained, merely being examined to check whether they required mailing at a higher rate when the obscene material was discovered (Nehls 1957–59, 3:311). Lawrence's explosion of rage—it could and should be shown, he protested, that "he [the home secretary] is a *liar,* and he did open my sealed and registered *letter*" (D. H. Lawrence 1993b, 227)—is an outburst of a kind so familiar it is possible to miss what sparked his rage. The detonator was the secretary of state's mendacity rather than the opening of the letter. Inured during the war to having his letters tampered with by military authorities (Worthen 2005, 193), Lawrence responded with skeptical calm, in December 1928, when Lahr (who helped distribute *Lady Chatterley* as well as publish *Pansies*) passed on his possibly well founded suspicions that their correspondence was being "touched" (D. H. Lawrence 1993b, 44). Yet in 1929, the banning of *Lady Chatterley's Lover* took up relatively few column inches in London journals and newspapers. It was after the *Pansies* seizure that Letters to the Editor columns began to carry stories from readers of how their sealed letters to publishers on the Continent had been opened. A growing number of authors—including Lytton Strachey, Leonard Woolf, Victor Gollancz, Rebecca West, John Hobson, Havelock Ellis, Arnold Bennett, Edward Garnett, Virginia Woolf, and E. M. Forster—complained of the violation of His Majesty's mail, of the curb imposed on free speech and creativity, of the ad hoc procedures of state censorship, and of their fear that the interception of a writer's book *before* publication was a reversion to the censorship methods of the ancien régime (Pollnitz 2005, 60–62). Conscious of public relations, the Home Office undersecretaries must have realized that the confiscation of the typescripts had been a public relations disaster. Yet Lawrence himself, never a devoted reader of London journals, remained unaware of the tide of opinion flowing in his direction. While he knew of the banning of Radclyffe Hall's *Well of Loneliness* (D. H. Lawrence 1993b, 132), the *Pansies* controversy only exacerbated his sense of isolation. If he was not the sole scapegoat, he saw himself, with some justice, as the preeminent target of the British censorship regime.

The postal officer who first read a *Pansies* type-copy would have adjudged it as obscene, not for the poems, but for the introduction with its defense of "the so-called 'obscene' words" (D. H. Lawrence 1929b, [4]).[26] Subsequently, the Home Office turned its attention to the unexpurgated edition of *Pansies* in which the introduction defiantly reappeared, but doubts arose as to whether a successful prosecution could be mounted against an edition sold by subscription and so restricted to the privileged class of collectors. "D" Division forwarded a copy of the edition to the DPP for an advice. Bodkin made a digest of the book's supposedly obscene parts by reading only those *pensées* Lawrence had instructed Lahr to asterisk in the table of contents—the poems Martin Secker had required Lawrence to exclude, for fear his trade edition would be subject to censorship. Reading these, Bodkin wrote an advice (reprinted in James T. Boulton's article on state censorship) that the poems were of "the nauseous and disgusting kind rather than . . . the corrupting and immoral kind"; they were, that is, unlikely to be prosecuted successfully (Boulton 2000, 8). Thus it was that a complete edition of *Pansies*, which included the offending introduction, as well as further skits on Britain's self-censoring and self-stifling conservatism—satires not included in the "grossly indecent" early type-copies[27]—threaded its way past Scotland Yard, the postal sorters, Jix, and the DPP. Neither the home secretary nor Sir Archibald was guilty of censoring poems that stigmatized them "as stale old dogs who pretend to guard / the morals of the masses" (D. H. Lawrence 1929b, 62); the responsibility for such omissions was Martin Secker's. While Lawrence was still battling to hammer out a compromise with Secker, it was against the publisher that he vented his ire for outdoing the job of the state censors, "outjixing jix" (1993b, 249) and outslashing Bodkin.

The cut that goaded Lawrence to coin "outjixing" was one Secker insisted on in "True Democracy," a *pensée* that begins, "I wish I was a gentleman / . . . / to pee in the eye of a police-man" (1929, 10). If the second line is "beyond all bearing," Lawrence suggested, "then put 'To—— in the eye etc.' But would you scrap that good sarcastic little poem for the mere three letters 'pee'" (1993b, 249)? Eventually, with the experience of *Lady Chatterley* behind him, Lawrence bypassed his publisher's objections to particular words and poems, securing both copyright and an ill-proofed but complete text of *Pansies* with the private edition. As he vainly tried to argue Secker out of his timidity, Lawrence was arguing over ground he had already assayed in the introduction to *Pansies*. In this and other analyses of censorship in 1929, Lawrence attributes the compulsion to censor to a denial of common sense and of the body. While this approach may lead him to an at-times crude literalism (reducing speech act to body part or body function), it has the benefit of distributing the responsibility for censorship among all participants in literary communication—the state censor, the publisher, the author who allows his scope of representation and inquiry to be restricted, and the reader who complacently accepts preprocessed reading matter. All are engaged in denying physical, psychological, and social truths, and the denial is no healthier if the hypocrisy is repressed or unconscious. The censorious consciousness "hates certain parts of the body, and makes the [taboo] words representing these parts scapegoats. It pelts them out of the consciousness with filth. . . . So that a man turns himself into a thing of shame and horror. And his consciousness shudders with horrors that he has made for himself" (1929, [5]). The imbecility to which the self-censoring consciousness half-voluntarily reduces itself, as well as the social contradictions and psychological ills of censorship, would become a central theme of *Nettles*, the volume that Lawrence extracted from his penultimete verse notebook.

From the Florence publication of *Lady Chatterley's Lover* until his death, Lawrence's relations with the Home Office censors and the literary journalists who backed state censorship partook of the ethics of feud, revenge attack following hard upon retaliatory raid. The July 5, 1929, raid on the Warren Gallery, from which the police carried off thirteen of the twenty-five Lawrence paintings on exhibition, was a coalition of "D" Division, the conservative justiciary, and the conservative press getting even for the castigation they had suffered over *Pansies*. Lawrence believed that it had been his inveterate foe, J. C. Squire, whose review of the paintings had precipitated the police raid (D. H. Lawrence 1993b, 376),[28] and in *Nettles* he fired off satires like "London Mercury" against Squire and his class. In "My Little Critics," he attributes Squire's review to a fit of "hysterics" (1930, 22). Faber and Faber were willing to publish broadsides like these in their pamphlet of Lawrence's *Nettles*, but were not immune to nervous bowdlerizing. "Daddy-Do-Nothing" and "Question"—two "nettles" on the Victorian statesman William Ewart Gladstone—poked fun at Gladstone's imprudent habit of walking London streets at night, approaching prostitutes, and offering them the means to find salvation. Lawrence included both in the typescript of *Nettles*, Roberts E266c, but Faber omitted them from the pamphlet, perhaps fearing a libel rather than an Obscenity Act prosecution. Yet color is lent to the notion this *was* political censorship by a third omission. In "British Sincerity" Lawrence launches a direct assault on the mores of Britain's censors, the "Jixery":

> They tell me that these British moral birds
> all the great Jixery up in the fixery
> are "perfectly sincere"
> and "perfectly honest"

If it is perfectly sincere to deny your own make-up
and perfectly honest to pretend to be unbegotten
may I ask you then, where insincerity and dishonesty begin.

The Jixery perhaps never picked a man's pocket
but my god, they sneak-thiefed his very genitals
  away from him:
going a bit further than his pocket, what?

And the poor man never knew he was jixed
fixed, jixed, fixed!

(1932, 242)

This version of the "nettle" was included in the "More Pansies" section of Secker's *Last Poems.*[29] By 1933, a skit too sensitive to be published in 1930 had become acceptable political comment.

In 1925, an American journalist, Kyle Crichton, put the question to Lawrence, Why did he write? John Worthen, in *Life of an Outsider,* finds a revelation of the author of *The Plumed Serpent* in Lawrence's hesitant answer (Worthen 2005, 325–26). In this context, I shall divide Crichton's "bright" question (Nehls 1957–59, 2:414) into two others: For whom did Lawrence write? And why was he unable, or unwilling, to write works passable by censors and palatable to a wider public? Lawrence's answers to such questions change at turning points in his writing career. The young novelist, awaiting publication of *Sons and Lovers* and assured his major theme was "a re-adjustment between men and women," wrote for "English folk" because he wanted them "to alter, and to have more sense" (D. H. Lawrence 1979b, 544). With *The Rainbow* banned and *Women in Love* unpublishable, Lawrence was less clear about his readership or his ambitions: "But a work of art is an act of faith, as Michael Angelo says, and one goes on writing, to the unseen witnesses" (1981a, 602). His conviction was now that it was not "English folk" he wrote for: "I'm not going to squat in a cottage feeling their fine feelings for them, and flying for them a flag that only makes a fool of *me*" (1984, 288).[30] In the later war years, the Lawrence who writes to unsettle his readers and break down their prejudices, rather than confirm them in a new social or spiritual vision, was emerging.

Having passed through the near-death experience of finishing *The Plumed Serpent,* he was equally sure he did not write for American folk. His answer to Crichton's question was solipsistic, then esoteric, then obscure: "You don't write for anybody; you rather write from a deep moral sense—for the race, as it were" (Nehls 1957–59, 2:414). After returning to Europe, publishing *Lady Chatterley's Lover,* and sending Christmas *pensées* to Charles Wilson's colliers (D. H. Lawrence 1993b, 98–104), Lawrence again began revolving the questions of why, and for, and against whom he wrote.

The questions were better defined when he debated censorship with Joynson-Hicks in Faber's Criterion Miscellany series, Jix taking the affirmative in *Do We Need a Censor?* and Lawrence the negative in *Pornography and Obscenity.* Joynson-Hicks concluded his argument by positing a utopia with a consensual morality so total—"the day will come when no form of censorship will be needed, when there will be no prosecutions or breaches of the law . . . because the people themselves will have attained . . . cleanness of heart" (Joynson-Hicks 1929, 34)—as to guarantee sociopolitical stasis. Abandoning the working-class nostalgia that makes itself felt in parts of *Lady Chatterley* and some later poems, Lawrence thinks of his writing as targeted, not at the working class or any mass audience, but at a "minority . . . which has its own dynamic ideas about pornography and obscenity" (D. H. Lawrence 2004e, 252). Had Lawrence cut his sentence short at a "minority" with "its own dynamic ideas," he might have seemed to be moving toward a Marxist alignment, a faith in carefully provoked class conflict as the engine for dialectical change. By adding "ideas about pornography and obscenity," he rather specifies that his late work is pitched for readers who can extract from literature ideas that transform both their self-conceptions and social expectations. Yet in *Pornography and Obscenity* Lawrence avoids any implication that he writes merely in order to oppose sexual censorship; he evades such a charge by correlating the power to rethink sexuality with the potential for moral, social, and (to a lesser extent in this pamphlet) religious change and renewal.

Adam Parkes, in an article comparing Lawrence's paintings with those of a contemporary, Federico Beltrán Massés, starts from the premise that, whereas a number of the paintings Beltrán planned to exhibit in London were pornographic —or at least pandered to a dominant male, upper-class eroticism—it is a mistake to "read" Lawrence's paintings in this way. Lawrence had been distressed to learn that those queuing to view his exhibition at the Warren Gallery had come expecting pornographic images:

> And they blushed, they giggled, they sniggered, they leered,
> or they boiled and they fumed, in fury they sneered
>
> and said: Oh boy! I tell you what,
> look at that one there, that's pretty hot!—
>
> And they stared and they stared, the half-witted lot
> at the spot where the fig-leaf just was not!
>
> But why, I ask you? Oh tell me why?
> Aren't they made quite the same, then, as you and I?
>
> Can it be they've been trimmed, so they've never seen
> the innocent member that a fig-leaf will screen?
>
> . . . .
>
> I tell you, there must be something wrong
> with my fellow-countrymen; or else I don't belong.
>
> (D. H. Lawrence 1930, 17–18)

The "nettle" is entitled "13,000 People," roughly the number who came to see the exhibition. Against the thirteen thousand, Parkes produces one contemporary reviewer of the exhibition who was not titillated, outraged, or disappointed by the paintings, but read them symbolically. For Stuart Fletcher, Lawrence's paintings, unlike those of Beltrán, envisage "a world where people are in no way dependent upon a commercial civilisation. The beauties of nature and the mysteries of sex are their birthright, which they refuse to sell for any mess that a Henry Ford or an Alfred Mond can concoct" (qtd. in Parkes 2000, 12).[31] *Ut pictura poesis:* Lawrence's poetry, no less than his fiction and painting, resists being read as pornography. However confrontational its account of sexuality, the representation occurs in a discourse that extrapolates it politically and religiously. Ernst and Seagle's categories of religious, political, and sexual censorship, while serving as a guide to the motivations of censors, break down before a literature committed to surmounting such distinctions.

The "flag" that Lawrence ran up was commitment to a literature that probed and reformed his readers' sexual, political, and religious identities. Throughout the vacillations of his commitments and disillusionments as a writer, such a discourse continued to define what he took his vocation to be. Lawrence's conviction in his authorial role was impressive; what was exaggerated was his sense of isolation in pursuing that role. Put another way, he had no confidence, even though in *Pornography and Obscenity* he posited the existence of such a class of readers, that he had any such reader as Stuart Fletcher. What was true of Lawrence's readers was also true of younger writers like Rhys Davies, the Welsh working-class novelist and admirer with whom Lawrence felt himself in sympathy. Yet when he "rapped out" at Davies, "All you young writers have me to thank for what freedom you enjoy, even as things are," Davies would have known other modernist champions of literary freedom (Davies 1940, 203). Lawrence nonetheless thought of himself as a lone scout—a lone ranger—carrying his flag into alien territory.

I have described Lawrence as "a pioneer, pushing back the frontiers of literary prohibition." But the "frontier" formula has come to offend my sensibilities as a white Australian, a descendant of a white-settler society still struggling to achieve a measure of postcolonial reconciliation with Australia's indigenous people. How anti-Lawrentian, though, to abandon a metaphor for its political incorrectness, for the mere risk of giving offence! In his self-conceived vocation, Lawrence is a frontier scout pushing into a *terra nullius* (here the metaphor complicates) made up of all that we, his readers, harbor as our unknowns. We are the indigenous people *he* invades, apparently blind to our rights, our very presence. Although we have been and continue to be appalled by causes he seems to espouse, once we grasp that those of his works which appear to claim empire over us, men and women, are works of literature, we should not fear his invasion. Instead, we should prepare for that most taxing and rewarding of negotiations—not reacting to his works with trembling and indignation like "censor-morons," but *reading* them.

Notes

1. Ernst and Seagle style Lawrence an "especial martyr" of sexual censorship, in Britain for *The Rainbow,* in America for the sequel: "[H]is *Women in Love* left British prudery unmoved while it stirred the New York Society for the Suppression of Vice to action—quite unsuccessful despite the supporting crusade of Justice Ford, who was shocked to discover the book in his unmarried daughter's hands. Thus a book which failed to move British authority to prosecution led to the founding of the Clean Books League in New York" (1928, 46).

2. To avoid censoring what Heinemann did with the poems, and what Lawrence said of Heinemann, the context of Lawrence's remark in his August 22, 1912, letter to Garnett should be supplied: "Heinemann sent me back my poems, without a word except 'Your manuscript is herewith returned'—and that after keeping them for six months. De la Mare says he strongly recommended them to Wm H.—and that Atkinson had done so. But I suppose the verses also shocked the modesty of his Jewship. Will Duckworth have them?"—(D. H. Lawrence 1979b, 442). Anti-Semitic aspersions are not uncommon in Lawrence's letters but are mostly directed against individuals who have provoked the author. Of a sometime friend and agent whose anti-Semitism was pronounced, Lawrence commented: "[H]e is one of those irritating people who have generalised detestations: his particular ones being Jews, Germans and Bolshevists. So unoriginal" (1987a, 113).

3. De la Mare's authorship of the review was established via the *TLS Centenary Archive,* accessed courtesy of the University of New South Wales Library.

4. Lawrence urged Edward Garnett to add poems with the sexual and social realism of "Lightning" and of "Violets" (1979b, 443). The father then handed on the enlarging of *Love Poems* to his son, and Lawrence's friend, David Garnett. The twenty-year-old David may have included the explicit "Lilies in the Fire," and he evidently made the odd choice of "Red Moon-Rise": "At Edward's request I had been responsible . . . for choosing the selection published in *Love Poems and Others* . . . I knew that, at his best, Lawrence was a very fine and very original poet. 'Snapdragon,' which was not among those from which I could choose in 1913, was, I was certain, a very great poem and 'Red Moonrise,' which I thought the best of those in *Love Poems and Others,* an extraordinarily exciting and original one" (Garnett 1955, 54–55).

5. By contrast to De la Mare in his review of *Love Poems,* Edward Garnett in a 1916 review of *Amores* for the *Dial* wrote in praise of a "poet-psychologist of instincts, emotions, and moods that it is needless to try and moralize." As if recalling Lawrence's difficulties with Heinemann

and De la Mare, Garnett added, "The moralists will be very wroth with him" (qtd. in Draper 1964, 114).

6. Cf. D. H. Lawrence 1928, 2:87–88. In the note Lawrence drafted for *Collected Poems,* he misremembered Chatto and Windus as having "objected to [his] mixing love and religion," not in the titles of "Eve's Mass" and "Candlemas," but in the last stanza of "Song of a Man Who Is Loved." "But surely," he continued, "there are many eternities" (*Poems* 852).

7. For the *Georgian Poetry* text of "Meeting Among the Mountains," see D. H. Lawrence 1972, 224–26; for Frieda's explanatory comment, see 992–93 and Moore 1954, 128–29.

8. For argument that Lawrence had the *Tagebuch* with the *Look!* poems beside him when he assembled *Collected Poems,* see Pollnitz 2003, 17–19. It was fortunate that, in *Not I, But the Wind . . .* Frieda recorded the poems omitted by Chatto and Windus; unfortunate that, then or thereafter, she lost the entire notebook.

9. See 1972, 992–93; and Kinkead-Weekes 1996, 360. Kinkead-Weekes objects, not to the poem's restoration in *Look!*, but to its insertion out of sequence. As late as 1923, Lawrence still planned to reinstate "Meeting Among the Mountains": "I enclose in this letter the two poems which were omitted from *Look We Have Come Through!,* and which I would like included in any future edition" (D. H. Lawrence 1987a, 378). These copies were, however, sent to Thomas Seltzer and were irrecoverable in 1928. In five years, Lawrence changed his mind, perhaps because the *Tagebuch* version of "Meeting Among the Mountains" that he had to hand in 1928 (see F. Lawrence 1935, 48–49) referred more nakedly to the Weekley–Frieda–Lawrence triangle than did the *Georgian Poetry* version.

10. A complete account of Lawrence's financial condition during the later years of the war can be found in John Worthen's chapter, "Poverty: 1917–19" (see specifically Worthen 1989, 73–74).

11. The closest Lawrence came to disputation was a comment to his agent on Secker's removal of "Late in Life": "I don't care if Secker leaves out the poem—but I don't want to hear his literary criticisms" (D. H. Lawrence 1984, 278). Nobody has ever cared much about "Late in Life"—there is nothing worth censoring in it—but it is not quite accurate to describe it as unpublished (283 n. 1). Under the title "Love Comes Late," an early version of the poem is in print (*Poems* 861).

12. A shorter, manuscript version of "All of Us," entitled "Bits," is available (*Poems* 749–59).

13. Lawrence translated Schäfer's German translations of the fellaheen songs in December 1910, to have some mildly amorous love poems to send his fiancée, Louie Burrows (see "Love Message" to "Sympathy," and "At Midnight" to "Two-Fold," in 1972, 881–83, 884–85). Neither the poems to Louie nor the "All of Us" sequence was well understood before David Cram's discovery that they were translations or imitations of Heinrich Schäfer's *Die Lieder eines ägyptischen Bauern* (see Cram and Pollnitz 2001, 133–50).

14. An exception should be made for Cushman 1988.

15. For the account here of Lawrence and Seltzer's differences over *Birds, Beasts and Flowers,* the indispensable bibliographical narrative re-

mains G. Thomas Tanselle's synopsis of the "Seltzer Imprint." Edward de Grazia's distinction between the civil and criminal actions mounted against Seltzer has been essential to my outline, as has Worthen's *Literary Life*. Hints have been gleaned from Gerald M. Lacy's discussion of Lawrence's letters to the Seltzers, and Gertzman and Squires's discussion of Seltzer and Robert Mountsier's letters to Lawrence.

16. Seltzer informed Lawrence that Pecora was not prosecuting him over *Women in Love*, but for having published the two other works seized by Sumner: Schnitzler's *Casanova's Homecoming* and the anonymous *A Young Girl's Diary*.

17. Two other books for which Lawrence also corrected proofs during his visit to New York and sojourn in New Jersey were *Kangaroo* and his translation of Verga's *Mastro-don Gesualdo*.

18. References in this form are to the manuscripts section in Roberts and Poplawski 2001.

19. Because of the erasures, one must travel to Cornell to observe these markings on E47d.

20. Lawrence corrected "Figs" to "Fig" in E47d, but not in E47e. In the American edition of *Birds, Beasts and Flowers* the poem is entitled "Fig," whereas in the English edition and *Collected Poems* the title is "Figs." In the Cambridge *Poems* Lawrence's preferred title, "Fig," will be restored. Cf. D. H. Lawrence 1923a, 18; and 1923b, 5.

21. The typescript of "Fig" that Lawrence received as part of E47d is now located in the composite manuscript-typescript of *Birds, Beasts and Flowers*, E47c. E47c was the manuscript Lawrence sent to Seltzer on February 7, 1923 (D. H. Lawrence 1987a, 378) so that the type-copies E47d and E47e could be prepared. Presumably Seltzer returned both E47c and E47d to Lawrence on March 14, 1923. Lawrence must have corrected the latter and posted both back to Seltzer, perhaps when he left Taos on March 18. Lawrence himself may have mistakenly inserted "Fig" from E47d in E47c, but it seems more likely that Seltzer, in view of his doubts about the poem, removed "Fig" from E47d to E47c so that it was not set up in proof. Whether this removal was intended to abet or prevent further discussion of the poem can hardly be decided. The two lines Seltzer bowdlerized were nevertheless carried by Secker's edition, which followed the text of E47e without alteration, and hence the lines were transmitted to *Collected Poems*.

22. Thanks are owed to Peter Preston for checking the "Fig" typescript at the University of Nottingham. That it was not Lawrence's intention to delete the last two lines of the stanza (lines 15–16 in *Collected Poems*) is confirmed by an autograph manuscript of "Fig," E130.5a, which appears among Seltzer's galley proofs (E47f) in Des Moines, Iowa. Lawrence drafted E130.5a with the possible intention of forwarding it to Secker, along with a duplicate set of corrected galley proofs, so that the text of the English edition would approximate to that of the American edition. E130.5a was not sent to Secker, however, and the text of "Figs" in the English edition, being based on E47e, included lines cut by Seltzer.

23. Cf. "The American Eagle," in D. H. Lawrence 1923a, 206; and 1923b, 179. In Seltzer's galley proofs, Roberts E47f, the hand in which the alter-

ation was made is neither Seltzer's nor Lawrence's—hence, the deduction that Seltzer passed the proofs on to one of his staff.

24. For another Lawrentian reference to the three feathers, see "Magnificent Democracy" (1972, 587).

25. On their return visit, the detectives also announced that "Introduction to These Paintings" was being held—potentially a more serious loss for Lawrence, since it was the "original Manuscript" of which he had "no copy" (D. H. Lawrence 1993b, 148). The essay was, however, returned.

26. See 1972, 418–21, for the "obscene" discussion of "obscene" words in the *Pansies* "Introduction."

27. Sir William Joynson-Hicks's description of the type-copies to the Commons, in Nehls 1957–59, 3:312.

28. Squire's review in his "Editorial Notes" (Squire 1929, 229–30) had called for "the interference of the police" to close the exhibition, though he was not alone in making such a call. Squire's incitement led Lahr to send a cutting from the *London Mercury* to Lawrence. While "D" Division did collect and act upon the comments of conservative literary journalists like Squire, the Home Office file on the Warren Gallery raid (HO 442.565—held at the Public Records Office at Kew) includes other reviews, not Squire's. What is plausible is that the new home secretary, Labour's J. R. Clynes, was asked to approve of the raid by "D" Division undersecretaries who gained prominence during the reign of Jix. Joynson-Hicks himself, under his new title of Lord Brentford, commended Clynes's taking the action he did (Joynson-Hicks 1929, 17).

29. The version of "British Sincerity" in the *Nettles* typescript will be published for the first time in the Cambridge *Poems*.

30. For Worthen, this declaration is "the culmination of his hatred, and rejection, of English society" (2005, 201).

31. Parkes's reference for Stuart Fletcher is "Raise the Scarlet Fig-Leaf High!" *Sackbut* 10, no. 3 (October 1929): 73–76.

Lawrence's De-patterning of America and Magical Realism

Jamie Jung Min Woo

D. H. LAWRENCE IS ALREADY ASSOCIATED WITH THE LATIN AMERican form of "magical realism" that privileges indigenous mythology over colonizing narratives from Europe. Writers such as Carlos Fuentes and Octavio Paz, whose influences on this genre were immense, have referred to Lawrence as one of their literary predecessors. And according to Arnold Odio, Lawrence's way of seeking beyond the Euro-American veneer of Mexico in *The Plumed Serpent* (1926) offers yet another aspect of his multifaceted "thought-adventures."[1] Early in the twentieth century, tourists and the Mexican elite thought of Mexico chiefly in terms of its Spanish cultural overlay, but Lawrence turned to the country's ancient American Indian roots as a source of national identity. Main characters in his novel are cast, in various degrees, as "emblematic manifestations of Aztec deities," occupying "a threshold location between two cultures" and moving back and forth between the "real world" and the "world of ritual" (1987b, 176–77). It is possible to see these juxtapositions as beginning in the first version, called *Quetzalcoatl,* and increasing in the final version with its greater insertion of mythological and political dimensions (some of the very aspects that made it unpopular in its time). We can learn much about Lawrence's Mexican work by relating it further to the international movement of magical realism, which originally referred to a postexpressionist style in visual art, taking mundane objects and scenes for its subject.

The phrase was first introduced in the German art critic and historian Franz Roh's 1925 essay "Magical Realism: Post-Expressionism." Roh's idea of this form is based on a

1920s artistic trend, which departs from both realist objectivity and expressionist abstraction, and embraces and transcends both impressionism and expressionism. According to Roh, magical realist art represents the possibility of making the object stand out from the empty background, which he calls "the last frontier, absolute nothingness, absolute death."[2] The intensity of the crystallized object, he argues, emerges from the void, not from the referential and detailed background description but from the consciously emptied space. In the analysis of postexpressionism, Roh suggests that the contemporary magical realist artists create a "new objectivity," which corresponds to the Weimar's Republic's *neue Sachlichkeit,* and which attempts to unite the opposition between rationality and spiritual experience, "as if by a miracle," "like voices from another world" (21). In 1949, Roh's idea is substantially referred to by the Cuban novelist Alejo Carpentier. However, Carpentier's interest is somewhat different, and the magically emerging new object is no longer the main point. Instead of the magical and miraculous, Carpentier coins the new term "the marvellous real." Initially the preface to *El reino de este mundo* (*The Kingdom of This World,* 1949), the essay "Lo real maravilloso americano" ("The Marvellous Real in America") contains perhaps the most frequently visited reference to magical realism. The essay was further elaborated in 1975. Here Carpentier significantly distinguishes "the Marvellous Real" from Roh's analysis of postexpressionism: magical realism not only encompasses the postexpressionist European artistic trend, but more significantly differentiates Latin America's art, history, and reality from Eurocentric modernism. For this reason, magical realism on the whole has often been regarded as regionally restricted to the anti- and postcolonial Latin American condition, particularly as this relates to its history of European colonialism. Another important writer in this tradition was Miguel Ángel Asturias of Guatemala, who used mythology from the Mayan Popol-Vuh extensively and whose espousal of magical realism gained prominence because he was (like Fuentes) a recipient of the prestigious Nobel Prize.[3]

Indeed, the development of theories of magical realism has been very dependent not only on such myth and ideology but also on a Latin American sense that magic lies within nature. Lois Parkinson Zamora and Wendy B. Faris in *Magical Realism: Theory, History, Community* point out this view: "[T]he fantastic is not to be discovered by subverting or transcending reality with abstract forms and manufactured combinations of images, . . . [but] inheres in the natural and human realities of time and place, where improbable juxtapositions and marvellous mixtures exist by virtue of Latin America's varied history, geography, demography, and politics—not by manifesto" (1995, 75). However, even though Latin America has been the prime source of the form and still has stronger voices there than elsewhere, magical realism is not merely a Latin American phenomenon but also an international one; its essence lies in its cross-cultural subversiveness as part of postmodern and postcolonial traditions that are broader than any regional artistic trend. This subversiveness, what Zamora and Faris call "in-betweenness" and "all-at-onceness" (6), combines literary, political, historical, and cultural diversity; it broadens the boundaries of reality while keeping the distinction between major and minor worlds. Thus, it represents a universal tradition, with a wide-ranging history and significant influence on the literatures of the world (including Eastern Europe, Asia, North America, Africa, the Caribbean, and Australia, over and above Latin America). It is a catalyst in the development of new comparative literatures, but it can even be a revitalizing force for the appreciation of more authoritarian (or canonical) narrative traditions. Indeed, it is a useful and meaningful literary mode that encompasses the incomprehensibility and unpresentability of a world in which many languages and modes of living coexist.

Lawrence's Mexican writings (comprising his novel, the poems in *The Plumed Serpent*, essays, and some letters, if not all his writings throughout his career) seem to correspond to some of the descriptions of the new art as "magical realist." Both Roh and Lawrence would agree that the art should initiate a miracle in which objectivity lives in eternally mobile and vibrating space: both use the word "flux" to emphasize an organic wholeness that embraces objectivity and subjectivity. As we will see, Lawrence surpasses the synthetic European trend to anticipate the Latin American or "marvellously real" trend.

Both Lawrence's Mexican writings and Carpentier's "The Marvellous Real in America" have similar interests in showing the contradictory yet coexisting polarities of the indigenous, mythic culture of the Native American and the economically, politically, and socioreligiously powerful European colonizing force. Works by Asturias and others are also in this tradition. In the essay "Landscape and the Novel in Mexico," Octavio Paz writes that the theme of Lawrence's *The Plumed Serpent* is "the construction of a magic space . . . a nature that has recovered its innocence, a celebration of the reconciliation of Heaven and Earth" (1987, 585–86).

Lawrence's patterning of Mexico's magical or "marvellously real" setting had been developing ever since he had planned to leave Europe for America during World War I; he did not arrive until September 1922. During such a long journey to get to his dreamworld, his imagination and expectation were inconsistent with reality, sometimes even contradictory to it. On the whole, his first idea of the American continent and history seems "unfinished," fantastical, and far from objective. He was not alone among Europeans in seeing aboriginal America as a fantasy world. The modernist writer Franz Kafka (1883–1924) in "Meditation" (published in *Metamorphosis and Other Stories*) introduces a very short piece entitled "Longing to Be a Red Indian." "Oh to be a Red Indian, instantly prepared, and astride one's galloping mount, leaning into the wind, to skim with each fleeting quivering touch over the quivering ground, till one shed the spurs, for there were no spurs, till one flung off the reins, for there were no reins, and could barely see the land unfurl as a smooth-shorn heath before one, now that horse's neck and horse's head were gone" (Kafka 2000, 31). First of all, it is very much Kafka's personal style that there is no single narratorial position here: his picture of the American Indians seems to fit his modernist aesthetics. He imagines an American Indian galloping without reins, "leaning into the wind" rather than against it, on the spreading plain, but we may question the extent of his ability to capture the "otherness" of the aboriginal American: a man riding freely on horseback is another stereotypical European fantasy of the aboriginal, primitive, uncultivated world. It may be true that it is a mere fantasy. However, the value of fantasy is not to be underestimated. Fantasy lies in opposition to conventional forms of scientific and rational analysis; it originally referred to a musical style with a free form and often an improvisatory style, and thus it is at the very core of the artistic, imaginary, and improvised (Becket 1997, 68). The European fantasy of the American Indian, though habitually stereotypical and biased,[4] fed by European Wild West shows and popular westerns in pulp literature, was based on the human need to disentangle imagination and feeling from the mechanical order that manifested itself in modern Europe.

Lawrence acknowledges the fantastic and imaginary qualities in his perception of the American and Mexican "other." In "Indians and an Englishman," he writes about the Apache Indian festival in New Mexico, which he attended immediately after his arrival in Taos, New Mexico, just ten years after New Mexico ceased to be one of the frontier territories and gained statehood: "To my heart, born in England and kindled with Fenimore Cooper," he says, "it was the nomad nations gathering still in the continent of hemlock trees and prairies" (D. H. Lawrence 1936a, 94). The language of the ceremonials and the elder's stories was Apache, an Athapascan tongue which he could not understand. The America of the Indian turns out to be non-America (or at least not like most of the United States), not only geographically but also culturally and emotionally "other." (He knew that the Pueblos had many affinities with Mexico, the neighboring country, home of major mythologies like the Aztec and the Mayan ones.) The sounds of the Apache dance and music seem virtually indescribable: "Almost a pre-animal sound, full of triumph in life, and devilment against other life, and mockery, and humorousness, and the pat-pat, pat-pat of the rhythm" (95). He continues in the essay, combining "nostalgia," "unbearable yearning for something," "a sickness of the soul," "humanness," "playfulness," "mockery," and "diabolical, pre-human, pine-tree fun" of violence: "So I felt. I may have been all wrong, and other folk may feel much more natural and reasonable things. But so I *felt*. And the sadness and the nostalgia of the song-calling, and the resinous continent of pine trees and turkeys, the feet of birds treading a dance, far off, when man was dusky and not individualised" (95; my emphasis). This, he says, "of course, may just be the limitation of my *European fancy*" (96).[5] Nevertheless, he is undoubtedly trying to record what he really "felt." There he stands "still" and "uncommunicative," waiting to see "a further development" but there is "none." The people circle around the fire during the "pat-pat" of the dance, with its cry "Hie! Hie! Hie! Hy-a! Hy-a! Hy-a! . . . Ay-away-away-a!" and with its hum and "tum-tum" music; then they listen quietly to the voice of an elder whose face is like a bronze mask: "[T]hey kept silent, and the voice of the old reciter went on blindly." No one seems to be paying attention consciously to what is going on. The people there are "listening without listening," Lawrence observes. And yet, "There was a deep pathos, for me, in the old, mask-like, virile figure, with its metallic courage of persistence, old memory, and its twanging male voice. So far, so great a memory. So dauntless a persistence in the piece of living red earth seated on the naked earth, before the fire; the old bronze-resonant man with his eyes as if glazed in old memory, and his voice issuing in endless plangent monotony from the wide, unfurled mouth" (98).

To a modern reader, this may seem to be the very depiction of the "marvellously real" in which the known world borders directly upon the mythic. The juxtaposition of many different aspects of this Apache experience—the untranslated stories, the elder's masklike face, the sounds of the dance, the past and the present, myth and reality, the attractive and the grotesque—all suggest aspects of the future genre. In the end, Lawrence asks no more, for he realizes that he cannot cross the barrier of the unknown but stands outside it: "As for me, standing outside, beyond the open entrance, I was no enemy of theirs; far from it. The voice out of the far-off time was not for my ears. Its language was unknown to me. And I did not wish to know. It was enough to hear the sound issuing plangent from the bristling darkness of the far past, to see the bronze mask of the face lifted, the white, small, close-packed teeth showing all the time. It was not for me, and I knew it. Nor had I any curiosity to understand" (98–99).

For Lawrence, exploring the American continent was in some ways a symbolic journey for one who wished to get "out of the world," like one of the characters in *St. Mawr* (1983, 143). To Lawrence, America began as a dream, the ideal place to be "a hermit." He had written in Taormina to Brewster on October 1921 that "the desire to be away from the body of mankind—to be a bit of a hermit—is paramount" (1987a, 95). Unmistakably, "the body of mankind" signified culture and civilization as Lawrence knew them. What he sought away from "the world"—*his* world—was to acquire the vision to "see" cultural difference, to speak the language of the "other," and to make a "contact" with local people native to America. Nevertheless, now when the dream becomes a visible reality at the Apache festival, he realizes the impossibility of understanding "its language";[6] this is not surprising, since he did not know the Apache tongue, but of course Lawrence refers to more than the spoken word. This account of his quest to understand the Apache "other" can serve as a kind of paradigm of his later quest in Mexico.

It is obvious that Lawrence's fascination with the aboriginal American was still high when he composed *Quetzalcoatl,* the first version of his Mexican novel *The Plumed Serpent.* First written at Chapala in 1923, it remained a long time unfinished, only "half finished" or "two-thirds done" despite his high spirits to write (D. H. Lawrence 1989a, 75, 128). He originally saw the setting as "paradise" but, seeing it again on a later trip without his wife, Frieda, he admitted that Lake Chapala did not seem as "paradisal" as before, for "something," perhaps Frieda, was gone (1987a, 519–20). However, Frieda's absence may not be the only reason for this change of perspective, for it is not an uncommon pattern for him, during his writing trips, to restructure his sketch of the world before the actual painting. Writing *The Plumed Serpent* is another example of this.

When Lawrence and Frieda finally got back to Mexico together, they settled at Oaxaca, and in November 1924 he started the half-finished novel again. Despite the change of his personal location, the novel's setting remains the village of "Sayula," or Chapala, on the shore of the beautiful lake of the same name. If it includes a more detailed sense of Mexico's suffering in the wake of its recent revolution, and indeed through ages of exploitation, this is because he learned increasingly more about his surroundings. The land's regeneration, in the final novel, is shadowed with such grim history, yet it also emerges as a new Atlantis or "world before the Flood" (1987b, 414–15).

Lawrence's intervening short visit to England and Europe, between his two periods of writing, had reassured him of the decline of the West. Now his dream of the new world met even more forcefully than ever with the challenge of Mexican religious myth and political reality, the combined power of which he believed could bring about a revolution. The novel became an increasingly experimental combination of political, sociological, theological, mythic, and artistic representations that contained most of the earlier version as its core. It represented in part what Lawrence himself called a "thought-adventure." Louis L. Martz points out in the introduction to *Quetzalcoatl* that "in *The Plumed Serpent* the additional mythic and transcendent elements—sermons, ruminations, expanded hymns, expanded ritual—tend to dominate the landscape and local detail preserved from the early version; in the new context these exist as a thin transient layer of temporal life, lying between two greater modes of being" (D. H. Lawrence 1995, xxix). It was somewhat unusual for Lawrence to take such a long time to write a novel. John Worthen points out that "unlike . . . his six-week novel *Kangaroo,* or later *Lady Chatterley's Lover,* also written in six weeks, the new book proved exhausting to write, although it built on its predecessor *Quetzalcoatl*" (2005, 318–19). Despite the unusually long composition period, some critics believe that this work remains his most awkward, that it lacks the fluidity for which Lawrence is usually noted. They think it shows too little connection between the symbolic world and ordinary, mundane, or everyday life, even less than in the first version: in other words, the revised and lengthened final version is heavily weighted with material concerning a Mexican religio-political mass movement, partly based on actual turmoil of its period and partly drawing from Mexican legend and history. As Virginia Hyde points out in her introduction to the Penguin edition of *The Plumed Serpent,* the "paramount concern of the novelist" is to represent the "greater modes of being"—

the sacred dimension of our life—not just in a "realistic" mimetic sense but "in all its protean magnificence" (Hyde 1995, xv). Although this is true in both versions, it can be shown that *The Plumed Serpent* is more overt in the search for the "sacred," while *Quetzalcoatl* remains limited to a more conventionally "realistic" level. Both have strong realistic scenes, and both allow the mundane objects of life to contain "magical" properties: landscapes sometimes gleam with glory, people sometimes represent gods, animals sometimes suggest enchanted ancient art, and myths sometimes merge with narrative details of the plotlines. But there is more of everything in *The Plumed Serpent,* particularly more ritual that Lawrence tries to reproduce from indigenous Indian models, both from the Southwest of the United States (since Cipriano has learned "northern" dances there) and from Mexico. It is these insertions—the very mixture of symbolism and reality, the abrupt shifts from the local to the transcendental and religious ceremonies—that make *The Plumed Serpent* so notable for sharp juxtapositions between "worlds." And for this reason, the novel often "reads like translation" (Worthen 2005, 319), something foreign and unconventional. Lawrence, engrossed in his own religio-political mode, pushes his new writing to extremes of intense unreality, which in turn creates a new mode of reality or "magical reality" in the Latin American style. The earlier version, depending more upon real-world scenes and objects for its "magic," seems more in the postexpressionist mode that Roh favored, generally avoiding overt supernaturalism but suggesting a spiritual content within everyday objects themselves. But the final novel, for all of its unwieldiness, has an epic mythic scope.

In patterning Mexican magical reality, Lawrence witnesses the extraordinary transformation of his imaginary Mexico, seen through the female protagonist's (Kate's) eye. Kate is a conqueror in some sense, a well-traveled woman from Europe, physically taller and bigger than some Mexican men such as Cipriano, and above all glowing with her freedom and independence; she is the most human character in both versions of the novel. She is free to be near the men's territory (for example, during her political and religious conversations with Ramón), perhaps because she is a foreigner; such status sometimes guarantees free entry to otherwise restricted activities—male or female, ruling or ruled. However, at some point, she seems to fall into the role of a victim, perhaps for the same reason that, being a foreigner, she never belongs to any category. "To Stay or Not To Stay" foreshadows Kate's apocalypse. Feeling "pulled down" by Mexico's "snake-like" power, Kate makes the decision to stay "in spite of the sense of doom on her heart" (D. H. Lawrence 1987b, 72–80). Despite her acute fear of all-encompassing destruction, she also gets the sense of a new world that is being reborn from the old. Ramón explains the positive side of the "downward" pull, for he believes the people in Mexico are "part of the Tree of Life" whose "roots go down to the centre of the earth." Kate generally welcomes his doctrine of regeneration, but there are times when it sounds to her like a self-important man's speech, and she continues to struggle with "the strange doom-like sound of the man's words" (80). As a result, this novel may not seem so much a weaving of Mexico's soul as the new identity of Kate the foreigner in a new land, transcending her paradoxical situation of being both conquering and conquered. In other words, *The Plumed Serpent* is meant as a story of an Irishwoman deconstructing—and reconstructing—her soul through realization of the mythic "other" of race and nationality in Ramón, Cipriano, and Teresa; she is seeking to develop an inner dimension of herself, "her greater womanhood" (131–32), which Lawrence equates with her deepest sacred identity, herself as goddess.

To appreciate Kate's deconstruction and renewal on a larger scale—that is to say, to read this novel bearing in mind discourses of cultural difference and national identity —it is necessary to understand a key metaphor about the weaving done by Navajo Indians of the Southwest. Lawrence's own aesthetic principle of open-endedness is embodied in this metaphor. The relevant passages originate in *Quetzalcoatl,* but they have versions as well in *The Plumed Serpent.* In the chapter "Cipriano and Kate," Cipriano explains the beauty of the Mexican pattern that remains unfinished, as compared to the English and European pattern that prefers completion: "You know the Navajo women, when they weave a blanket, leave a little place for their soul to come out, at the end: not to weave their soul into it.—I always think England has woven her soul into her fabrics, into all the things she has made. And she never left a place for it to come out. So now all her soul is in her goods, and nowhere else" (234). Kate tries to resist Cipriano's Mexico: "But Mexico has no soul," said Kate. "She's swallowed the stone of despair, as the hymn says." Then, Cipriano bounces back, "Ah! You think so? I think not. The soul is also a thing you make, like a pattern in a blanket. It is very nice while all the wools are rolling different threads and different colours, and the pattern is being made. But once it is finished—then finished. It has no interest any more. Mexico hasn't started to weave the pattern of her soul. Or she is only just starting . . ." (234). Immediately after the pattern discussion, Kate is asked to marry Cipriano and "become" a Mexican goddess called Malintzi. She at first cannot help being startled by such a sudden and bizarre suggestion, and says, "Mexico is *really* a bit horrible to me" (235). Then Cipriano answers, "Why not? . . . Horror is real. Why not a bit of horror . . . ? . . . You feel a bit of horror for me too—But why not? Perhaps I feel a bit of horror for you too, for your light-coloured eyes and your strong white hands. But that is good." The mutual otherness, even with its initial sense of horror, is the "real," and this difference acts as a catalyst for deconstructing and reformulating Mexican reality. Kate comes to accept Cipriano as her husband only in *The Plumed Serpent,* whereas she cannot bring herself to do so in *Quetzalcoatl* because of his different race.

But the novel's first version, where the above passage originates, supports the postcolonial theme by introducing not only the weaving metaphor but also a focus on "the unknown": "The pattern is very beautiful, while there are threads into the unknown, and the pattern is never finished. The Indian patterns are never *quite* complete. There is a flaw at the end, where they break into the beyond—nothing is more beautiful to me than a pattern which is lovely and perfect, when it breaks at the end imperfectly on to the unknown—" (1995, 163). This quotation provides not only a foundation for cultural comparison between England and Mexico but also shows Lawrence's fundamental way of balancing power games between characters by making them play a game of *dialogues*. The oxymoronic vocabulary—imperfection becomes perfection, flaw becomes beauty, and end becomes a going beyond—is a reminder of Birkin and Ursula's dialogue in *Women in Love*, as Kate struggles to preserve the notion of her Britishness against Cipriano's assertions that the "soul is greater than any circumstance, of nationality or even race. That is the unfinished end of the pattern," and because her soul no longer "wants" her British past, "the pattern breaks" (164). Then, in response to Kate's effort to affirm her connection with her "people," her "country," Cipriano brings his argument to a close by speaking through the powerful image of weaving: "No, the pattern is broken for you. Your soul can weave your life no longer in the English or Irish pattern. That pattern is finished. And the loose ends lead into the beyond. Lead into the unwoven pattern of Mexico and America. The loose ends of your life lead into the Mexican pattern—the pattern of unwoven America." And finally to her resistant assertion, "I must go home," Cipriano "passionately" responds, "You have no home" (164).

The above dialogical language game shows the tension of repulsion and attraction between Kate and Cipriano, and of cultural differences between England and Mexico. Whatever "magic" is present, it inheres in the objects and the characters, not in their impersonation of deities.

Not only do word games suggest transformation; even the Mexican animals seem transformed to Kate. A bull introduced in the first chapter ("The Bullfight") is a symbol of bloody violence, enacted upon it by figures of dominant, aggressive Mexican masculinity. But, at the end, another bull appears in the "paradisal" lake of Chapala, later Sayula (1995, 321; 1987b, 431–32). To Kate's eye it is dreamy, mysterious, and more than real, like a Greek *kolossos* of Herodotus: "a colossus of a bull standing perched motionless on the wall, broadside, a passive monster spangled with black, low-aloft" (1995, 322): "It all happened so quietly, no noise save the thud of hoofs at one moment; so softly and unviolently, with the loose pauses and the casual, soft-balanced rearrangements at every pause. And now the boat was softly on the water, with her white sail in a whorl like the boat of Dionysos, going across the lake. There seemed a certain *mystery* in it. When she thought of the great dappled bull upon the waters, it seemed mystical to her" (323; my emphasis).

Again, the novel's first version originates this scene, although both contain it. The change in the image of the bull, from a bloody, brutalized creature in the first chapter to a massive but tamed and friendly mammal in the last, implies that Kate's view of Mexico is gradually changing. When "myth" appears from within nature itself, as it does here, there is neither Ramón nor Cipriano, and no need to mention Mexican politics and revolution. The last part of this novel demonstrates the discovery of the "marvellously real" in the Mexican locality behind the political life and agenda of the country, and the scene goes on into *The Plumed Serpent* with much of the same significance. (The difference is that it is surrounded in this final version with other scenes of mythic and political import.) Perhaps such "realistic" scenes contain no "magic" to the locals, as they represent their common lives. Odio points out that Lawrence's description of Mexico is "accurate" by quoting numerous critics who have known Mexico, such as Barber, Ortiz de Montellano, Castro Leal, and Martha Diaz de Leon (1999, 168).[7] To foreigners like Kate as well as Lawrence, the place seems bigger than real, "mysteriously" real; but to the natives, the "magical real" may just be the real-life mode of life.

The novel is also a prime result of Lawrence's own search for his ideal world, sought in the culturally and geographically remotest place he could find ("the ultimate place *out of the world*"). "The physical nature of Mexico—a cruel, devouring, sunbaked landscape" that captured and confused Lawrence as a writer and as a man—is, as Carlos Fuentes said in 1967, "filled with portents of magical distraction" (1967, 128).[8] And Fuentes went on to say that, like Lawrence, the Mexican artist "has seldom been able to act outside the demands of the all-encompassing myth." Mexico's legacy, in other words, is that objective observation and optical exactness are hardly possible because of the "unseeability" of Mexican nature.

Lawrence corrected the typescript of his final Mexican novel (prepared by Dorothy Brett) when he returned to Taos. Brett had accompanied the Lawrences to Mexico on this final trip, but they had parted there because of conflict between her and Frieda.[9] When going through the typed pages, Lawrence may have recalled such discord, along with other difficulties of the time in Mexico. He wrote that he felt "nausea" and "doubt" about ever returning there (D. H. Lawrence 1989a, 254). Half a month later, however, he realized that *The Plumed Serpent* was "*different* from [his] other books: and to [him], the one that mean[t] most to [him]" (1989a, 260; my emphasis). It was not the first time he felt a new book seemed so "new" and "different": *The Rainbow* was like a novel written in a foreign language he did not know, and he also felt *The Trespasser* and *Women in Love* were revolutionarily different from his other works. Although he now declared *The Plumed Serpent* his greatest work, he also had a rather sickly feeling about it, for it awakened a memory of the illnesses he had suffered (tuberculosis, malaria, near-death experiences, cultural and religious shock), "a bad turn," so to speak (1989a, 254). But his reaction was probably not primarily from personal misfortune.

The fundamental "difference" in the final Mexican novel lies in its more elaborate socioreligious, mythlike rituals, its increased political awareness, and Kate's different decisions. Lawrence's first Kate decides to return to Europe (and is packing in the last chapter), whereas the later Kate has prospects that are left somewhat fluid but far more committed to the new world:[10] she is poised to stay in Mexico, having embraced the Zapotec Indian Cipriano as her husband and having engaged in the effort to create a new Mexico. When Lawrence started the new version, he was seeing Mexico from a more macropolitical point of view (unlike the somewhat naïve tourist view in the earlier version). He knew that violence was continuing in the aftermath of the Mexican War (1910–17): a leading general (Pancho Villa) was assassinated shortly after the Lawrences' first departure from Mexico, and one shore of Lake Chapala itself was the site of a decisive battle in 1924, soon after his second visit there. Vera Cruz, where he had sailed for England, was caught up in the same militarism.

It is not surprising that some literary and artistic representations of modern Mexico turned out to be mythically, rather than realistically, real. The tradition of mythic / magical / marvellously real "realism" became the core of a Latin

American cultural development in which myth and reality were one. During the long conflict, peasants and natives had banded together under the leadership of figures such as Villa and Emiliano Zapata to reject the old order's dictatorship, to enable democracy, and to claim Mexico for the everyday man and woman. In the first decade of the revolutionary period, an estimated two million people were killed; even in the less turbulent twenties and thirties the country remained a land of bloodshed, rebellion, and repression. In such a chaotic situation, people may require particular narratives, rituals, and faiths embracing and painfully assimilating the cruelty of the real. The circumstances, perhaps recalling the violence of pre-Columbian sacrifice and warfare, called for legendary and historic models of heroism.

It would be misleading, however, to assume that violence, modern or pre-Columbian, was the main reason for Lawrence and many other foreign writers (such as Aldous Huxley, Evelyn Waugh, Graham Greene, and Malcolm Lowry) to be drawn to Mexico after the revolution. For Lawrence, Mexico was initially an extension of aboriginal America, and here he saw the continued power of the indigenous people to resist the homogenization of the American continent; heroes of the Mexican conflict had included the great Zapotec and other Indian leaders, and thus Mexico could seem the antithesis of the United States. Even the modern revolutionary propaganda of Mexico, as in the art of Diego Rivera and José Clemente Orozco—whom Lawrence met—interested the sojourning writer, who was hungry for new material (although he criticizes them in the novel). Thus, Lawrence tried to create a cultural "other" in his Mexican setting out of the historically marginalized desire (the "dragon") of the native Mexican.

In his new genre, "the modern Spirit" of Western Europe contrasts with the native Indian's "Soul" with its inexplicable relation to "the blood."[11] In the seventh chapter, "The Plaza," he refers to a "curious, radical opposition of the Indians to the thing we call the Spirit" as represented by young urban revelers. Here we see "strangers," coming from modernized hotels and outdoor cafés, contrasting with the peons on the other side of the public space, "sitting immobile on the seats in the background" (D. H. Lawrence 1987b,

114). The city people, "Fifis and flappers," in flannel and frocks, bring the modern world to Sayula, with their motor-cars and contemporary jazz music:

> It is Spirit which makes the flapper flap her organdie wings like a butterfly. It is Spirit, which creases the white flannel trousers of the Fifi and makes him cut his rather pathetic dash. They try to talk the elegancies and flippancies of the modern Spirit.
>
> But *down* on it all, like a weight of obsidian, comes the passive negation of the Indian. He understands Soul, which is *of the blood.* But Spirit, which is superior, and is the quality of civilisation, this, in the mass, he darkly and barbarically repudiates. Not until he becomes an artizan or connected with machinery does the modern Spirit get him.
>
> And perhaps it is this ponderous repudiation of the modern Spirit which makes Mexico what it is.
>
> But perhaps the automobile will make roads even through the inaccessible soul of the Indian. (116; my emphasis)

Through Kate's eye, Lawrence describes a Mexican destiny that faces the overwhelming modern zeitgeist. In the virgin land of Sayula (Chapala in *Quetzalcoatl*), as Kate observes, "men used to want a horse and a sword, now they want a car," "a machine" (112). As in *Quetzalcoatl,* Kate projects Lawrence's own position: she is a multicultured nomad, who feels at home everywhere and nowhere. However, in contrast to the first version, where her conflict with Mexico is more abstract, in *The Plumed Serpent* the source of the tension is quite tangible as the unmodernized, immobilized primordial world meets the new force of auto-mobilization. The polarity between the old and the new is without compromise (115). As Walker points out, the plaza scene is the most effective representation of "frontier" experience in the novel: this scene dramatizes "Kate's sense of being in a kind of frontier or neutral zone between opposite poles" (1978, 87). Furthermore, the significance of the plaza lies in the fact that it epitomizes not only the regional conflict of Mexico but also a more universal problem of different worlds occupying the same space.

It may be unfair to satirize a particular art form like modern jazz, but Lawrence's target is really the "culture industry" that foists its choices upon a deceived population—

the action that various contemporary theorists, including Theodor Adorno, detested. Adorno stated (in 1944), "Automobiles, bombs, and movies keep the whole thing together until their levelling element shows its strength in the very wrong which it furthered. It has made the technology of the culture industry no more than the achievement of standardization and mass production" (Adorno and Horkheimer 2002, 121). In the same way as Adorno, Lawrence feels that modernity, or its "culture market," is floppy, soft, flamboyant, like a fluttering creature. The Fifis' arms are slim, and their faces are soft with their smiles; and the flappers are whitened, "suggestive of a victim's luxuriousness" (D. H. Lawrence 1987b, 115).

The opposition to the butterfly-like softies is the peons, "under their big, heavy, poised hats," whose dark eyes are full of "a will to ignore" the strangers. The negation is not one-sided: the Fifis also "steer as best as they might, to avoid the heavy relentless passage of the young peons": both parties are "never touched, never jostled" (116), and the space is divided into two different worlds. And here, Kate remains in between: "Kate was at once attracted and repelled. She was attracted, almost fascinated by the strange nuclear power of the men in the circle. It was like a darkly glowing, vivid nucleus of new life. Repellant the strange heaviness, the sinking of the spirit into the earth, like dark water. Repellant the silent, dense opposition to the pale-faced spiritual direction" (122).

Despite the undeniable magnetic centripetal attraction of the ancient culture, at this stage the protagonist clings to the tourist-persona, "prefer[ring] to be on the fringe, sufficiently out of contact," much as the novelist describes himself in "Indians and an Englishman." However, there comes a moment of brief mingling when Kate participates in the circle dance with a dark-skinned stranger; she later recalls the experience as the "living mystery" of having the greater self, or womanhood. But the moment the dance ends, she hurries back home to regain individual space, suggesting a recurring vacillation between accepting and refusing Mexico. Her marriage to Cipriano contains fluctuations, as well.

Struck by modern Mexico's dichotomy, she accepts his drastic proposal, becoming, or performing, the goddess

Malintzi herself, the consort to his Aztec identity as the war-god Huitzilopochtli. In the earlier version, Kate does not want to be a goddess; and, of course, she does not easily give in to such an alien culture, even in *The Plumed Serpent*. She cries,

> "For heaven's sake let me get out of this, and back to simple human people. I loathe the very sound of Quetzalcoatl and Huitzilopochtli. I would die rather than be mixed up in it any more. Horrible, really, both Ramón and Cipriano. And they want to put it over me, with their high-flown bunk, and their Malintzi. Malintzi! I am Kate Forrester, really. I am neither Kate Leslie nor Kate Tylor. I am sick of these men putting names over me. I was born Kate Forrester, and I shall die Kate Forrester. I want to go home. Loathsome, really, to be called Malintzi.—I've had it put over me." (371)

Having many names, through her marriages, traditional and otherwise, she yearns intensely for a fundamental I-ness, as she was born "Kate Forrester." However, once wearing the mask of Malintzi, her European identity rapidly disappears, and it becomes more obvious that Kate is, though passively, willing to go through the death of the original—European, female, merely human—identity in order to fulfill her new role of goddess. Unlike Kate in the first version—who remains considerably skeptical of the deification, though caught between the European and the native Mexican—Kate in the second version shows psychological complexity as she is torn between resistance and willingness to join in the mythic rituals.

It remains a question whether Lawrence succeeds in avoiding sentimental mysticism in making Kate over in this way. His Mexican novel may be a failure, in the sense of traditional English fictional narrative. Indeed, the author seems quite lost in translating the other, as well as in translating himself and his own characters. But the old land Mexico, for Lawrence, is a virgin land of new possibility for the future civilization. And in this naïveté of a foreigner's observation, which generally involves sentimental excitement, is a perspective that the local people would not have for themselves.

In conclusion, although Lawrence does not present Mexican reality as other realist novels show, his Chapala novel reveals the ambitious possibility of reviving Mexican mythology for a modern zeitgeist through a foreign woman's (Kate's) eyes. Ironically, Kate is supposed to fail to *see*, for myth, Lawrence insists, is not to be seen by curious, eager-to-know eyes. The book tells us, in Kate's words, about the ritual of closing "*seeing* eyes": the "itching, prurient, *knowing*, imagining eye" (184). What she wants, instead, is to have eyes to feel, like the unfathomable obsidian-dark Indian eyes. Such eyes look out upon life from the opposite side of any "establishment," like those of the Indians in the Mexican plaza. Their strength is not superficial—not visual nor verbal, but deeper. "The words did not matter," Kate realizes: "Any verse, any words, no words, the song remained the same: a strong, deep wind rushing from the caverns of the breast, from the everlasting soul!" (127) Here, "Unable to *know*, Kate [and also Lawrence in *Quetzalcoatl*] "went away, unable to forget it" (D. H. Lawrence 1995, 320) but lingers around later in *The Plumed Serpent* as if trying to find a magic recipe, "a voice from another world," for the Mexican consciousness. The last line in *The Plumed Serpent* may contain a strong note of submission: "You won't let me go" (1987b, 444). However, what makes her stand still in the midst of her horror at the patronizing voices of Ramón and Cipriano is the awareness and acceptance of the "magical real," the mythical state of being unable to see. One cannot be fused with or dissolved in the other in Lawrence's world, but one "still can stand a little way off," as Kate stood a little way off when she first heard the strange sound of the "tum-tum" music. The "unbridgeable gap"[13] between people may represent a bitter failure, but it is an unavoidable consequence of the beautifully unfinished step of a traveler crossing frontiers.

Notes

1. See Odio 1999, 165–92.
2. See Zamora and Faris 1995, 20.
3. See Odio 1999.

4. Lawrence shows his knowledge of the circuslike "Wild West" shows in his novel *The Lost Girl* (1920) with its theatrical troupe of "Indian" impersonators who are in fact Europeans.

5. Indeed, it does have some of the remoteness and exoticism that Edward Said has shown as features of the "Orientalism" that distances itself from "otherness." Said, in his landmark work in postcolonial cultural studies, applies the term somewhat generally to stereotypical concepts of cultures that have been marginalized by the West.

6. It also reminds us of Wittgenstein's argument that a private language is not possible, since language is a product of relationship. Lawrence's pattern discourse—the discourse of deconstructing pattern—values Wittgenstein's rule of language, in which individuality intersects with the other, creating new language within the context of mutual life experiences.

7. See also the chapter "The Man and the Continent," in Clark 1964, 16–50, relating *The Plumed Serpent* to its real-life settings and characters and thus showing its literal realism.

8. See also Walker 1978, 12.

9. See "Frieda to Dorothy Brett" [Spring 1925], 47, 49 in Irvine and Kiley.

10. Hyde and Clark (1993–94) show, from the multiple manuscripts of the last scene, the two primary end formats: one in which Kate chooses to leave the Mexican "utopia" she has entered and one in which she chooses to stay, based significantly upon her interracial marriage to Cipriano (in the final novel).

11. But Lawrence does not rule out the "soul" here, for he holds a pre-Socratic philosophy that distinguishes "spirit" from "soul." The "spirit" he often associates with excessive self-consciousness, but the "soul" can be considered an aspect of "the blood itself," he says (D. H. Lawrence 1979, 189, 136).

12. Theresa Thompson also finds that these "painted faces of the urban Mexicans are, of course, revelatory of how invading Europeans have colonized Mexican cultural practice" (2001, 224).

13. See Kinkead-Weekes 2001, 69.

How to Live?—
The End of Lawrence's Quest

Keith Sagar

I.

"Dare to be a Daniel. Dare to stand alone."[1] The fiercely independent spirit of nonconformism was so thoroughly absorbed by Lawrence (and so closely fitted his temperament) that by the time he was twenty-two he was refusing to conform to any organized religion, writing to the Eastwood Congregational minister Robert Reid that every man had an obligation to formulate his own religion, slowly and painfully, subjecting it to constant modification (see D. H. Lawrence 1979b, 40). He remained true to that belief throughout his life. His works are that process of constant modification, eventually embracing much of what we today would call "deep ecology" as part of a global perspective.

The prewar novels could all be said to be about the process Jung called "individuation." Ursula in *The Rainbow* calls it discovering how the life that is in you wants to be lived. *The Rainbow* and *The Lost Girl* in particular are existentialist novels. The individual must struggle to live authentically, which means to resist the constant pressures of the extant social world to impose inauthentic, secondhand life modes.

After Lawrence's death Frieda called him "the only rebel worthy of the name." We can see what she means. It is easy to describe Lawrence in these terms, and it is true as far as it goes. But it does not go very far. It leaves out of account at least three other Lawrences we can think of: Lawrence the married man and priest of love; Lawrence the utopian socialist; and Lawrence the pantheist. I have referred elsewhere to this last aspect of Lawrence in terms of "deep ecology," the biocentric consciousness he related to Pan (Sagar 2001, 156).[2]

We admire the first Lawrence as free spirit, thought-adventurer, traveler, challenger, forerunner, lonely explorer always forging ahead at the frontiers . . . but we must remember that these are the very terms Lawrence himself used, with heavy irony, for his baby tortoise. The arrogant baby tortoise is doomed to discover all too soon that isolation is not its birthright. By the time he wrote that letter to Robert Reid, Lawrence had already been "crucified into sex": "Doomed, in the long crucifixion of desire, to seek his consummation beyond himself. / Divided into passionate duality. . . ." Though he eventually found a worthy mate, became a "priest of love," and gave a high place to sex in his personal religion, he never lost sight of the cost, the humiliation, entailed: "Doomed to make an intolerable fool of himself / In his effort toward completion again" ("Lui et Elle," in D. H. Lawrence 1972, 361).

Is not a large part of *Women in Love* Birkin's doomed attempts, through his "star-equilibrium" (D. H. Lawrence 1987c, 319) and whatnot, to have his cake and eat it, to admit his absolute need for the woman while desperately, rather absurdly, trying to hang on to his "free, proud singleness" (254)? As Connie Chatterley was to reflect, complete freedom would mean that one must "evaporate" into nothingness. (The man who loved islands was to do just that.)

If the second Lawrence is Lawrence the married man, who would, as he himself claimed, have been nothing without Frieda, a third Lawrence is the Lawrence who believed, with Birkin, that marriage cannot be an end in itself, is no more than "égoïsme à deux" unless it involves at least "a few other people" (1987c, 318). While writing *Women in Love* Lawrence wrote: "My individual self is all right, but it seems quite cut off and isolated, as if it had no connection and no relation with anybody, beyond Frieda. . . . There is a gnawing craving in oneself, to move and live not only as a single, satisfied individual, but as a real representative of the whole race" (1984, 63). Birkin and Ursula cut themselves off from family, community, jobs, nation, culture, civilization itself, and find themselves at the end of *Women in Love* isolated in an icy wilderness. This problem was still unresolved by Mellors and Connie.

Lawrence was gregarious. As a youth he had always been the life and soul of the party, the leader of the Pagans in their excursions into the surrounding countryside, bringing more life, greater awareness, to others through his ability to communicate his own enthusiasms, knowledge, and insights, as later through his schoolteaching and his works. This is the Lawrence who, living through the dehumanization of the industrial system in the days before unions, imbibed an idealistic utopian socialism that led him to Willie Hopkin as his mentor.

Lawrence told Reid that his own religion would involve an awareness of the sufferings of "multitudes of brothers," and that "true Socialism" *was* religion. The proposed constitution of Rananim was that of a socialist utopia. In 1918 Lawrence told his friend S. S. Koteliansky that he wanted to make contact with several of the leading members of the Independent Labour Party, to escape from his "rather meaningless isolation." For a few years Lawrence's utopianism was diverted into the cul-de-sac of leadership, but he seems to have left that behind him when he returned to Europe from America in 1925. On his last visit to England in 1926 he wrote: "Curiously, I like England again, now I am up in my own regions. It braces me up: and there seems a queer, odd sort of potentiality in the people, especially the common people. One feels in them some odd, unaccustomed sort of plasm twinkling and nascent. They are not finished. And they have a funny sort of purity and gentleness, and at the same time, unbreakableness, that attracts one" (1989a, 519–20).

It was this feeling that generated the first version of *Lady Chatterley's Lover.* In May 1929 Lawrence cheered the victory of the Labour Party in the general election, and a few weeks later he wrote:

> And though the pomegranate has red flowers
> outside the window
> and oleander is hot with perfume under the
> afternoon sun
> and I am "il Signore" and they love me here,
> yet I am a mill-hand in Leeds
> and the death of the Black Country is upon me
> and I am wrapped in the lead of a coffin-lining,
> the living death of my fellow men.
> ("We Die Together," in D. H. Lawrence 1972, 630)

There remains a fourth Lawrence, a Lawrence who would not have been satisfied even had he found perfect "self-effectuation" within a perfect marriage within a perfect community. Such a life would require for its completeness a larger context still, that of nature and ecological concerns: of birds, beasts and flowers, and of the wheeling cosmos. For those of us who live in cities, especially in that tight little island across the Atlantic, simply coming to New Mexico gives us a glimpse of what Lawrence called the Greater Day, a landscape of huge horizons that dwarfs humanity, and a landscape bristling with its own untamed vitality, a vitality Lawrence also called Pan. I need not elaborate on this here. It has been much written about, and is the theme of a chapter—"Lawrence and the Resurrection of Pan"—in my most recent book.[3]

These, then, are my four Lawrences. Like his baby tortoise, perhaps like all male human beings, Lawrence had a "cross-wise, cloven psyche." The four corners are in perpetual conflict with each other. The striving for self-effectuation comes into conflict with the demands of sexual love for self-abnegation, culminating in the "little death," the ego-death of coition. Self-effectuation and marriage both come into conflict with what Trigant Burrow called "the societal instinct." Lawrence firmly believed that the instinct to work shoulder to shoulder with one's fellow men in building a civilization, or at least a model of one, was as basic as the sexual and survival instincts. And all of these come into conflict with the attractions of the nonhuman world. In 1917 Lawrence wrote: "As for republics, they are the imaginary chickens of an addled egg. Nothing will save us now; we must lapse sheer away from the extant world, reject it all, become indifferent, and listen beyond" (1984, 139). He told Koteliansky that his Rananim idea was "the true one. Only the people were wrong. But to go to Rananim *without* the people is right" (23). During his wartime "nightmare" this split caused him not only to envisage a colony without people, but a world without people—just, in Birkin's words, "uninterrupted grass, and a hare sitting up" (1987c, 127).

It seemed that humanity and nature could not be reconciled. The Great Goddess demands that man should suspend what seems to define him as human in order to comply with her laws. As Ted Hughes wrote: "The ego's extreme alternatives are either to reject her and attempt to live an independent, rational, secular life or to abnegate the ego and embrace her love with 'total, unconditional love,' which means to become a saint, a holy idiot, possessed by the Divine Love. . . . Man will always choose the former, simply because once he is free of a natural, creaturely awareness of the divine indulgence which permits him to exist at all, he wants to live his own life, and he has never invented a society of saints that was tolerable" (1962, 392–93).

In my first book, *The Art of D .H. Lawrence,* forty years ago, I spoke of Lawrence's work as falling into four phases, roughly corresponding to the four Lawrences I have just described. Now I think it is probably more accurate to speak of these not as consecutive phases, but as coexisting, from his adolescence onward. The tension between them generates those phenomenal creative energies. His lifelong quest is to try to reconcile them so that these energies can be directed into a coherent and constructive life mode and "metaphysic." The vocation of the great writer is to be a healer, to bring gifts of healing truths. But before he can perform this task, he must heal himself. The work enacts or reenacts the struggle for atonement and completion, and the reader's participation in this struggle is itself a healing experience.

Ursula's perception of the self as a "supreme gleaming triumph of infinity" in *The Rainbow* (D. H. Lawrence 1989c, 409) has to be painfully superseded by her recognition of the self's total dependence on the whole spectrum of relationships, human and nonhuman, material and spiritual, symbolized by the rainbow itself, a symbol that adumbrated for Lawrence, as it had for Blake, the complete life that was his ultimate goal.

II.

As L. D. Clark demonstrated in his beautiful book *The Minoan Distance,* by far the most important image in relation to Lawrence's life or work is that of travel—travel, of course, as quest. The quest is simultaneously an inner quest for the idea of a complete life and an outer quest for a real place in which such a life might be found or founded. The fact that England, possibly the whole of Europe, is rotten does not necessarily imply that there is nowhere in the wide world where men live saner lives, in good faith. Lawrence's "savage pilgrimage" was a search for such a place.

Virtually imprisoned in England during the war, Lawrence was obliged to look for some alternative to travel as the main enacting of his quest. He chose during his "nightmare" to write off all existing societies and cultures, and to start a new one with a few handpicked like-minded souls. In his recent biography of Lawrence, John Worthen argues that Lawrence was never wholly serious about it (see Turner and Worthen 1999, 135–71) and never really intended to put it into practice. I disagree. His reluctance seems to me to signify quite the opposite—that the idea was so precious to him that he feared to put it to the test. Had he ever gotten so far as to set up his community, we can have little doubt that it would have collapsed for the same reason such experiments almost always collapse: the inability of people to subject their own egos to the higher needs of a community. When the candidates included such sizeable egos as those of Murry, Russell, Huxley, and Heseltine, the idea was a nonstarter. And of course Lawrence's own ego would have been the main problem, since he assumed that every community had to have a leader, and that he himself would automatically fill that role. Gonzalo's commonwealth in *The Tempest* abolishes kingship, yet could be instituted only if he were king. Half of Lawrence alerted him to these dangers, and deeply frustrated the deep desire of the other half to take the plunge.

After the war the Brewsters persuaded him to try Ceylon, but it nauseated him. In Australia he responded very strongly to the bush, but felt that to "go bush" would be to betray his Englishness. The South Sea Islands, so attractive to Paul Gauguin and Robert Louis Stevenson, were more lessons in disillusion. Always at the back of his mind, often at the front, had been America, the last frontier.

The culture of the American Indians was at first very alien to Lawrence, but he came to understand it and admire it deeply. It was right for them, their race, their spirit of place, but it was not in him to cluster to the drum. After his brush with death in Mexico, Lawrence's recovery at the ranch was a literal resurrection. He was happy there and as healthy as he was ever again likely to be. Why then did he choose to abandon it, on his fortieth birthday, to return to Europe? It was, in effect, an abandonment of the idea that travel might bring him to some promised land. As he was to say of Connie Chatterley, "She had no faith in the newness of new countries. It was exile, always exile." It was also a feeling that he could not justify his personal happiness if it were at the expense of turning his back on Europe and opting out of the fight he felt was his "business" both as man and writer. He could justify the peace and happiness of the ranch only in terms of *reculer pour mieux sauter:* as a brief withdrawal from the world to recoup his energies for another assault on it—the world, that is, of his own people, of Europe.

For health reasons, living in England was not an option. Lawrence's infallible instinct for beautiful places took him first to the Villa Bernarda at Spotorno, then to the Villa Mirenda. Perched in the Tuscan hills above Florence, the Mirenda was almost as far removed from the world of industry and politics and strife as the ranch had been. The Lawrences' neighbors, the Wilkinsons, had chosen to live there for that very reason, and marveled that Lawrence seemed determined to import the world's problems. In fact, Lawrence was at least as attracted to escaping from the world as they were. It is often assumed that after *The Plumed Serpent* Lawrence dropped Rananim. He dropped the name, certainly, and rejected Rolf Gardiner's invitation to join his relatively practical scheme—but he still oscillated between the claims of the "societal instinct" and the needs of the individual. The "extant social world," now he was back in Europe, filled him with rage and nausea. He felt an absolute need to cut himself off from it for his very survival. He began to feel that perhaps even Frieda was one too many "other people." The temptation was great to become a hermit, a temptation he had to exorcise in "The Man Who Loved Islands" and "The Man Who Was Through With the World."

In stories such as these Lawrence could state very strongly the case against the isolated "individual consciousness." In essays such as "The Individual Consciousness v. the Social Consciousness" and "John Galsworthy" he could state equally strongly the case against the repressive "social consciousness." But in more ambitious works where he sought to heal that split, he floundered. The difficulty is evident in the fact that three of the works in which this may have been the intended theme were left unfinished—"The Flying Fish," "The Man Who Was Through with the World," and "A Dream of Life," not to mention *Lady Chatterley's Lover,* which, after three attempts, still leaves Mellors and Connie dangling at the end, and *The Escaped Cock,* which, as I shall argue, needed a part 3, and might have had one if Lawrence's health had been up to another piece of sustained fiction.

III.

"A Dream of Life" is a revealing failure, and *The Escaped Cock* is the story in which it seems to me Lawrence came nearest to achieving his quest. First, consider these two passages:

> A sunlit glade at the southern foot of a thickly wooded hill. On the west side of it, the steps and columned porch of a dainty little classic temple. . . . A dance of youths and maidens is in progress. The music is provided by a few flute-players seated carelessly on the steps of the temple. . . . Some of the youths have beards. Their dress, like the architecture of the theatre and the design of the altar and curved seats, resembles Grecian of the fourth century B.C., freely handled. They move with perfect balance and remarkable grace, racing through a figure like a farandole.

Second:

> It was a big gateway of yellow stone, and inside was a clear space, paved mostly with whitish stones, and around it stood buildings in the yellow stone, golden-looking, with pavement arcades supported on yellow pillars. . . . The crowd had gathered in order, a cluster of men on the left, in grey, grey-and-scarlet, and pure scarlet, and a cluster of women on the right, in tunics of all shades of blue and crocus lilac. In the vaulted porticoes

were more people. And the red sun shone on all, till the square glowed again. . . . Yet the dance swept into swifter and swifter rhythm, with the most extraordinary incalculable unison. (D. H. Lawrence 2004, 63, 64)

Both these passages might be attempts to re-create some Etruscan ceremony. In fact, both are set in England in the distant future. The first passage is George Bernard Shaw's vision of life in the year 31,920, in the stage direction to part 5 of *Back to Methuselah.* The second is Lawrence's vision of life in the year 2927, in his only futuristic fiction, which I have called "A Dream of Life." (It is printed in the Cambridge Edition as "Autobiographical Fragment.")

Shaw published *Back to Methuselah* in 1921. Lawrence must have read it, or been somehow apprised of it, immediately, since he refers to it in *Fantasia of the Unconscious,* written in that same year: "Our leaders have not loved men: they have loved ideas, and have been willing to sacrifice passionate men on the altars of the blood-drinking, ever-ash-thirsty ideal. Has President Wilson, or Karl Marx or Bernard Shaw ever felt one hot blood-pulse of love for the working man, the half-conscious, deluded working man? Never. Each of these leaders has wanted to abstract him away from his own blood and being into some foul Methuselah or abstraction of a man" (2004a, 141)

The two passages I juxtaposed, despite their apparent similarity, are serving exactly opposite purposes. The main thrust of Lawrence's late works—particularly *Lady Chatterley's Lover, Etruscan Places, The Escaped Cock,* and his paintings—can be seen as his attempt to refute *Back to Methuselah* and substantiate an exactly opposite vision of life.

Shaw believed in what he called Creative Evolution. He believed that evolution did not happen by chance, but by will; that men could will themselves to become almost anything. What had prevented man in the past from perfecting himself was the shortness of his life span and fear of death, so the first stage in our future evolution must be to will ourselves to live much longer. Methuselah was supposed to have lived for nine hundred years. The final section of *Back to Methuselah* is called "As Far as Thought Can Reach." It envisages a time when man has evolved a body that dies only by accident. Early development and learning have been accelerated to the point where childhood and youth are compressed into about four years. After that men become Ancients, and are able to put away childish things and concentrate entirely on developing the one truly mature and fully human thing—thought. To this end they are willing themselves not to need bodies at all.

One would have thought that such projects had already been thoroughly discredited by Shaw's compatriot Jonathan Swift, with his Laputians, Struldbruggs, and Houyhnhnms, but Shaw seems to have lacked entirely Swift's common sense and humanity. Since his Ancients have already divested themselves of all forms of love, all relationships, and are no longer subject to the needs, desires, instincts, and pleasures of the body, there seems little need to dispense with that body; but Shaw seems to have felt that mind is invariably tainted, degraded, by its close association with body, even with brain, and would be more free and powerful as a disembodied "vortex." Nowhere in the play or extensive preface does Shaw tell us what, having shed so much, there would be to think *about*.

In the passage with which we began, Shaw is evoking precisely that kind of art which Lawrence most admired, as closest to nature, expressing the very shapes and rhythms of life in song and dance, clothing, architecture; it was like the art of the Etruscans, which did not seek to defeat time, leaving "burdens on the face of the earth" like the Romans, but celebrated the ephemeral, the passing seasons and cycles: an art not "cooked in the artistic consciousness," like most of modern art: an art that was communal but not civic, not walled off from the surrounding woods.

Shaw puts all this in his stage direction, suggesting a Lawrentian utopia, only to reject it all as merely childish. First one of the older maidens (aged four) announces to the youth who loves her that she is bored with all the songs and dances, with art and love, and finds the Ancients more interesting: "They are fascinating, just fascinating. I want to get away from our eternal dancing and music, and just sit down by myself and think about numbers." Then two of the Ancients (of opposite sex, though this seems to make no difference: they are both bald and "without sexual charm") attempt to explain to the "children" how their own lives are superior. The explanation consists entirely of negatives—what is childish about everything other than thinking. What is so wonderful about thinking is apparently a secret the children are not yet old enough to be told.

The Ancients dismiss as worthless not only the body but also the whole of nature: "Your landscapes, your mountains, are only the world's cast skins and decaying teeth on which we live like microbes." They have "swept away the beasts of the garden, and made an end of the crawling things and the flying things and of all them that refuse to live for ever." The "final reality," says the She-Ancient (with an uncomfortable pre-echo of the "final solution") is "myself," detached from body and become immortal. One of the youths describes the Ancients as "unnatural, heartless, loveless, joyless monsters," and nothing in the play detracts from the accuracy of this description.

The final speech of the play is delivered by our first parent, Lilith, who claims that the only worthy goal for her offspring is "redemption from the flesh, to the vortex freed from matter, to the whirlpool in pure intelligence." The cosmos, she says, is a desert, but "my seed shall one day fill it and master its matter to its utmost confines."

If Lawrence read this play, we can imagine his increasing horror. However, Shaw was only taking to its logical extreme an attitude to the body and the whole physical world endemic in Western culture for two thousand years. This characteristic mind-set is evident even in a writer as sympathetic to Lawrence as Aldous Huxley, who wrote in his review of *Etruscan Places:*

> For the sake of the double flute and all it stands for, he [Lawrence] was prepared to sacrifice most of the activities upon which, for the last two thousand years or thereabouts, humanity, at any rate in the West, has set the highest value. The philosophy and practice of non-acceptance have made it possible for man to become, in some respects, more than human. But in the process he has had to sacrifice much of his former happiness; and while he has become spiritually and intellectually more, emotionally and physically he has, too often, degenerated and become less than human. (Huxley 1932)

Huxley's mind-set prevented him from reading what Lawrence had actually written in *Etruscan Places.* He is clearly unable to think in other than dualistic terms. Lawrence is not arguing that one distinct set of values should be sacrificed for the sake of another distinct set of values. He is arguing that the refusal to accept the given terms of life, the interdependence of man, flora, fauna, landscape, climate, and the fact of death, together with the hubristic impulse to become "more than human," had alienated man from his birthright, his atonement with the rest of life, including its creative energies. He does not want to go back to a childish or prelapsarian innocence (or ignorance); rather, he wants to develop a more selfless awareness, a holistic and biocentric consciousness, which would enable us to reaccept nature with that Blakean adult innocence which can only be attained on the far side of experience. He wants, above all, wholeness.

It is tempting to see *Etruscan Places* as the culmination of Lawrence's quest. After years of fruitless searching for the Holy Grail, Parzival is advised to cease his search, to relax and simply let the reins lie on his horse's neck. The horse takes him straight to the Grail. So with Lawrence it seems that no sooner had he given up his savage pilgrimage and relaxed into Tuscan insouciance than chance took him on his Etruscan tour. And there in the vivid frescoes of Tarquinia was the very life he had been searching for: "Behind all the dancing was a vision, and even a science of life, a conception of the universe and man's place in the universe which made men live to the depth of their capacity. To the Etruscan, all was alive: the whole universe lived: and the business of man was himself to live amid it all. He had to draw life into himself, out of the wandering huge vitalities of the world" (D. H. Lawrence 1992, 56–57).

Etruscan Places is perhaps the nearest Lawrence came to describing a utopia, but it does not really address the split, because, unlike a work of fiction, it carries no obligation to describe individuals and their relationships. They are just "the Etruscans," undifferentiated. Their art records only their communal life and religious rituals. And Shaw was surely right at least in his recognition that you cannot make a complete human life out of these elements alone. Lawrence would never have been content to spend his days in dancing, feasting, hunting, games, and lovemaking, however close that might have brought him to the sources of life. He was too thoroughly an heir of the romantic definition of life (in William Wordsworth's words from *The Prelude*) as "Effort and expectation and desire, / And something evermore about to be" (6.541-42). A utopia is not a place to inhabit. That would be a "Lotus Land." It is a state to strive for.

When, in "A Dream of Life," Lawrence tried a fictional transportation of Etruscan civilization to the English Midlands, he could not get beyond a description of the architecture, uniform costumes, and communal dances: "All the time the sun was slowly sinking, shadow was falling, and the dance was moving slower, the women wheeling blue around the obliterated sun. They were dancing the sun down, and dancing as birds wheel and dance, and fishes in shoals, controlled by some strange unanimous instinct. It was at once terrifying and magnificent. I wanted to die, so as not to see it, and I wanted to rush down, to be one of them. To be a drop in that wave of life" (D. H. Lawrence 2004c, 64).

In "The Flying Fish" Lawrence's image of "swift, laughing togetherness" had been a school of dolphins. Here it is a flock of birds. Why did Lawrence never finish the story? The problem is that birds and dolphins cannot achieve and maintain their marvelous togetherness, their complete unison, and at the same time be unique individuals. Ted Hughes was surely right in claiming that the "state of steady bliss" that he calls "the heaven of the animals" is neither achievable nor ultimately desirable for man. Much as he admired birds, dolphins, or Etruscans, Lawrence felt that modern Western man had come too far to submerge his individuality. He could not bring himself to abandon his belief in the sanctity of the unique individual. And how could fiction be written about individuals who had become indistinguishable from one another?

The difficulty is clearly stated by Lawrence in his review of Trigant Burrow's *The Social Basis of Consciousness:*

> [M]an is a prey to the division inside himself. Helplessly he must strive for more consciousness, which means, also, a more intensified aloneness, or individuality; and at the same time he

> has a horror of his own aloneness, and a blind, dim yearning for the old togetherness of the far past, what Dr. Burrow calls the preconscious state.
>
> What man really wants, according to Dr. Burrow, is a sense of togetherness with his fellow men, which shall balance the secret but overmastering sense of separateness and aloneness which now dominates him. (2005b, 333)

But if the delicate balance tips the other way, that can be suicidal: "As a matter of fact, the mass is more neurotic than the individual patient. This is Dr. Burrow's finding. The mass, the normals, never live a life of their own. They cannot" (334). The review ends with what is virtually the program of *The Escaped Cock:* "Men must get back into *touch.* And to do so they must forfeit the vanity and the *noli me tangere* of their own absoluteness: also they must utterly break the present great picture of a normal humanity: shatter that mirror in which we all live grimacing: and fall again into true relatedness" (336).

The man who had died begins the process of reestablishing "the living organic connections," but we are left in doubt as to how this will be achieved in relation to "mankind and nation."

There is no evidence to suggest that Lawrence knew much Blake, or was much influenced by him. But it seems to me that Lawrence ended up with a scheme that has much in common with Blake's idea of "fourfold vision." What Blake called "single vision and Newton's sleep" was, for Lawrence, the materialism of Western culture—what in *Lady Chatterley* he called "the din-din-dinning of books, schools, cinemas, clergymen, the whole national and human consciousness hammering on the fact of material prosperity above all things." It was also that hubris, man's "self-importance," which the ancient Greeks had recognized as the original sin (or perhaps genetic flaw) in man's makeup. Twofold vision is the recovery of the Energies, the charge of vitality that flows from a renewed connection with the larger life, the Greater Day, of the cosmos. One aspect of this charge is desire. Once "free from desire," the man who loved islands is already virtually dead. In contrast, the man who had died is painfully reborn into the world of clamorous desire embodied in the escaped cock.

His atonement with the phenomenal world frees the man to embark on his quest for a more complete human life than that of the self-sacrificing savior. His marriage to the priestess of Isis and subsequent fatherhood constitute his threefold vision, his recovery of primal innocence. This is not the vulnerable innocence of childhood, but the innocence on the far side of experience, an innocence that is well aware of the need to fight to maintain itself in a hostile world, and that sallies out into that world to confront its adversaries.

The man who had died rejects, first, the temptations of the hermit life, which is no better than the grave; then, the temptation to settle for domestic contentment with the woman of his choice and their child. He sails out at the end into the dangerous world where Rome rules. He will support himself as a healer, and return in due season to his family. What else will he do? The story cries out for a part 3 describing the complete life of a risen man, a man who has come through to fourfold vision. Though Lawrence never felt strong enough to undertake any more fiction, he did leave us in an essay called "The Risen Lord" what amounts to a sketch for a third part of the story.

> If Jesus rose in the full flesh, he rose to know the tenderness of a woman, and the great pleasure of her, and to have children by her. He rose to know the responsibility and the peculiar delight of children, and also the exasperation and nuisance of them. If Jesus rose as a full man, in the flesh, he rose to have friends, to have a man friend whom he would hold sometimes to his breast, in strong affection, and who would be dearer to him than a brother, just out of the sheer mystery of sympathy. And how much more wonderful, this, than having disciples! If Jesus rose a full man in the flesh he rose to do his share in the world's work, something he really liked doing. And if he remembered his first life, it would neither be teaching nor preaching, but probably carpentering again, with joy, among the shavings. If Jesus rose a full man in the flesh, he rose to continue his fight with the hard-boiled conventionalists like Roman judges and Jewish priests and money-makers of every sort. But this time, it would no longer be the fight of self-sacrifice that would end

> in crucifixion. This time, it would be a freed man fighting to shelter the rose of life from being trampled on by the pigs. (2004g, 271)

Etruscan Places, The Escaped Cock, and "The Risen Lord" are not about ancient history. Every age has its equivalent of the Romans, Philistines, and money changers. Lawrence identified them in his own day; they are not difficult to identify in ours. He knew that to drive the money changers from the temple was simply to license them to operate everywhere else; that to render unto Caesar that which is Caesar's is to give Caesar carte blanche. Lawrence loathed whiteness. Whiteness represented for him what remained when the multicolored diversity and potentiality of the rainbow had been extinguished.

If Lawrence were able to come back today, how might he need to modify his metaphysic? He would, of course, be appalled by the degradation and desecration of the earth, our only home, in the last three-quarters of a century, the triumph of Mammon, the fact that the multinational corporations now literally have the power (and, it seems, the will and the public support) to extinguish life; more specifically, by such things as the rape of the rain forests and the destruction of indigenous peoples. In his darker moments he would feel that our world simply confirmed what he said in his last work, *Apocalypse:* that man was doomed ultimately to destroy himself "in conflict with the cosmos" (1979, 200). But he might salvage some hope from the convergence of so many creeds and disciplines toward deep ecology (and the knowledge of how much he had himself contributed to that), and from the emergence of a worldwide network of individuals, groups, and organizations, of activists, conservationists, writers, educators, dedicated to preventing, or at least deferring a little longer, the extinction of the rose of life.

Notes

1. The words and music were by Philip P. Bliss (1873):

> Standing by a purpose true,
> Heeding God's command,

Honor them, the faithful few!
All hail to Daniel's band!

Refrain:
Dare to be a Daniel,
Dare to stand alone!
Dare to have a purpose firm!
Dare to make it known.

2. See my comments on "holistic thinking," "biocentric consciousness," and "deep ecology": "Ecology was, for Lawrence, a matter of a different consciousness, a wholeness, an atonement, a being in touch" (Sagar 2001, 147–48, 152).

3. See Sagar 2006.

References

Adams, Carol J. 2004. *The Sexual Politics of Meat: A Feminist-Vegetarian Critical Theory.* New York: Continuum.

Adelman, Gary. 2002. *Reclaiming D. H. Lawrence: Contemporary Writers Speak Out.* Lewisburg, PA: Bucknell University Press.

Adorno, Theodor W., and Max Horkheimer. 2002. *The Dialectic of Enlightenment.* Trans. Edmund Jephcott. Stanford, CA: Stanford University Press.

Agamben, Giorgio. 2004. *The Open.* Trans. Kevin Attell. Stanford, CA: Stanford University Press.

Arnold, Armin. 1958. *D. H. Lawrence and America.* London: Linden Press.

Baker, Paul G. 1983. *A Reassessment of D. H. Lawrence's "Aaron's Rod."* Studies in Modern Literature, no. 31, ed. A. Walton Litz. Ann Arbor, MI: UMI Research Press.

Barr, William R. 1976. "*Aaron's Rod* as D. H. Lawrence's Picaresque Novel." *DHLR* 9:213–25. Repr in. *D. H. Lawrence: Critical Assessments,* ed. David Ellis and Ornella de Zordo, 2:449–57. Mountfield, England: Helm Information, 1992.

Bataille, Georges. 1985. *Visions of Excess: Selected Writings 1927–1939.* Ed. Allan Stoekl. Minneapolis: University of Minnesota Press.

———. 1990. *On Bataille: Yale French Studies.* Ed. Allan Stoekl. New Haven, CT: Yale University Press.

Beal, Anthony, ed. 1955. *D. H. Lawrence: Selected Criticism.* London: Heinemann.

Becket, Fiona. 1997. *D. H. Lawrence: The Thinker as Poet.* London: Macmillan.

———. 1997–98. "Being There: Nostalgia and the Masculine Maternal in D. H. Lawrence." *DHLR* 27, nos. 2–3:255–68.

———. 2001. "Lawrence and Psychoanalysis." In Fernihough 2001, 217–33.

Beer, Gillian. 1983. *Darwin's Plots: Evolutionary Narrative in Darwin, George Eliot, and Nineteenth-Century Fiction.* London: Routledge and Kegan Paul.

Bell, Michael. 2004. *D. H. Lawrence: Language and Being.* Cambridge: Cambridge University Press.

———. 2006. *Literature, Modernism and Myth: Belief and Responsibility in the Twentieth Century.* Cambridge: Cambridge University Press.

———. 2007 "Lawrence and the 'Other' in Ideological Retrospect." *D. H. Lawrence Studies* (Korea) 25:1–20.

Bennett, Bruce, and Jennifer Strauss, eds. 1998. *The Oxford Literary History of Australia.* Melbourne: Oxford University Press.

Bentham, Jeremy. 1948. *An Introduction to the Principles of Morals and Legislation.* New York: Hafner/Macmillan.

Bloom, Harold, ed. 1986. *D. H. Lawrence.* Modern Critical Views. New York: Chelsea House.

Boies, Henry M. 1893. *Prisoners and Paupers.* New York: G. P. Putnam's Sons.

Booth, Howard. 2002. "D. H. Lawrence and Male Homosexual Desire." *Review of English Studies* 53, no. 209:86–107.

Boulton, James T. 2000. "D. H. Lawrence's *Pansies* and the State, 1929." *Journal of the D. H. Lawrence Society,* 5–16.

Bradbury, Malcolm. 1993. *The Modern British Novel.* London: Secker and Warburg.

Brewster, Earl and Achsah Brewster. 1934. *D. H. Lawrence: Reminiscences and Correspondence.* London: Martin Secker.

Brewster, Scott. 1997–98. "Jumping Continents: Abjection, *Kangaroo* and the Celtic Uncanny." *DHLR* 27, nos. 2–3:217–32.

Burack, Charles Michael. 2005. *D. H. Lawrence's Language of Sacred Experience: The Transfiguration of the Reader.* New York: Palgrave Macmillan, 2005.

Burwell, Rose Marie. 1970. "A Catalogue of D. H. Lawrence's Reading from Early Childhood" *DHLR* 3, no. 3:193–324.

Butler, Judith. 1997. *The Psychic Life of Power: Theories in Subjection.* Stanford, CA: Stanford University Press.

Caesar, Adrian. 1998. "National Myths of Manhood: ANZACS and Others." In Bennett and Strauss 1998, 147–65.

Carlson, Elof Axel. 2001. *The Unfit: A History of a Bad Idea.* New York: Cold Spring Harbor Laboratory Press.

Chase, Richard. 1969. *The American Novel and Its Tradition.* Baltimore: Johns Hopkins University Press.

Chaudhury, Amit. 2003. *D. H. Lawrence and Difference: Postcoloniality and the Poetry of the Present.* Oxford: Oxford University Press.

Chesterton, G. K. 2000. *Eugenics and Other Evils: An Argument Against the Scientifically Organized State.* With additional articles by his eugenic and birth control opponents. Ed. Michael W. Perry. Seattle: Inkling Books.

Childs, Peter. 2000. *Modernism.* London: Routledge.

Clarey, JoEllyn. 1986. "D. H. Lawrence's *Moby-Dick:* A Textual Note." *Modern Philology* 84 (November): 191–95.

Clark, L. D. 1964. *Dark Night of the Body: D. H. Lawrence's "The Plumed Serpent."* Austin: University of Texas Press.

Clarke, Bruce. 2001. *Energy Forms: Allegory and Science in the Era of Classical Thermodynamics.* Ann Arbor: University of Michigan Press.

Colacurcio, Michael J. 1975. "The Symbolic and the Symptomatic: D. H. Lawrence in Recent American Criticism." *American Quarterly* 27: 191–95.

Conor, Liz. 2004. *The Spectacular Modern Woman: Feminine Visibility in the 1920s.* Bloomington: Indiana University Press.

Cowan, James C. 2002. *D. H. Lawrence: Self and Sexuality.* Columbus: Ohio State University Press.

Cram, David, and Christopher Pollnitz. 2001. "D. H. Lawrence as Verse Translator." *Cambridge Quarterly* 30, no. 2:133–50.

Cushman, Keith. 1988. "*Bay:* The Noncombatant as War Poet." In *The Spirit of D. H. Lawrence,* ed. Gamini Salgado and G. K. Das, 181–98. London: Macmillan.

———. 1999. "DHL in the USA." In *The Reception of D. H. Lawrence Around the World,* ed. Takeo Iida, 133–63. Fukuoka, Japan: Kyushu University Press.

Cushman, Keith, and Earl G. Ingersoll, eds. 2003a. *D. H. Lawrence: New Worlds.* Madison, NJ: Fairleigh Dickinson University Press.

——— 2003b. Introduction to Cushman and Ingersoll 2003a, 15–21.

Daleski, H. M. 1965. *The Forked Flame: A Study of D. H. Lawrence.* London: Faber and Faber.

Darroch, Robert. 1981. *D. H. Lawrence in Australia.* Melbourne: Macmillan.

Davies, Rhys. 1940. "D. H. Lawrence in Bandol." *Horizon* 2 (October), 191–208.

Davis, Joseph. 1988. *D. H. Lawrence at Thirroul.* Sydney: Collins.

De Grazia, Edward. 1992. *Girls Lean Back Everywhere: The Law of Obscenity and the Assault on Genius.* New York: Random House.

de la Mare, Walter. 1913. Review of *Helen Redeemed,* by Maurice Hewlett, and *Love Poems and Others,* by D. H. Lawrence. *Times Literary Supplement,* March 13, 108.

Delany, Paul. 1978. *D. H. Lawrence's Nightmare: The Writer and His Circle in the Years of the Great War.* New York: Basic Books.

Deleuze, Gilles. 1989. *Masochism.* Trans. Jean McNeil. New York: Zone Books.

Deleuze, Gilles, and Félix Guattari. 1984. *Anti-Oedipus: Capitalism and Schizophrenia.* Trans. Robert Hurley, Mark Seem, and Helen Lane. London: Athlone Press.

———. 1987. *A Thousand Plateaus: Capitalism and Schizophrenia.* Trans. Brian Massumi. Minneapolis: University of Minnesota Press.

D'Emilio, John, and Estelle B. Freeman. 1988. *Intimate Matters: A History of Sexuality in America.* New York: Harper and Row.

Derrida, Jacques. 1978. *Writing and Difference.* Trans. Alan Bass. London: Routledge and Kegan Paul.

———. 1991. "'Eating Well,' or The Calculation of the Subject: An Interview with Jacques Derrida." In *Who Comes after the Subject?* ed. Eduardo Cadava, Peter Connor, and Jean-Luc Nancy, 96–119. New York: Routledge.

———. 1993. "On a Newly Arisen Apocalyptic Tone in Philosophy." In *Raising the Tone of Philosophy: Late Essays by Immanuel Kant, Transformative Critique by Jacques Derrida*, ed. Peter Fenves, 117–71. Baltimore: Johns Hopkins University Press.

———. 1994. "'To Do Justice to Freud': The History of Madness in the Age of Psychoanalysis." *Critical Inquiry* 20 (Winter): 227–66.

———. 2003. "And Say the Animal Responded." Trans. David Wills. In *Zoontologies: The Question of the Animal*, ed. Cary Wolfe, 121–46. Minneapolis: University of Minnesota Press.

Devall, William, and George Sessions. 1985. *Deep Ecology: Living as if Nature Mattered.* Layton, UT: Peregrine Smith Books.

Dixon, Robert. 1998. "Literature and Melodrama." In Bennett and Strauss 1998, 66–88.

Doherty, Gerald. 1987. "White Mythologies: D. H. Lawrence and the Deconstructive Turn." *Criticism* 29:477–96.

Donaldson, George, and Mara Kalnins, ed. 1999. *D. H. Lawrence in Italy and England.* New York: St. Martin's Press.

Draper, R. P. 1964. *D. H. Lawrence.* New York: Twayne.

———, ed. 1970. *D. H. Lawrence: The Critical Heritage.* London: Routledge and Kegan Paul.

Eggert, Paul. 2001. "The Biographical Issue: Lives of Lawrence." In Fernihough 2001, 157–77.

Einstein, Albert. 1961. *Relativity: The Special and the General Theory.* Trans. Robert W. Lawson. New York: Three Rivers Press.

Ellis, David. 1989. "Lawrence in Australia: The Darroch Controversy." *D. H. Lawrence Review* 21 (Summer): 167–74.

———. 1998. *D. H. Lawrence: Dying Game, 1922–1930.* Cambridge: Cambridge University Press.

Ernst, Morris L., and William Seagle. 1928. *To the Pure . . . : A Study of Obscenity and the Censor.* New York: Viking Press.

Falasca-Zamponi, Simonetta. 1997. *Fascist Spectacle: The Aesthetics of Power in Mussolini's Italy.* Berkeley: University of California Press.

Feldman, Mark. 2006. "The Physics and Metaphysics of Caging: The Animal in Late-Nineteenth-Century American Culture." *Mosaic* 39: 161–80.

Fernihough, Anne, ed. 2001. *The Cambridge Companion to D. H. Lawrence.* Cambridge: Cambridge University Press.

Fiedler, Leslie A. 1966. *Love and Death in the American Novel.* New York: Stein and Day.

Fjagesund, Peter. 1991. *The Apocalyptic World of D. H. Lawrence.* London: Norwegian University Press.

Fleishman, Avrom. 1990. "Lawrence and Bakhtin: Where Pluralism Ends and Dialogism Begins." In *Rethinking Lawrence,* ed. Keith Brown, 109–19. Milton Keynes, England: Open University Press.

Ford, George. 1965. *Double Measure: A Study of the Novels and Stories of D. H. Lawrence.* New York: Holt, Rinehart, and Winston.

Forstner, Lorne J., and John H. Todd, eds. 1971. *The Everlasting Universe: Readings on the Ecological Revolution.* Lexington, MA: Heath. (Contains "The Death of Pan," a reprinting from Lawrence's "Pan in America.")

Forter, Greg. 2003. "Against Melancholy: Contemporary Mourning Theory, Fitzgerald's *The Great Gatsby,* and the Politics of Unfinished Grief." *Difference* 14, no. 2:134–70.

Foucault, Michel. 1978. *The History of Sexuality, Volume I: An Introduction.* Trans. Robert Hurley. New York: Random House.

Freeden, Michael. 1983. "Eugenics and Ideology." *Historical Journal* 26, no. 4:959–62.

Freud, Sigmund. 1957. *The Standard Edition of the Complete Psychological Works of Sigmund Freud,* ed. James Strachey. 15 vols. London: Hogarth Press. (Contains "Civilization and Its Discontents" and "Mourning and Melancholy.")

Frost, Robert. 1949. *Complete Poems.* New York: Holt, Rinehart, and Winston.

Fuentes, Carlos. 1967. "Mexico's New Wave." *Venture* 3 (December–January).

Gadd, Tim. 2005. "Human-Animal Affiliation in Modern Popular Film." In Pollock and Rainwater 2005, 247–59.

Galton, Francis. 1883. *Inquiry into Human Faculty and Its Development.* London: Macmillan.

Garnett, David. 1955. *The Flowers of the Forest.* London: Chatto and Windus.

Gat, Azar. 1998. *Fascist and Liberal Visions of War: Fuller, Liddell Hart, Douhet, and Other Modernists.* Oxford: Clarendon.

Gertzman, Jay A. 1992. "Erotic Novel, Liberal Lawyer, and the 'Censor Moron': 'Sex for Its Own Sake' and Some Literary Censorship of the 1930s." *DHLR* 24, no. 3:217–27.

Gertzman, Jay A., and Michael Squires, eds. 1999. "New Letters from Thomas Seltzer and Robert Mountsier to D. H. Lawrence." *DHLR* 28, nos. 1–2:53–77.

Gilbert, Sandra M. 1985. "Potent Griselda: 'The Ladybird' and the Great Mother." In *D. H. Lawrence: A Contemporary Consideration,* ed. Peter Balbert and Phillip L. Marcus, 130–61. Ithaca, NY: Cornell University Press.

———. 1990. Preface to *Acts of Attention: The Poems of D. H. Lawrence.* 2nd ed. Carbondale: Southern Illinois University Press.

———. 2002. Foreword to *Reclaiming D. H. Lawrence: Contemporary Writers Speak Out,* by Gary Adelman. Lewisburg, PA: Bucknell University Press.

Girard, René. 1977. *Violence and the Sacred.* Trans. Patrick Gregory. Baltimore: Johns Hopkins University Press.

Granofsky, Ronald. 2000. "Modernism and D. H. Lawrence: Spatial Form and Selfhood in *Aaron's Rod.*" *English Studies in Canada* 26, no. 1:29–51.

———. 2003. *D. H. Lawrence and Survival: Darwinism in the Fiction of the Transitional Period.* Montreal: McGill-Queen's University Press.

Greenspan, Ezra, Lindeth Vasey, and John Worthen, eds. 2003. Introductionto D. H. Lawrence 2003b, xxiii–lxxix.

Griffin, Roger. 1995. General introduction to *Fascism,* 1–20. Oxford: Oxford University Press.

Haberstroh, Charles J., Jr. 1980. *Melville and Male Identity.* Rutherford, NJ: Fairleigh Dickinson University Press.

Henderson, Linda Dalrymple. 1983. *The Fourth Dimension and Non-Euclidean Geometry in Modern Art.* Princeton, NJ: Princeton University Press.

———. 2003. "Modernism's Quest for Invisible Realities." In *Make It New: The Rise of Modernism,* ed. Kurt Heinzelman, 135–39. Austin, TX: Harry Ransom Humanities Research Center.

———. 2005. *Duchamp in Context: Science and Technology in the "Large Glass" and Related Works.* Princeton, NJ: Princeton University Press.

Hough, Graham. 1956. *The Dark Sun: A Study of D. H. Lawrence.* London: Gerald Duckworth.

Hughes, Robert. 1991. *The Shock of the New.* New York: McGraw-Hill.

Hughes, Ted. 1962. *Shakespeare and the Goddess of Complete Being.* London: Faber and Faber.

Huxley, Aldous. 1932. Review of *Sketches of Etrusean Places,* by D. H. Lawrence. *Spectator,* November 4.

Hyde, G. M. 1990. *D. H. Lawrence.* London: Macmillan Education.

Hyde, Virginia. 1987. "*Aaron's Rod:* D. H. Lawrence's Revisionist Typology." *Mosaic* 20, no. 2:111–26. Repr. in *D.H. Lawrence: Critical Assessments,* ed. David Ellis and Ornella de Zordo. 2:468–82. Mountfield, England: Helm Information, 1992.

———. 1992. *The Risen Adam: D. H. Lawrence's Revisionist Typology.* University Park: Pennsylvania State University Press.

———. 1993. "To 'Undiscovered Land': D. H. Lawrence's Horsewomen and Other Questers." In *Women and the Journey: The Female Travel Experience,* ed. Bonnie Frederick and Susan H. McLeod, 170–89. Pullman: Washington State University Press.

———. 1994. "'Lost' Girls': D. H. Lawrence's Versions of Persephone." In *Images of Persephone: Feminist Readings in Western Literature,* ed. Elizabeth T. Hayes. Gainesville: University Press of Florida.

———. 1995. Introduction to *The Plumed Serpent,* by D. H. Lawrence, ed. L. D. Clark and Virginia Hyde, xv–xxxv. Harmondsworth, England: Penguin.

———. 2001. "Picking Up 'Life-Threads' in D. H. Lawrence's Mexico." In Sargent and Watson 2001a, 172–82.

———. 2003. "Mexican Cypresses: Myth and Multiculturalism in Lawrence's 'Novel of America.'" In Cushman and Ingersoll 2003a, 195–215.

———. 2004. "What the Parrots Said: Fable, Myth, and History in *Mornings in Mexico.*" *D. H. Lawrence Studies* 12, no. 2:105–34.

Hyde, Virginia, and L. D. Clark. 1993–94. "The Sense of an Ending in *The Plumed Serpent.*" *D. H. Lawrence Review* 25, nos. 1–3:140–44.

Iida, Takeo, ed. 1999. *The Reception of D. H. Lawrence Around the World.* Fukuoka, Japan: Kyushu University Press.

Ingersoll, Earl G. 1989. "The Failure of Bloodbrotherhood in Melville's *Moby-Dick* and Lawrence's *Women in Love.*" *Midwest Quarterly* 30, no. 4 (Summer): 458–77.

———. 1997. "Lawrence and Bloomsbury: The Friendship with David Garnett." *D. H. Lawrence Review* 26, nos. 1–3:1–27.

———. 2001. *D. H. Lawrence, Desire, and Narrative.* Gainesville: University Press of Florida.

———. 2004. "Review of D. H. Lawrence's *Studies in Classic American Literature.*" *English Literature in Transition* 47, no. 4:485–88.

Irvine, Peter L., and Anne Kiley, ed. 1976. "D. H. Lawrence and Frieda Lawrence: Letters to Dorothy Brett." *D. H. Lawrence Review* 9:1–116.

Jansohn, Christa, and Dieter Mehl. 2007. *The Reception of D. H. Lawrence in Europe.* London: Continuum.

Joynson-Hicks, William [Viscount Brentford]. 1929. *Do We Need a Censor?* Criterion Miscellany 6. London: Faber and Faber.

Kafka, Franz, 2000. *Metamorphosis and Other Stories.* Trans. Malcolm Pasley. London: Penguin.

Kermode, Frank.1973. *D. H. Lawrence.* London: Fontana.

Kevles, Daniel J. 1985. *In the Name of Eugenics: Genetics and the Uses of Human Heredity.* New York: Knopf.

King, Dixie. 1982. "The Influences of Forster's *Maurice* on *Lady Chatterley's Lover,*" *Contemporary Literature* 23, no. 1 (Winter): 65–82.

Kinkead-Weekes, Mark. 1996. *D. H. Lawrence: Triumph to Exile, 1912–22.* Cambridge: Cambridge University Press.

———. 2001. "Decolonising imagination: Lawrence in the 1920s." in Fernihough 2001.

Kurth, James. 1999. "War, Peace, and the Ideologies of the Twentieth Century." *Current History* 98 (January): 3–8.

LaChapelle, Dolores. 1996. *D. H. Lawrence: Future Primitive.* Denton: University of North Texas Press.

Lacy, Gerald M., ed. 1976. *D. H. Lawrence: Letters to Thomas and Adele Seltzer.* Santa Barbara, Cal.: Black Sparrow Press.

Lane, Christopher. 1995. *The Ruling Passion: British Colonial Allegory and the Paradox of Homosexual Desire*. Durham: Duke University Press.

Lawrence, D. H. 1913. *Love Poems and Others*. London: Duckworth.

———. 1916. *Amores*. London: Duckworth.

———. 1917. *Look! We Have Come Through!* London: Chatto and Windus.

———. 1918. *New Poems*. London: Secker.

———. 1923a. *Birds, Beasts and Flowers*. London: Secker.

———. 1923b. *Birds, Beasts and Flowers*. New York: Seltzer.

———. 1928. *Collected Poems*. 2 vols. London: Secker.

———. 1929a. *Pansies*. London: Knopf.

———. 1929b. *Pansies*. London: n. p.

———. 1929c. *Pansies*. London: Secker.

———. 1930. *Nettles*. London: Faber and Faber.

———. 1932. *Last Poems*. Ed. Richard Aldington and Giuseppe Orioli. Florence: G. Orioli.

———. 1936a. "Indians and an Englishman." In D. H. Lawrence 1936b, 92–99.

———. 1936b. *Phoenix: The Posthumous Papers of D. H. Lawrence*. Ed. Edward McDonald. New York: Viking.

———. 1972. *The Complete Poems*. Ed. Vivian de Sola Pinto and Warren Roberts. 3rd ed. London: Heinemann.

———. 1979a. *Apocalypse and the Writings on Revelation*. Ed. Mara Kalnins. Cambridge: Cambridge University Press.

———. 1979b. *The Letters of D. H. Lawrence: Volume I, 1901–13*. Ed. James T. Boulton. Cambridge: Cambridge University Press.

———. 1981a. *The Letters of D. H. Lawrence: Volume II, 1913–16*. Ed. George J. Zytaruk and James T. Boulton. Cambridge: Cambridge University Press.

———. 1981b. *The Lost Girl*. Ed. John Worthen. Cambridge: Cambridge University Press.

———. 1982. *The Trespasser*. Ed. Elizabeth Mansfield. Cambridge: Cambridge University Press.

———. 1983. *St. Mawr and Other Stories*. Ed. Brian Finney. Cambridge: Cambridge University Press.

———. 1984. *The Letters of D. H. Lawrence: Volume III, 1916–21*. Ed. James T. Boulton and Andrew Robertson. Cambridge: Cambridge University Press.

———. 1985a. "Art and Morality." In D. H. Lawrence 1985e, 161–68.

———. 1985b. "The Future of the Novel." In D. H. Lawrence 1985e, 151–55.

———. 1985c. "Morality and the Novel." In D. H. Lawrence 1985e, 169–76.

———. 1985d. "The Novel." In D. H. Lawrence 1985e, 177–90.

———. 1985e. *Study of Thomas Hardy and Other Essays*. Ed. Bruce Steele. Cambridge: Cambridge University Press.

———. 1985f. "Why the Novel Matters." In D. H. Lawrence 1985e, 193–98.

———. 1987a. *The Letters of D. H. Lawrence: Volume IV, 1921–24*. Ed. Warren Roberts, James T. Boulton, and Elizabeth Mansfield. Cambridge: Cambridge University Press.

———. 1987b. *The Plumed Serpent*. Ed. L. D. Clark. Cambridge: Cambridge University Press.

———. 1987c. *Women in Love*. Ed. David Farmer, Lindeth Vasey, and John Worthen. Cambridge: Cambridge: Cambridge University Press.

———.1988a. *Aaron's Rod*. Ed. Mara Kalnins. Cambridge: Cambridge University Press.

———. 1988b. "Aristocracy." In D. H. Lawrence 1988f, 367–76.

———. 1988c. "Books." In D. H. Lawrence 1988f, 195–200.

———. 1988d. "Education of the People." In D. H. Lawrence 1988f, 87–193.

———. 1988e. ". . . . . . Love Was Once a Little Boy." In D. H. Lawrence 1988f, 331–46.

———. 1988f. *Reflections on the Death of a Porcupine and Other Essays*. Ed. Michael Herbert. Cambridge: Cambridge University Press.

———. 1989a. *The Letters of D. H. Lawrence: V, 1924–27*. Ed. James T. Boulton and Lindeth Vasey. Cambridge: Cambridge University Press.

———. 1989b. *Movements in European History*. Ed. Philip Crumpton. Cambridge: Cambridge University Press.

———. 1989c. *The Rainbow*. Ed. Mark Kinkead-Weekes. Cambridge: Cambridge University Press.

———. 1992. *Sketches of Etruscan Places and Other Italian Essays*. Ed. Simonetta De Filippis. Cambridge: Cambridge University Press.

———. 1993a. *Lady Chatterley's Lover*. Ed. Michael Squires. Cambridge: Cambridge University Press.

———. 1993b. *The Letters of D. H. Lawrence: VII, 1928–30*. Ed. Keith Sagar and James T. Boulton. Cambridge: Cambridge University Press.

———. 1994. *Kangaroo*. Ed. Bruce Steele. Cambridge: Cambridge University Press.

———. 1995. *Quetzalcoatl: The Early Version of "The Plumed Serpent."* Ed. Louis Martz. Redding Ridge, CT: Black Swan.

———. 1997. *Sea and Sardinia*. Ed Mara Kalnins. Cambridge: Cambridge University Press.

———. 1998. *The First "Women in Love."* Ed. John Worthen and Lindeth Vasey. Cambridge: Cambridge University Press.

———. 2003. *Studies in Classic American Literature*. Ed. Ezra Greenspan, Lindeth Vasey, and John Worthen. Cambridge: Cambridge University Press.

———. 2004a. *Fantasia of the Unconscious*. In *Psychoanalysis and the Unconscious* and *Fantasia of the Unconscious*. Ed. Bruce Steele. Cambridge: Cambridge University Press.

———. 2004b. *Late Essays and Articles*. Ed. James T. Boulton. Cambridge: Cambridge University Press.

———. 2004c. "[Newthorpe] Autobiographical Fragment"; ["A Dream of Life"]. In D. H. Lawrence 2004b, 50–68.

———. 2004d. "Pictures on the Walls." In D. H. Lawrence 2004b, 257–64.

———. 2004e. *Pornography and Obscenity.* In D. H. Lawrence 2004b, 233–53.

———. 2004f. "The Real Thing." In D. H. Lawrence, 2004b, 304–10.

———. 2004g. "The Risen Lord." In D. H. Lawrence 2004b, 267–73.

———. 2005a. "Chaos in Poetry: Introduction to *Chariot of the Sun.*" In D. H. Lawrence 2005b, 109–16.

———. 2005b. *Introductions and Reviews.* Ed. Neil Reeves and John Worthen. Cambridge: Cambridge University Press.

———. 2005c. "*Memoir of Maurice Magnus:* Introduction to *Memoirs of the Foreign Legion.*" In D. H. Lawrence 2005b, 11–72.

———. 2006. *The Virgin and the Gipsy and Other Stories.* Ed. Michael Herbert, Bethan Jones, and Lindeth Vasey. Cambridge: Cambridge University Press.

Lawrence, Frieda. 1935. *"Not I, But the Wind . . ."* New York: Viking Press.

Leavis, F. R. 1994. *D. H. Lawrence: Novelist.* Harmondsworth, England: Penguin.

Lodge, David. 1990. "Lawrence, Dostoevsky, Bakhtin: Lawrence and Dialogic Fiction." In *Rethinking Lawrence,* ed. Keith Brown, 92–108. Milton Keynes, England: Open University Press.

Loran, Erle. 1946. *Cézanne's Composition: Analysis of His Form with Diagrams and Photographs of His Motifs.* Berkeley and Los Angeles: University of California Press.

Lucas, John. 1999. *The Radical Twenties: Writing, Politics, and Culture.* New Brunswick, NJ: Rutgers University Press.

Macintyre, Stuart. 1998. *The Reds.* Sydney: Allen & Unwin.

Maddox, Brenda. 1994. *D. H. Lawrence: The Story of a Marriage.* New York: Simon & Schuster.

Mazumdar, Pauline M. H. 1992. *Eugenics, Human Genetics and Human Failings.* London: Routledge.

Melville, Herman. 1957. *Moby-Dick.* New York: Rinehart.

———. 1960. *The Letters of Herman Melville.* Ed. Merrell R. Davis and William H. Gilman. New Haven, CT: Yale University Press.

———. 1993. *Correspondence.* Ed. Lynn Horth. Evanston, IL: Northwestern University Press.

Meyers, Jeffrey. 1977. *Homosexuality and Literature, 1890–1930.* Montreal: McGill-Queen's University Press.

———, ed. 1987. *The Legacy of D. H. Lawrence.* New York: St. Martin's Press.

Miller, Arthur I. 2001 *Einstein, Picasso: Space, Time, and the Beauty that Causes Havoc.* New York: Basic Books.

Miller, Edwin Haviland. 1975. *Melville.* New York: Braziller.

Milne, Drew. 2001. "Lawrence and the Politics of Sexual Politics." In Fernihough 2001, 197–215.

Mohanty, Satya P. 1997. *Literary Theory and the Claims of History: Postmodernism, Objectivity, Multicultural Politics.* Ithaca, NY: Cornell University Press.

Moholy-Nagy, László. 1947. *Vision in Motion.* Chicago: Paul Theobald.

Moore, Harry T. 1954. *The Intelligent Heart: The Story of D. H. Lawrence.* New York: Farrar, Straus and Young.

Mount, Ferdinand, ed. *TLS Centenary Archive.* September 28, 2005. http://www.tls.psmedia.com/member.asp.

Nakabayashi, Masomi. 2006. "Verbalising the Non-verbalisable: A Non-Native-English Reader's Approach of Self-consciousness and Unself-consciousness in the *Lady Chatterley* Novels." PhD diss., University of Nottingham.

Nehls, Edward, ed. 1957–59. *D. H. Lawrence: A Composite Biography.* 3 vols. Madison: University of Wisconsin Press.

Nietzsche, Friedrich. 1978. *Thus Spake Zarathustra.* Trans. R. J. Hollingdale. Harmondsworth, England: Penguin.

———. 1996. *On the Genealogy of Morals.* Trans. Douglas Smith. Oxford: Oxford University Press.

Nile, Richard. 1998a. "Literary Democracy and the Politics of Reputation." In Bennett and Strauss 1998, 130–46.

Nixon, Cornelia. 1986. *D. H. Lawrence's Leadership Politics and the Turn Against Women.* Berkeley and Los Angeles: University of California Press.

Nordau, Max. 1895. *Degeneration.* New York: D. Appleton.

Norris, Margot. 1985. *Beasts of the Modern Imagination: Darwin, Nietzsche, Kafka, Ernst, and Lawrence.* Baltimore: Johns Hopkins University Press.

Odio, Arnold. 1999. "D. H. Lawrence Among the Mexicans." In *The Reception of D. H. Lawrence Around the World,* ed. Takeo Iida, 165–92. Fukuoka, Japan: Kyushu University Press.

Ouspensky, P. D. 2004. *Tertium Organum: A Key to the Enigmas of the World.* San Diego, CA: Book Tree.

Parker, David. 2004. "Into the Ideological Unknown: *Women in Love.*" In *D. H. Lawrence: "The Rainbow" and "Women in Love;" New Casebooks,* ed. Gary Day and Libby Di Niro, 209–34. Basingstoke, England: Palgrave Macmillan.

Parkes, Adam. 2000. "D. H. Lawrence and Federico Beltrán Massés: Censorship, Obscenity, and Class." *DHLR* 29, no. 1:7–18.

Paxton, Nancy L. 1999. *Writing under the Raj: Gender, Race, and Rape in the British Colonial Imagination, 1830–1947.* New Brunswick, NJ: Rutgers University Press.

Paz, Octavio. 1987. "Landscape and the Novel in Mexico." In *Generaciones y semblanzas: Escritores y letras de México,* ed. Octavio Paz and Luis Mario Schneider, 585–86. Mexico City: Letras Mexicanas.

Phelps, Jim, and Nigel Bell, eds. 2007. *D. H. Lawrence Around the World: South African Perspectives.* Empangeni, South Africa: Echoing Green Press.

Pickering-Iazzi, Robin. 1997. *Politics of the Visible: Writing Women, Culture, and Fascism.* Minneapolis: University of Minnesota Press.

Pollnitz, Christopher. 2003. "Watermarks in a Cigar Box: Findings in D. H. Lawrence's Manuscript Verse." *DHLR* 31, no. 2:5–23.

———. 2005. "The Censorship and Transmission of D. H. Lawrence's *Pansies:* The Home Office and the 'Foul-Mouthed Fellow.'" *Journal of Modern Literature* 28, no. 3 (Winter): 44–71.

Pollock, Mary Sanders, and Catherine Rainwater. 2005. *Figuring Animals: Essays on Animal Images in Art, Literature, Philosophy, and Popular Culture.* New York: Palgrave Macmillan.

Radford, Andrew. 2002. "Strange Gods Beneath the Post-war Rubble in *Kangaroo.*" *DHLR* 31, no. 1:51–65.

Richardson, Angelique. 2003. *Love and Eugenics in the Late Nineteenth Century: Rational Reproduction and the New Woman.* Oxford: Oxford University Press.

Robb, George. 1996. "The Way of All Flesh: Degeneration, Eugenics, and the Gospel of Free Love." *Journal of the History of Sexuality* 6, no. 4: 589–602.

Roberts, Neil. 2004. *D. H. Lawrence, Travel and Cultural Difference.* New York: Palgrave Macmillan.

Roberts, Warren, and Paul Poplawski. 2001. *A Bibliography of D. H. Lawrence.* 3rd ed. Cambridge: Cambridge University Press.

Roh, Franz. 1995. "Magical Realism: Post-Expression" in Zamora and Faris, 15–31.

Rohman, Carrie. 2003. "'Demonish Maturity': Identity, Consumption, and the Discourse of Species in *The Plumed Serpent.*" In Cushman and Ingersoll 2003a, 216–29.

———. 2005. "Burning Out the Animal: The Failure of Enlightenment Purification in H. G. Wells's *The Island of Dr. Moreau.*" In Pollock and Rainwater 2005, 121–34.

———. 2007. "On Marrying a Butcher: Animality and Modernist Anxiety in West's 'Indissoluble Matrimony.'" *Mosaic* 40:27–43.

Ruderman, Judith. 1984. *D. H. Lawrence and the Devouring Mother: The Search for a Patriarchal Ideal of Leadership.* Durham, NC: Duke University Press.

———. 1991. "D. H. Lawrence and the 'Jewish Problem': Reflections on a Self-Confessed 'Hebrophobe.'" *DHLR* 23, nos. 2–3 (Fall): 99–109.

———. 2003. "'An Englishman at Heart'? Lawrence and the National Identity Debates." In Cushman and Ingersoll 2003a, 50–67.

Sagar, Keith. 2001. "The Resurrection of Pan: Teaching Biocentric Consciousness and Deep Ecology in Lawrence's Poetry and Late Nonfiction." In Sargent and Watson 2001a, 146–56.

———. 2006. *Literature and the Crime Against Nature.* London: Chaucer Press.

Said, Edward. 1979. *Orientalism.* New York: Vintage.

Sargent, M. Betsy, and Garry Watson, eds. 2001a. *Approaches to Teaching the Works of D. H. Lawrence.* New York: MLA.

———. 2001b. "D. H. Lawrence and the Dialogical Principle: 'The Strange Reality of Otherness.'" *College English* 63, no. 4 (March): 409–36.

Schaffer, Kay. 1988. *Women and the Bush: Forces of Desire in the Australian Cultural Tradition.* Cambridge: Cambridge University Press.

Searle, G. R. 1976. *Eugenics and Politics in Britain, 1900–1914.* Science in History, ser. 3. Gen, ed. G. L'E. Turner. Leyden: Noordhoff International Publishing.

Shaw, George Bernard. 1947. *Back to Methuselah.* Oxford: Oxford University Press.

Sheehan, Paul. 2002. *Modernism, Narrative and Humanism.* New York: Cambridge University Press.

Siegel, Carol. 1991. *Lawrence Among the Women: Wavering Boundaries in Women's Literary Traditions.* Charlottesville: University Press of Virginia.

Smith, Julie A. 2005. "Sensory Experience as Consciousness in Literary Representations of Animal Minds." In Pollock and Rainwater 2005, 231–46.

Soloway, Richard A. 1995. *Demography and Degeneration: Eugenics and the Declining Birthrate in Twentieth-Century Britain.* Chapel Hill: University of North Carolina Press.

Squire, J. C. 1929. "Editorial Notes." *London Mercury* 20 (July): 229–30.

Squires, Michael, and Lynn K. Talbot. 2002. *Living at the Edge: A Biography of D. H. Lawrence and Frieda von Richthofen.* London: Robert Hale.

Steele, Bruce. 1991. "*Kangaroo:* Fact and Fiction." *Meridian* 10 (May): 19–34.

Steiner, Gary. 2005. *Anthropocentrism and Its Discontents: The Moral Status of Animals in the History of Western Philosophy.* Pittsburgh: University of Pittsburgh Press.

Steven, C. J. 1988. *Lawrence at Tregerthen (D. H. Lawrence in Cornwall).* Troy, NY: Whitston Press.

Stone, Chuck. 1992. "The Censor-Morons of the World: Ubiquitous Usurpers of the Four Literary Freedoms." *DHLR* 24:203–16.

Stone, Dan. 2002. *Breeding Superman: Nietzsche, Race and Eugenics in Edwardian and Interwar Britain.* London: Liverpool University Press.

Sylvester, David, ed. 1975. *Interviews with Francis Bacon.* London: Thames & Hudson.

Tanselle, G. Thomas. 1964. "The Thomas Seltzer Imprint." *Papers of the Bibliographical Society of America* 58:380–448.

Templeton, Wayne. 1996. "'Indians and an Englishman': Lawrence in the American Southwest." *D. H. Lawrence Review* 26:14–34.

Thompson, Theresa Mae. 2001 "Unlearning Europe: Postcolonial Questions for Teaching *The Plumed Serpent.*" In Sargent and Watson 2001a 221–225.

Thomson, Mathew. 1998. *The Problem of Mental Deficiency: Eugenics, Democracy, and Social Policy in Britain, c. 1870–1959.* Oxford: Clarendon.

Thornycroft, Rosalind. 1991. *Time Which Spaces Us Apart.* Batcombe, England: privately printed.

Torgovnick, Marianna. 1990. *Gone Primitive: Savage Intellects, Modern Lives.* Chicago University of Chicago Press.

———. 2001. "Narrating Sexuality: *The Rainbow.*" In Fernihough 2001, 33–48.

Turner, John F., and John Worthen. 1999. "Ideas of Community: Lawrence and 'Rananim.'" *D. H. Lawrence Studies* (Korea) 8:135–71.

Vine, Steven. 1995. "Introduction: D. H. Lawrence's Exodus." In *Aaron's Rod,* ed. Mara Kalnins, xv–xxxvi. Harmondsworth, England: Penguin.

Vivas, Eliseo. 1964. *D. H. Lawrence: The Failure and the Triumph of Art.* Bloomington: Indiana University Press.

Walker, Ronald. 1978. *Infernal Paradise: Mexico and the Modern English Novel.* Berkeley and Los Angeles: University of California Press.

Wallace, Jeff. 2005. *D. H. Lawrence, Science, and the Posthuman.* Basingstoke, England: Palgrave Macmillan.

Weaver, Raymond. 1961. *Herman Melville: Mariner and* Mystic. New York: Pageant Books.

Webster, Charles. 1977. "Eugenic Sterilisation: Europe's Shame." *Health-Matters* 31 (Autumn). Rpt. http://www.healthmatters.org.uk/issue31/eugenicshame.

Wells, H. G. 1924. "The Invisible Man." In vol. 3 of *The Works of H. G. Wells.* New York: Scribner's and Sons.

Whitworth, Michael H. 2004. *Einstein's Wake: Relativity, Metaphor, and Modernist Literature.* Oxford: Oxford University Press.

Wicks, Izumi. 2003. "Lawrence to Joyce: Lawrence, Joyce, Modernist Fiction to Cubism." In *D. H. Lawrence to Modernism no Sakkatachi,* ed. Shunji Suzuki and Izumi Wicks, 65–96. Tokyo: Eihosha.

Williams, Linda Ruth. 1993. *Sex in the Head: Visions of Femininity and Film in D. H. Lawrence.* Detroit: Wayne State University Press.

Wittgenstein, Ludwig. 1961. *Tractatus Logico-Philosophicus.* Trans. D. F. Pears and B. F. McGuiness. London: Routledge.

Wolfe, Cary. 2003a. *Animal Rites: American Culture, the Discourse of Species, and Posthumanist Theory.* Chicago: University of Chicago Press.

———. 2003b. *Zoontologies: The Question of the Animal.* Minneapolis: University of Minnesota Press.

Wood, David. 2004. "Thinking with Cats." In *Animal Philosophy: Essential Readings in Continental Thought,* ed. Peter Singer, Matthew Calarco, and Peter Atterton. London: Continuum.

Worthen, John. 1979. *D. H. Lawrence and the Idea of the Novel.* London: Macmillan Press.

———. 1989. *D. H. Lawrence: A Literary Life.* London: Macmillan.

———. 1991. *D. H. Lawrence: The Early Years, 1885–1912.* Cambridge: Cambridge University Press.

———. 2003. "Lawrence's Theater of the Southwest." In Cushman and Ingersoll 2003a, 243–57.

———. 2005. *D. H. Lawrence: The Life of an Outsider.* London: Allen Lane; New York: Counterpoint.

Wussow, Helen. 1998. *The Nightmare of History: The Fictions of Virginia Woolf and D. H. Lawrence.* Bethlehem, PA: Lehigh University Press.

Young, Richard O. 1980. "'Where Even the Trees Come and Go': D. H. Lawrence and the Fourth Dimension." *DHLR* 8:30–44.

Zamora, Lois Parkinson, and Wendy B. Faris. 1995. *Magical Realism: Theory, History, Community.* Durham, NC: Duke University Press.

Žižek, Slavoj. 2001. *Enjoy Your Symptom! Jacques Lacan in Hollywood and Out.* New York: Routledge.

Contributors

GERALD DOHERTY retired some years ago as a senior lecturer at the University of Turku, Finland. He has published widely in modernist studies, especially on the work of James Joyce and D. H. Lawrence, in *PMLA, Modern Fiction Studies, Style,* the *James Joyce Quarterly, and* the *D. H. Lawrence Review.* He is the author of *Theorizing Lawrence* (1999), *Oriental Lawrence* (2001), and *Dubliners' Dozen* (FDUP, 2004). He is presently at work on a book tentatively entitled "Lawrence Among the Animals."

KUMIKO HOSHI is a doctoral candidate at Tokyo Woman's Christian University in Japan, where she is working on her dissertation, "D. H. Lawrence's Representations of Relativity: With Special Reference to the Cultural Climate before Einstein."

VIRGINIA HYDE is a Professor of British Literature, which she has taught at Washington State University for thirty-five years. She is the author of *The Risen Adam: D. H. Lawrence's Revisionist Typology* (1992) and has published on a number of literary figures in books and journals such as the *D. H. Lawrence Review, Contemporary Literature, Mosaic, Yeats Annual,* and *Victorian Poetry.* She is editor of *Mornings in Mexico and Other Essays* (Cambridge Edition, 2009), and, with L. D. Clark, published a Penguin edition of *The Plumed Serpent* (1995). She has served as president of the D. H. Lawrence Society of North America, and in 2005 she received the Harry T. Moore Award for lifetime achievement in Lawrence studies.

EARL G. INGERSOLL is a Distinguished Professor and Distinguished Teaching Professor of English, Emeritus, at the State University of New York, College at Brockport, and a past president of the D. H. Lawrence Society of North America. He has published widely in twentieth-century British and Irish literatures, including *Waiting for the End: Gender and Ending in the Contemporary Novel* (FDUP, 2007) and *Engendered Trope in James Joyce's "Dubliners"* (1996). In addition to a dozen articles and essays on Lawrence, he has published *D. H. Lawrence, Desire, and Narrative* (2001) and co-edited *D. H. Lawrence: New Worlds* (FDUP, 2003) with Keith Cushman.

NANCY L. PAXTON, Professor of English at Northern Arizona University, has published *George Eliot and Herbert Spencer: Feminism, Evolutionism, and the Reconstruction of Gender* (1989) and *Writing under the Raj: Gender, Race, and Rape in the British Colonial Imagination, 1830–1947* (1999), as well as *Outside Modernism: In Pursuit of the British Novel, 1900–1930* (2000), co-edited with Lynne Hapgood. She is the editor of the *D. H. Lawrence Society of North America Newsletter*, and she is working on a book on censorship in the 1920s, with a chapter on Lawrence.

CHRISTOPHER POLLNITZ is a senior lecturer at the University of Newcastle, Australia. In addition to his interests in contemporary Australian literature, particularly poetry, he is a specialist in modernist studies, especially Lawrence. He is preparing the critical edition of Lawrence's poetry, which will complete the series begun by Cambridge University Press over a quarter century ago.

KEITH SAGAR has lived in "Lawrence country," teaching at Manchester University and the University of Nottingham. From *The Art of D. H. Lawrence* (1966) to his volume of Lawrence's letters (Cambridge Edition, with James T. Boulton, 1993) and his collection of *D. H. Lawrence's Paintings* (2004), he published over 20 books on Lawrence and Ted Hughes. His *Literature and the Crime Against Nature* (2005) is a wide-ranging study of British literature that includes ecological perspectives. In 2004 he published his collected poems *Mola*. Sagar has lectured widely in the United States and (for the British Council) in Yugoslavia, India, China, and elsewhere. He has received the Harry T. Moore Award for lifetime achievement in Lawrence studies.

Theresa Mae Thompson is Professor of twentieth-century British literature and postcolonial theory at Valdosta State University, Georgia. She is co-editor of *Imagining the Worst: Stephen King and the Representation of Women* (with Kathleen Lant, 1998) and a contributor to MLA's *Approaches to Teaching the Works of D. H. Lawrence* (2001). She has spoken widely on Lawrence from postcolonial and feminist perspectives.

Jamie Jung Min Woo has been teaching in Korea since she received her PhD from the University of Warwick in England in 2006. She has published several essays on Lawrence in *D. H. Lawrence Studies*, the journal of the D. H. Lawrence Society of Korea, and in *Études Lawrenciennes*. She is an editor of *D. H. Lawrence Studies*.

John Worthen is Emeritus Professor of D. H. Lawrence Studies at the University of Nottingham. He is the author of *D. H. Lawrence: The Early Years 1885–1912*, the first volume of the three-volume Cambridge biography, and *D. H. Lawrence: The Life of an Outsider* (2005). He is also the editor of numerous texts in the Cambridge University Press critical editions of Lawrence's writings. In addition, he has published landmark work on Coleridge and the Wordsworths (2001). He has received the Harry T. Moore Award for lifetime achievement in Lawrence studies.

Index

Adams, Carol, 97 n. 13
Adelman, Gary, 9, 10, 18 n. 4
Adorno, Theodor, 203
Arnold, Armin, 48 n. 10
Asquith, Lady Cynthia, 28, 29, 170
Asturias, Miguel Ángel, 188, 190
Auden, W. H., 18 n. 4

Bacon, Francis, 66
Baker, Paul G., 106, 117 n. 7
Bakhtin, Mikhail, 9, 10, 18 n. 6, 102, 116 n. 2
Balla, Giacomo, 109; *Dynamism of a Dog on a Leash,* 109
Barr, William R., 106
Bataille, Georges, 70, 72, 84, 95, 96 n. 7
Baynes, Rosalind, 56
Beal, Anthony, 48 n. 11
Becket, Fiona, 140, 163 n. 1
Beer, Gillian, 96 n. 3
Bell, Clive, 23
Bell, Michael, 10, 18 n. 6, 139, 150
Bell, Nigel, 9
Bennett, Arnold, 175–76
Bennett, Bruce, 163 n. 3
Bentham, Jeremy, 76, 78, 97 n. 12
Beresford, J. D., 24
Blake, William, 211, 218, 220
Bliss, Philip B., 222 n. 1
Bloom, Harold, 9
Bodkin, Sir Archibald, 174, 176, 177
Boies, Henry, 119–20, 126; *Prisoners and Paupers,* 119–20, 126
Booth, Harold, 148, 164 n. 12
Boulton, James, 176
Braque, Georges, 102, 108
Brett, Dorothy, 199–200, 206 n. 9
Brewster, Earl, and Achsah Brewster, 60, 193, 212
Brewster, Scott, 140, 163 n. 1
Brontë, Charlotte; *Jane Eyre,* 144
Burack, Charles, 146
Burrow, Trigant, 210, 219, 220; *The Social Basis of Consciousness,* 219–20
Burrows, Louie, 184 n. 13
Burwell, Rose Marie, 47 n. 4
Butler, Judith, 14–15, 141, 142, 145, 147, 157, 160, 162, 164 n. 6; *Bodies that Matter,* 141; *The Psychic Life of Power,* 141

Caesar, Adrian, 163 n. 3
Cannan, Mary, 52, 53
Carlson, Elof Axel, 120, 123, 124, 126, 129, 130, 134, 136 nn. 4 and 5, 137 n. 6; *The Unfit,* 123
Carpentier, Alejo, 188, 190; *The Kingdom of This World,* 188
Carswell, Catherine, 23
Cézanne, Paul, 106, 108–9, 111; *Still Life with a Fruit Basket,* 109
Chaplin, Charlie, 101
Chase, Richard, 48 nn. 9 and 11
Chaudhury, Amit, 10
Childs, Peter, 101, 103, 116 n. 2
Clarey, JoEllen, 44, 48 n. 11

Clark, L. D., 18 n. 10, 206 nn. 7 and 10, 211; *The Minoan Distance,* 211
Clarke, Bruce, 100, 105, 106
Clynes, J. R., 186 n. 28
Colacurcio, Michael J., 48 n. 11
Coleridge, Samuel Taylor, 23
Columbus, Christopher, 25
Conor, Liz, 158, 164 n. 5
Conrad, Joseph, 154; *Heart of Darkness,* 154
Cowan, James C., 11; *D. H. Lawrence: Self and Sexuality,* 11
Cram, David, 184 n. 13
Crichton, Kyle, 179, 180
Crosby, Harry, 60; *Chariot of the Sun,* 60
Cushman, Keith, 18 n. 5, 63, 184 n. 14

Daleski, H. M., 117 n. 4
Dana, Richard Henry, 21, 22, 30, 41–42
Darroch, Robert, 163 n. 2, 164 n. 8
Darwin, Charles, 9, 96 n. 5, 122
Davies, Rhys, 182
Davis, Joseph, 163 n. 2, 164 n. 13
De Grazia, Edward, 185 n. 15
De la Mare, Walter, 167, 183 nn. 2, 3, and 5, 184 n. 5
Delany, Paul, 18 n. 3, 23, 25, 49 n. 12, 163 n. 4
Deleuze, Gilles, 8, 9, 13, 18 n. 1, 76, 80, 90, 97 nn. 8, 16, and 20, 98 nn. 20 and 22
D'Emilio, John, 164 n. 5
Derrida, Jacques, 9, 13, 70, 72, 76, 82, 90, 96 n. 7, 97 n. 18, 121
Descartes, René, 70, 74, 75, 82, 92, 97 n. 11
Devall, William, 10
Dixon, Robert, 163 n. 3
Doherty, Gerald, 10, 13, 16
Doolittle, Hilda ("H.D."), 18 n. 4
Douglas, Norman, 51, 52, 53, 55, 61
Draper, R. P., 117 n. 4, 184 n. 6
Drysdale, Alice Vickery, 136 n. 3
Duchamp, Marcel, 13, 102, 106, 108, 109; *Nude Descending a Staircase, No. 2,* 13, 108, 109

Eder, David, 47 n. 6
Eggert, Paul, 18 n. 7
Einstein, Albert, 8, 14, 99, 100, 101, 102, 103, 104, 116, 117 n. 3; *Theory of Relativity,* 100, 101, 104
Eliot, T. S., 158; *The Waste Land,* 158
Ellis, David, 163, 163 n. 2, 164 n. 12, 171
Ellis, Havelock, 175
Ernst, Morris, 166, 181, 183 n. 1

Fabian Society, 124, 125
Faris, Wendy B., 189, 205 n. 2; *Magical Realism,* 189
Feldman, Mark, 97 n. 9
Fiedler, Leslie, 33, 48 n. 11; *Love and Death in the American Novel,* 48 n. 11
Fitzgerald, F. Scott, 142, 158; *The Great Gatsby,* 142, 149, 158
Fjagesund, Peter, 121
Fleishman, Avrom, 18 n. 6
Fletcher, Stuart, 181, 182, 186 n. 31
Ford, George, 22; *Double Measure,* 22
Ford, Henry, 181
Forster, E. M., 29, 30, 47 n. 3, 69, 176; *Maurice,* 47 n. 3; *A Passage to India,* 69
Forstner, Lorne J., 10
Forter, Greg, 142, 145, 149, 156
Foucault, Michel, 18 n. 1
Freeman, Estelle, 164 n. 5
Freud, Sigmund, 28, 29, 77, 86, 90, 96 n. 6, 140, 141, 145, 150, 155, 157, 162, 163; *Mourning and Melancholy,* 150
Frost, Robert, 18 n. 4; "The Road Not Taken," 53, 68 n. 2
Fuentes, Carlos, 15, 187, 188, 199

Gadd, Tim, 96 n. 5
Galton, Francis, 122, 123, 136 nn. 4 and 5
Gardiner, Rolf, 213
Garnett, David, 47 n. 1, 51, 68 n. 1, 167, 183 n. 4

Garnett, Edward, 67, 113, 122, 142, 166, 167, 176, 183 nn. 2, 4, and 5
Gauguin, Paul, 212
Geddes, Patrick, 136 n. 5
Gertzman, Jay A., 164 n. 9, 165, 185 n. 15
Gilbert, Sandra, 10–11
Ginsberg, Allen, 18 n. 4
Girard, René, 72, 96 n. 7
Gladstone, William Ewart, 178
Gleizes, Albert, 108
Gollancz, Victor, 175
Granofsky, Ronald, 105, 117 n. 5
Grant, Duncan, 47 n. 1
Greene, Graham, 201
Greenspan, Ezra, 40, 47 n. 7, 48 nn. 8 and 11
Griffin, Roger, 120
Guattari, Félix, 8, 18 n. 1, 90, 97 nn. 8 and 16, 98 n. 22

Haberstroh, Charles, 30
Hall, Radclyffe: *The Well of Loneliness,* 176
Haviland, Edwin, 30
Hawthorne, Nathaniel, 21, 30, 31, 36–38, 39, 40, 41, 43, 45, 46, 49 n. 12; *Mosses from an Old Manse,* 30, 31; *The Scarlet Letter,* 36–38, 39
Heaney, Seamus, 18 n. 4
Hegel, Georg Wilhelm Friedrich, 96 n. 7
Heinemann, William, 167, 183 nn. 2 and 5
Henderson, Linda, 102, 103
Herodotus, 198
Heseltine, Philip, 212
Hitler, Adolf, 122
Hobson, John, 175
Hocking, William Henry, 46, 49 n. 12, 53, 68 n. 1
Hopkin, Sally, and Willie Hopkin, 65
Horkheimer, Max, 203
Hough, Graham, 117 n. 4
Hughes, Billy, 152–53
Hughes, Ted, 211, 219
Huxley, Aldous, 18 n. 4, 201, 212, 217, 218
Hyde, G. M., 117 n. 6
Hyde, Virginia, 18 n. 10, 105, 120, 140, 206 n. 10

Iida, Takeo, 9
Ingersoll, Earl G., 10, 11, 18 n. 5, 47 n. 5, 97 n. 10

Jansohn, Christa, 9
Joyce, James, 69, 102, 116 n. 2; *Ulysses,* 69
Joynson-Hicks, Sir William, 174, 175, 177, 180, 186 n. 27 and 28
Jung, Carl, 207

Kafka, Franz, 190; "Meditation," 190–91; *Metamorphosis and Other Stories,* 190
Kermode, Frank, 117 n. 4
King, Dixie, 47 n. 5
Kinkead-Weekes, Mark, 10, 18 n. 7, 23, 24, 46, 49 n. 12, 53, 54, 64, 103, 120, 130, 131, 163 n. 4, 184 n. 9, 206 n. 13
Koteliansky, S. S., 26, 61, 100, 104, 122, 209, 210
Kristeva, Julia, 140; *Black Sun,* 140

Lacan, Jacques, 9, 10, 34, 86, 97 n. 18
LaChapelle, Dolores, 10
Lahr, Charles, 174, 175, 176
Lane, Christopher, 149, 164 n. 11
Lawrence, Arthur John, 162, 163
Lawrence, D. H.: and censorship, 122, 124, 165–86; cubism, 13; eco-criticism, 10, 16, 207–8; eugenics, 14, 119–21, 122, 124, 135, 136 n. 1; health, 24–25, 26; magic realism, 15, 187–89; quest, 7, 16, 25, 207–23; reputation, 9; specieism, 13, 69–98; thought-adventures, 7, 16, 22, 32, 44, 65–66, 187; travel, 7, 25, 50–67; windows to the sun, 7–8, 9, 14, 16, 17, 21, 116, 140, 156, 162
–Works: *Aaron's Rod,* 7, 13–14, 56, 104–17; "Adolf," 46; "All of Us,"

Lawrence, D. H.
—Works (*continued*)
170, 184 nn. 12 and 13; "The American Eagle," 173, 185 n. 23; *Amores,* 167, 183 n. 5; *Apocalypse,* 222; "A Propos of *Lady Chatterley's Lover,*" 18 n. 8; *Bay,* 170; *Birds, Beasts, and Flowers,* 46, 170, 171, 184 n. 15, 185 n. 20; "Birth Night," 168; "Bits," 184 n. 12; *The Boy in the Bush,* 67, 140; "British Sincerity," 178–79; "Candlemas," 184 n. 6; *Collected Poems,* 169, 173, 184 n. 8, 185 nn. 20, 21, and 22; *Complete Poems,* 169, 174, 184 nn. 11 and 12; "Cypresses," 173; "Daddy-Do-Nothing," 178; "A Dream of Life," 214, 219; "Education of the People," 17; "Elephant," 173, 174; *The Escaped Cock,* 214, 215, 220, 222; *Etruscan Places,* 7, 215, 217, 218–19, 222; "Eve's Mass," 184 n. 6; *Fantasy of the Unconscious,* 7, 37, 66, 104, 114, 138, 155, 163, 215; "Fig," 172, 185 nn. 20, 21, and 22; *The First "Women in Love,"* 170; "Fish," 64; "Flying Fish," 214, 219; "The Future of the Novel," 8; "The Hands of the Beloved," 167; "Indians and an Englishman," 191–92; "The Individual Consciousness v. the Social Consciousness," 214; "Introduction to These Paintings," 186 n. 25; *Introductions and Reviews,* 63; "John Galsworthy," 214; *Kangaroo,* 7, 12, 14–15, 49 n. 12, 68 n. 1, 100, 103, 104, 138–64, 185 n. 17, 194; *Lady Chatterley's Lover,* 15, 23, 46, 47 n. 3, 54, 67, 166, 174, 175, 177, 178, 180, 194, 208, 209, 213, 214, 215, 220; "Last Words to Miriam," 167; "Late in Life," 184 n. 11; "Lightning," 183 n. 4; "Lilies in the Fire," 183 n. 4; "London Mercury," 178; *Look! We Have Come Through!* 168, 169, 184 nn. 8 and 9; *The Lost Girl,* 7, 14, 52, 112, 118–37, 206, 207; "Love Comes Late," 184 n. 11; "Love Message," 184 n. 13; *Love Poems and Others,* 166, 183 nn. 4 and 5; "Love Was Once a Little Boy," 115; "Lui et Elle," 208; "Magnificent Democracy," 186 n. 24; "The Man Who Loved Islands," 213; "The Man Who Was Through with the World," 213, 214; *The Married Man,* 18 n. 11; "Meeting Among the Mountains," 168, 169, 184 nn. 7 and 9; *Memoir of Maurice Magnus,* 7, 11–12, 50–64; *Mr. Noon,* 37; "My Little Critics," 178; "My Naughty Book," 174; *Nettles,* 178, 186 n. 29; *New Poems,* 170; *Pansies,* 18 n. 9, 101, 166, 174, 175, 176, 186 n. 26; "Pictures on the Wall," 100; *The Plumed Serpent,* 7, 15, 16, 67, 96 n. 1, 131, 179, 180, 187, 189, 190, 193, 194, 195–205, 206 n. 7, 213; *Pornography and Obscenity,* 180, 182; *Psychoanalysis and the Unconscious,* 140, 163; "Question," 178; *Quetzalcoatl,* 15, 187, 193, 194, 195, 197, 202, 205; *The Rainbow,* 11, 22–23, 23–24, 28, 36, 96 n. 4, 113, 120, 168, 169, 179, 183 n. 1, 200, 207, 211; "Reading a Letter," 170; "Red Moon-Rise," 183 n. 4; "Relativity," 101; "Rex," 46; "Scent of Irises," 167; "Snapdragon," 183 n. 4; "Song of a Man Who Is Loved," 168, 169; *Sons and Lovers,* 22, 29, 167, 179, 207; *St. Mawr,* 193; *Studies in Classic American Literature,* 7, 11, 21–22, 26, 34–39, 40, 41, 42, 45, 46, 47 nn. 4 and 7, 48 n. 11, 60, 66; "Surgery for the Novel–or a Bomb," 18 n. 2; "Sympathy," 184 n. 13; "13,000 People," 181; "To Clarinda," 174; *The*

Trespasser, 110–11, 200; "True Democracy," 177; *Twilight in Italy*, 63; "Two-Fold," 184 n. 13; "Valentine's Night," 168; "Violets," 183 n. 4; "Whales Weep Not," 46; *The White Peacock*, 167; *Women in Love*, 7, 13, 14, 21, 25, 27, 28, 30, 34–35, 41, 43, 44, 46, 47 n. 1, 63, 66, 69–98, 100, 104, 116 n. 1, 120, 141, 169, 171, 179, 185 n. 16, 198, 200, 208; "The Young and Their Guardians," 174
Lawrence, Frieda, 11, 25, 26, 29, 47 n. 1, 52, 54, 159, 161, 162, 168, 184 nn. 7, 8, and 9, 193, 200, 207, 208; *Not I But the Wind . . .* 168, 184 n. 7
Lawson, Henry, 142
Leavis, F. R., 117 n. 6
Lombroso, Cesare, 134
Loran, Paul, 108–9
Low, Barbara, 26, 28
Lowry, Malcolm, 201
Lynd, Robert, 25

MacCarthy, Mary, 47 n. 1
Macintyre, Stuart, 152, 164 n. 16
Maddox, Brenda, 18 n. 11, 24
Magnus, Maurice, 51–64; *Dregs*, 55, 57, 60
Malthus, Thomas, 126, 137 n. 6
Mansfield, Katherine, 24
Marey, Étienne-Jule, 103
Martz, Louis L., 194
Marx, Karl, 180, 215
Massés, Federico Beltrán, 180–81
McKenzie, Compton, 40, 54
Mehl, Dieter, 9
Melville, Herman, 7, 11, 21–22, 26, 27, 28–29, 30–34, 35, 36, 39, 40, 41, 42, 45, 46, 47 n. 2, 48 n. 8; *Billy Budd*, 46; *Mardi*, 29, 48 n. 8; *Moby-Dick*, 11, 22, 26, 27, 28, 30, 31, 32–33, 39, 41, 42–43, 44–45, 46, 47 n. 2, 48 nn. 10 and 11; *Omoo*, 29; *Pierre*, 48 n. 8; *Redburn*, 29; *Typee*, 29, 40; *White-Jacket*, 29
Metzinger, Jean, 108
Meyers, Jeffrey, 18 n. 4, 164 n. 12
Michelangelo Buonarroti, 28
Miller, Arthur I., 99, 101
Miller, Henry, 11
Millett, Kate, 10; *Sexual Politics*, 10
Milne, Drew, 10
Mohanty, Satya, 146
Moholy-Nagy, László, 109
Mond, Alfred, 181
Moore, Harry T., 184 n. 7
Morrell, Lady Ottoline, 23, 25, 26, 28, 29, 30, 47 n. 1, 59
Morrison, Nellie, 64
Mountsier, Robert, 104, 148, 164 n. 9
Muir, John, 10
Murry, John Middleton, 24, 25, 46, 68 n. 1, 97 n. 20, 212
Mussolini, Benito, 136 n. 1

Nakabayashi, Masomi, 68 n. 11
Nehls, Edward, 175, 179, 180, 186 n. 27
New Age, 126, 136 n. 5
Newton, Sir Isaac, 101, 220
Nietzsche, Friedrich, 13, 73, 79, 80, 82, 88, 97 n. 14; *Also Sprach Zarathustra*, 79, 97 n. 14
Nile, Richard, 163 n. 3
Nin, Anaïs, 11
Norris, Margot, 96 n. 5; *Beasts of the Modern Imagination*, 96 n. 5

Oates, Joyce Carol, 18 n. 4
Odio, Arnold, 16, 187, 199, 205 nn. 1 and 3
Orioli, Giuseppe (Pino), 174
Orozco, Jose Clemente, 201
Ouspensky, P. D., 105; *Tertium Organum*, 105

Parker, David, 97 n. 15
Parkes, Adam, 180, 181, 186 n. 31
Paxton, Nancy, 14, 164 n. 11
Paz, Octavio, 15, 187, 190
Pecora, Ferdinand, 171, 185 n. 16
Phelps, Jim, 9

Picasso, Pablo, 13, 99, 100, 102, 108, 109, 116; *Les Demoiselles d'Avignon,* 99, 108, 116
Pinker, J. B., 170
Pinto, Vivian de Sola, 169
Plato, 17
Poe, Edgar Allan, 37
Pollinger, Laurence, 174
Pollnitz, Christopher, 15, 18 n. 9, 174, 176, 184 nn. 8 and 13
Poplawski, Paul, 172, 185 n. 18; *A Bibliography of D. H. Lawrence,* 172
Preston, Peter, 185 n. 22
Proust, Marcel, 102, 116 n. 2

Radford, Andrew, 164 n. 15
Renoir, Pierre-Auguste, 100
Rivera, Diego, 201
Robb, George, 123, 130
Roberts, Neil, 10
Roberts, Warren, 169, 171, 172, 178, 185 nn. 18 and 23; *A Bibliography of D. H. Lawrence,* 172
Roh, Franz, 187–88, 189
Rohman, Carrie, 96 n. 1
Röntgen, Wilhelm Conrad, 114
Ruderman, Judith, 138, 146, 163 n. 1, 164 n. 7
Russell, Lord Bertrand, 30, 312

Sagar, Keith, 10, 16, 184 n. 13, 223 nn. 2 and 3; *The Art of D. H. Lawrence,* 211; *Literature and the Crime Against Nature,* 10, 211; "The Resurrection of Pan," 10
Said, Edward, 206 n. 5
Schäfer, Heinrich, 170, 184 n. 13; *Lieder,* 184 n. 13
Schnitzler, Arthur, 185 n. 16; *Casanova's Homecoming,* 185 n. 16
Seagle, William, 166, 182; *To the Pure . . . ,* 166
Secker, Martin, 169, 175, 176, 177, 184 n. 11, 185 n. 22
Sedgwick, Eve, 164 n. 11
Seltzer, Thomas, 40, 45, 66, 148, 164 n. 9, 171, 172, 173, 184 nn. 9 and 15, 185 nn. 16, 21, 22, and 23
Shaffer, Kay, 139, 142, 163 n. 3; *Women and the Bush,* 142
Shakespeare, William; *The Tempest,* 212
Shaw, George Bernard, 214, 215, 216, 218; *Back to Methuselah,* 214–16, 216–17
Siegel, Carol, 11
Simpson, George, 171
Skinner, Molly, 140
Socrates, 206 n. 11
Soloway, Richard A., 125, 127, 128, 133, 136 n. 3
Spencer, Herb, 129
Squire, J. C., 25, 178, 185 n. 28
Squires, Michael, 56, 68 n. 4, 164 n. 9, 185 n. 15
Steele, Bruce, 158, 163 n. 2, 164 n. 10
Steiner, George, 71, 78, 97 n. 12
Stevenson, Robert Louis, 212
Stone, Chuck, 125, 165
Stopes, Marie, 136 n. 3; *Married Love,* 136 n. 3
Strachey, Lytton, 30
Strauss, Jennifer, 163 n. 3
Sumner, John, 171, 185 n. 16
Swift, Jonathan, 216; *Gulliver's Travels,* 216
Sylvester, David, 66

Talbot, Lynn K., 56, 68 n. 4
Tanselle, G. Thomas, 185 n. 15
Thompson, Theresa M., 14, 206 n. 12
Thoreau, Henry David, 10
Tiziano Vecelli (Titian), 100
Todd, John T., 10
Torgovnick, Marianna, 10
Townsend, General Charles, 170
Turner, John F., 212
Twain, Mark (Samuel Langhorne Clemens), 33, 47 n. 4; *Huckleberry Finn,* 33, 47 n. 4; "The Mysterious Stranger," 47 n. 4

Van Gogh, Vincent, 106
Vasey, Lindeth, 40, 47 n. 7, 48 nn. 8 and 11
Villa, Pancho, 200–201
Vine, Stephen, 117 n. 7
Vivas, Eliseo, 117 n. 4

Walker, Ronald, 202, 206 n. 8
Wallace, Alfred Russel, 124–25
Wallace, Jeff, 98 n. 23
Watteau, Jean-Antoine, 77
Waugh, Evelyn, 201
Weaver, Raymond, 31, 40–41, 45, 46; *Herman Melville: Mariner and Mystic*, 40, 45
Weekley, Ernest, 169, 184 n. 9
Wells, H. G., 102, 106, 113, 114, 116; *The Invisible Man*, 106, 113; *The Time Machine*, 106, 113
West, Benjamin, 42
West, Rebecca, 175
Whitman, Walt, 21, 24, 38–40, 41, 43, 45, 60, 153; "The Bathers," 39; "Calamus," 39
Whitworth, Michael, 100
Wicks, Izumi, 116 n. 1
Williams, Linda Ruth, 38, 76
Wilson, Charles, 180
Wilson, Woodrow, 215
Wittgenstein, Ludwig, 64, 68, 206 n. 6; *Tractatus*, 68 n. 7
Wolfe, Cary, 83, 90, 96 n. 1, 97 n. 16
Wood, David, 70
Woolf, Leonard, 175
Woolf, Virginia Stephen, 23, 26, 29, 69, 102, 116 n. 2, 176; *Mrs. Dalloway*, 69
Wordsworth, William, 219; *Prelude*, 219
Worthen, John, 11–12, 18 n. 7, 40, 47 n. 7, 48 nn. 8 and 11, 53, 116, 122, 125, 135, 136 n. 2, 171, 175, 179, 184 n. 10, 185 n. 15, 186 n. 30, 194, 195, 212; *Literary Life*, 184 n. 10, 185 n. 15; *Outsider*, 50, 179, 185 n. 15
Wussow, Helen, 18 n. 3, 163 n. 4, 164 n. 14

Yeats, W. B., 136; "Sailing to Byzantium," 136
Young, Richard O., 105

Zamora, Lois Parkinson, 189, 205 n. 2; *Magical Realism*, 189
Zapata, Emiliano, 201
Žižek, Slavoj, 89
Zohar, 146